THE BATTLE IS NOT YOURS, IT'S GOD'S

BIBLE BATTLES

ROY R. BROWN

WINEPRESS **WP** PUBLISHING

WinePress Publishing (PO Box 428, Enumclaw, WA 98022) functions only as book publisher. As such, the ultimate design, content, editorial accuracy, and views expressed or implied in this work are those of the author.

ISBN 1-57921-854-7
Library of Congress Catalog Card Number: 2005903523

DEDICATION

This book is dedicated to my children, Carolyn (deceased), Sylvia-Jean, Roy Jr., Alan, and my three grandchildren; Stephanie, AJ, and Jocelyn, with a prayer that they will be ever mindful that Jesus won the battle; therefore, The Battle Is Not Yours, It's God's.

TABLE OF CONTENTS

PREFACE

Bookstores all around the world have books that speak of God's love, miracles, grace and a thousand and one features and characteristics. This book will speak about God's involvement in battle/war. It will approach the matter from the divine-human relationship. Righteousness by faith will run like a golden thread throughout its pages. This is how it all began.

I received a telephone call from my daughter who resides in California one bright summer day. It appeared that some clouds attempted to blot the sunshine of God's radiant love from her sky. She was deeply concerned over a discussion that had occurred in her Bible class at the church she attends. She wanted an immediate answer to satisfy her knowledge that God was indeed a God of love. She said, "Daddy, we had this rather engaging discussion today which centered on the wars in the Old Testament. In these battles, God was the prime mover, and He killed or allowed Israel to participate in destroying thousands of men, women, children, animals, and property. It was God who said, 'Thou shalt not kill.' How do we reconcile the massive carnage in Scripture with a God of love and His command not to kill?" She was careful to assure me that her love for God had not lessened, nor did doubts prevail. She just wanted a justifying biblical response. I explained as best I possibly could the dilemma we face in an area that could be deemed a paradox.

Well, what do you know? For years my wife had encouraged me to write a book but I never got around to doing so. I served as the director of communications for nine years with the Southeastern Conference of Seventh-day Adventists in Florida. I recalled how the task of writing a feature for the *Southern Tidings* was like giving birth to barbed wire. After some coaching and encouragement we mutually agreed upon the approach. It was only a few weeks before my daughter posed the question that I had begun writing. What seemed so coincidental was that her question happened to be the very topic the book would be about. As a result of that conversation, I gave greater energy to the writing of this book, dealing with some of the battles in the Bible.

The purpose is to explain, although in a limited sense, the love and justice and mercy of the great and awesome God we serve. It will be seen that whereas there seems to be a distinct conflict with the love and justice of God, after careful review, and although some aspects may be hazy, there is perfect reconciliation between both. The righteousness of God will surface and it will be discovered that the battle is really the Lord's. Whether a spiritual or physical war, the fact is God is in charge and victory is His. In the various conflicts addressed, lessons will be extracted which hopefully will lift our admiration of God; yes, even cause our faith to rise higher than the Himalayas.

The battles at Jahaz and Edrei, started by Sihon and Og, Amorite kings against Israel, will be instructive as they deal with wars authorized by God. However, these battles will lay a foundation for why wars were permitted. Those that are to follow will rest on the same foundation, although each will be different.

Webster's New Twentieth Century Dictionary, defines war as: open armed conflict between nations or states, or between parties in the same state, carried on by force of arms for various purposes; a conflict of arms between hostile parties or nations. The profession, science, or art of military operations, or military operations as a department of activity. Any state of violent opposition or contest; act of opposition; inimical act or action; hostility; strife; a battle.

Webster's definition of a war does not pertain to God or the battles He fights. Two important characteristics of God, His love and His justice, are not considered in the definition, for only God knows how to demonstrate both fully at the same time. God is an unchanging God.

He was willing to sacrifice His only Son to rescue all mankind. That act alone encompasses love, mercy, and justice. A true picture of God is not one that is bloodthirsty, nor does He delight in the death of any of His children.

> Say unto them, As I live, saith the LORD GOD, I have no pleasure in the death of the wicked; but that the wicked turn from his way and live: turn ye, turn ye from your evil ways; for why will ye die, O house of Israel?
>
> —Ezekiel 33:11

We are led to conclude, based upon Ezekiel's testimony, that there are reasons, eternal reasons, divine prerogatives behind every war, every conflict we read about. In God-authorized warfare there are vaster considerations than the human mind can conjure up. When we read about the wars in the Bible, their devastating effects, the great loss of life and limb, property, cities, and animals, we are prone to make moral judgments based upon our limited human viewpoint. Our moral considerations on the matter are stained and saturated with, colored by the nearsightedness of only the moment or the day, which is all we possess as far as time is concerned. We have serious limitations. We do not possess the long view of the eternal significance. We are so imperfect that the conclusions drawn are warped and defective. At our best shining moment we are compelled to admit a bias. In fact, we must admit we just do not know. Solomon said,

> Then I beheld all the work of God, that a man cannot find out the work that is done under the sun: because though a man labour to seek it out, yet he shall not find it; yea further; though a wise man think to know it, yet shall he not be able to find it.
>
> —Ecclesiastes 8:17 KJV

> No matter how hard a man tries, he can never fully understand why things happen the way they do and why God permits certain things and not others. Even a very wise man can't come up with the answers to everything.
>
> —Ecclesiastes 8:17 The Clear Word.

But God, the God of the universe, knows everything, the end from the beginning, and His judgments are pure, perfect, and right.

The wars in the Bible are all different in their scope and operation. God sent an angel to conduct the midnight massacre of all the firstborn in Egypt over whose houses there was no blood. He had the sun and the moon stand still until Joshua completed the military conflict in which no survivor was left. Earthquakes and hailstones at His command do a work of annihilation. Yet there is never a battle in which God is not glorified.

We live in the Christian dispensation. Christians should do to others what they expect others should do to them. We are shocked almost beyond recovery when we read in the Bible of the wholesale destruction done by an angel, the elements, or man, any or all of which are God's appointed agencies. The most disturbing aspect is that the destruction God orders or allows occurs because of His permissive will; it is not the easiest full cup of water to carry without spillage. At that juncture we are compelled to repose in a wisdom that is higher than our own, a goodness that is greater. If not, we will chafe under our inability when we try to place our views of sin and destruction on the same plane with God and expect that they will be equal to God's or at least be understandable. We should always remember that God does not depend upon man's will, ideas, efforts, or plans but only on His own measure of justice and mercy. Therefore, He can exercise His will in whatever form it may take and He will always be right and a loving God.

ACKNOWLEDGMENTS

Special thanks to my wife, "Ms. Daisy," for her support and encouragement over the years to write a book and for her patience in reading every chapter for the hundredth time, my daughter Jeannie for asking the question, "Where is God in war?" and Roy Jr. for his keen mind and insightful comments.

INTRODUCTION

Roy Brown, preacher, teacher, administrator and cosmopolitan personality, has in this volume poured out his heart in a stimulating review of God's purposes in allowing and sometimes (as in Old Testament days) ordering human conflict.

The reader will note throughout Pastor Brown's love for the dramatic and at the same time his admirable attention to process and detail. His fluid, descriptive style is that of a preacher turned author–a combination of arresting presentation and accurate documentation.

I fully expect that, *The Battle Is Not Yours It's God's,* will be a favorite of all Christians and non-Christians alike who read it seriously and will take its place in the Pantheon of literary works.

This book has special appeal to all racial and religious groups. Its message is as broad as the gospel itself. That is because, our brother of high faith and culture has put it all together in a way that makes us all proud and all the better for the years of research and creative energy that this project has required.

Those who in their mature years are able to focus on a mission that challenges their own intellect and faith while stimulating the same in others, do so to the benefit of all who listen. Only long years of personally battling and overcoming in one's own real-life situations can provide such encouragement. Roy Brown has discovered and fulfilled that confluence of faith and experience and has given, in the analysis of battles common and cosmic that this book contains, an inspirational blueprint capable of helping each of us to conquer in the practical everyday struggles of life.

Calvin B. Rock, Ph.D.
Retired Vice-President,
General Conference of Seventh-day Adventists
Silver Spring, Maryland

Chapter 1

GOD'S SAY-SO

(Based on Numbers 21:21–35; Deut. 2:26–36; 3:1–10)

The cities of Heshbon and Bashan, weighed on God's scales and found wanting, were guilty of iniquities that had separated them from God. The hands of the inhabitants were defiled with blood. The tongues of the multitudes were loosed in wild blasphemies and profanities that held not God in awe and reverence. The people ran with the multitudes to evil. They loved that which God hated, and clung to evil. Judgment was turned away. Justice stood afar off. There were none that sought after God. None of them did that which was good. They had turned deaf ears to God's voice and His will. The voice they knew, or should have known, they rejected. They had a choice. The cup of their iniquity was about to run over. God had a decision to make concerning them. They had well-nigh obliterated the image of God in themselves. Even civility and human kindness found no place in the hearts of their kings, Sihon and Og. The kings were on the verge of meeting God's people who were about ready to realize their long-deferred hope.

Israel's forty years of wandering in the wilderness had come to an end. The barriers to the entrance, unbelief and distrust, were raised by Israel. They disallowed an earlier entry. Be it far from any of us that we will come to the borders of God's kingdom, and fail to enter in because of our unbelief or lack of faith. As Israel stood on the edge of the Promised Land, they forgot that it was not their readiness, their search

15

of the land by the twelve spies that entitled them to take possession of it. It was their faith in the divine promise. It was the covenant and God's say-so. The land of Canaan would be theirs as soon as they disposed of all those nations God spoke about to Abraham. But Israel, lured by the life of relative ease in Egypt, the leeks and garlic, all the meat and food they wanted to eat, concerned about the way being too difficult and the sons of Anak, stood discouraged on the verge of the Promised Land. What a sad picture. Can you imagine a child of God with immortal life beckoning, going back to the far country and the swine troughs?

God knew that Israel could not inhabit Canaan unless the people were destroyed. The battles with the two Amorite kings, Sihon and Og, whom we will consider, and their countries were not part of the promise made to Abraham. I am sure God included them for other reasons. First, two and a half of the twelve tribes, the half tribe of Manasseh, Reuben and Gad,[1] would inherit that land. Second, it could be considered that Moses took Israel into the Promised Land although God had said Moses would not enter. Without question, the territories belonging to the kings of Heshbon and Bashan[2] were located on the other side of the Jordan. But the loving God we know has a thousand ways to help us without contradiction to His Word. His directives to Moses were clear and concise: "I have given into thine hand Sihon the Amorite king of Heshbon, and his land: begin to possess it, and contend with him in battle."[3] A similar message was given concerning King Og.[4] The destruction was complete.[5] The nations had opposed God's will. Like the antediluvian world, they made God to have had regrets concerning the creation of man and a saddened heart.[6] Had Israel inhaled the sulfuric fumes from the morally bankrupt religious atmosphere that surrounded them, it would have spiritually suffocated them. By then God's grace and tolerance had come to an end. He authorized the destruction.

Throughout the Old Testament especially, we observe a lot of sorrow, devastation, and destruction of multitudes of people and property as demanded by God. Be ever so careful not to question God's actions, the authenticity of the Bible, or its inspiration. If the reading of all these wars taxes, disturbs, perplexes, and annoys, if you feel like running away from those encounters or yielding to doubt and unbelief, hold on. Take another good look. Have you read Deuteronomy 29:29? Read it again.

When we discuss the battles at Jahaz and Edrei, you will see they were two conflicts of total extermination required by God and with good reasons. Don't forget that,

> The secret things belong unto the LORD our God: but those things which are revealed belong unto us and to our children for ever, that we may do all the words of this law.[7]

Without question the ordered death of men, women, children, animals, and property is like a high mountain to scale in the Christian walk. But when we cannot explain or understand God's ways which are past finding out, the saner senses must quickly allow God to be God. Even when a matter has been carefully reasoned out and concluded, and the findings are right, and those right conclusions are on God's side, still there are acts of the infinite God that will never be clearly understood. But some day in glory God will unfold what were His sacred designs. Now we see only through a glass[8] that is so deeply tinted it is impenetrable.

However, until that day comes it will be helpful to catch an angel's attitude:

> In the year that King Uzziah died I saw the Lord sitting upon a throne, high and lifted up, and His train filled the temple. Above it stood the seraphims: each one had six wings; with twain he covered his face, and with twain he covered his feet, and with twain he did fly.[9]

Seraphims with 20/20, clear, piercing, strong heavenly vision do not presume to pierce the glory of God. Two wings cover the face. They are content to know that God does all things well and right. They do His bidding irrespective of its nature. If they can and do trust and obey Him unquestioningly, then with humility of heart, mortals should bow and believe. Although one's sensibilities are shocked beyond description due to what is read and cannot be fathomed, the best posture to take is "Just and true are Thy ways, Thou King of saints."[10]

God is the sovereign Judge of the entire universe. Consequently, in all places and under all circumstances, God will make perfect and appropriate judgments and punishments. It is God alone, and none other, who sees the intricate bearings of all that transpires, the sins of nations, and what continued existence as a people would mean. His permissive will or direct involvement has righteousness attached.

There have been a number of wars in our crumbling world. Two world wars, the Viet Nam war, the Korean conflict, the Civil War, the Gulf War, war on terrorism, wars in places like Bosnia, Africa, Ireland, Palestine, and all over the globe. It appears that at one time or another, nations have resorted to settling their affairs, their differences, disputes, or disagreements by violence. A careful scrutiny of all wars reveals selfishness as the prime cause. However, God has a separate motivation. In all the recorded conflicts He had specific reasons. While we will never fully comprehend the reasons why God fights or permits disaster, a thorough view of His commands will increase our faith and trust, and will help us acknowledge that God's ways are right.

THE COVENANT

God made a covenant with Abraham. A review of that covenant will make it clear whether war was warrantable or not. The battles involving Kings Sihon and Og involved the covenant. They will be central to that understanding, and used as examples as to why God acted as He did. Those two pivotal conflicts at Jahaz and Edrei directly involved the covenant relationship God had with His children:

> And He said unto Abram, Know of a surety that thy seed shall be a stranger in a land that is not theirs, and shall serve them; and they shall afflict them four hundred years; And also that nation, whom they shall serve, will I judge: and afterward shall they come out with great substance. And thou shalt go to thy fathers in peace; thou shalt be buried in a good old age. *But in the fourth generation they shall come hither again: for the iniquity of the Amorites is not yet full.* And it came to pass, that, when the sun went down, and it was dark, behold a smoking furnace, and a burning lamp that passed between those pieces. In the same day *the LORD made a* covenant *with Abram*, saying, Unto thy seed have I given this land, from the river of Egypt unto the great river, the river Euphrates:[11]

Territory in this covenant was important. Abraham's seed was given the land from the river of Egypt to the River Euphrates. The geographical area called the Promised Land was God's gift. However, not until the days of David and Solomon were those borders realized. The Mediterranean shore was the western border and Egypt the southern border of Solomon's realm. His father David, by force of arms, defeated the nations that occupied those lands. Solomon, his wise son maintained peace during his reign by good administration, government, and policy.[12] God fulfilled the covenant.

Since a covenant was made, we ought to consider the agreements reached in the contract. It was not a covenant between equals. It was not a covenant drawn up after serious negotiations. God alone drew up a document which Israel did not have to sign and then have notarized. It was all God's doing. He is a God of righteousness, truth, justice, and mercy. We give Him glory for sensing our need even before we recognized that a Promised Land was necessary.

A covenant is a binding and solemn contract between two persons. The covenant was between God and the seed of Abraham. Yet, God need not sign the document. Why not? God never changes. He is not a man that He should lie. He does not alter the things He has said.[13] The dependability of God need not be ratified. The covenant will be ratified if men will have faith as did Abraham, who believed what God said and it was counted to him for righteousness; who went out at God's command, not knowing where he was going;[14] and if they will be obedient to God as Abraham was. A covenant and God does not sign on? God the Covenanter does not sign the document? Great mystery isn't it?

Thus far we have not considered all the matters concerning this covenant and we are baffled. How does a document requiring two signatures receive only one? Can you imagine the great God and finite man in contract? What it is and how it is being fulfilled we do not know. This simply calls for a faith in a divine plan and a reverent submission to the Almighty whose ways we cannot comprehend. It calls for an explicit submission to the Majesty of heaven and earth, and an absolute trust in all the methods of His providence in His dealings with us, the children of men. When we wade into the doings of the Most High, as we are attempting to do here, when we fail to find an adequate expression of our innermost feelings, we can only declare, "Oh, the depth and richness of the unsearchable wisdom and knowledge of God! How far beyond our human understanding are His gracious decisions and His ways of carrying them out!"[15]

To be in a covenant relationship is to embark upon a transaction with a God who cannot fail, who is omnipotent, who will assist the other side in the contractual agreement to be eminently successful and the recipient of every proffered blessing. His ways are inexplicable and His greatness beyond our reach.

Moses knew the covenant promises made to Abraham. He cherished the thought of leading Israel into the Promised Land. His study of the history of God's people led him to believe that the fruition of those promises would be fulfilled in his day. He spoke of the activity of God in the fulfillment of the covenant to Abraham, and the stipulations that ought to be heeded.

> When the LORD thy God shall bring thee into the land whither thou goest to possess it, and hath cast out many nations before thee, the Hittites, and the Girgashites, and the Amorites, and the Canaanites, and the Perizzites, and the Hivites, and the Jebusites, seven nations greater and mightier than thou; And when the LORD thy God shall deliver them before thee; thou shalt smite them, and utterly destroy them; thou shalt make no covenant with them, nor shew mercy unto them: Neither shalt thou make marriages with them; thy daughter shalt thou not give unto his son, nor his daughter shalt thou take unto thy son. For they will turn away thy son from following me, that they may serve other gods: so will the anger of the LORD be kindled against you, and destroy thee suddenly. But thus shall ye deal with them; ye shall destroy their altars, and break down their images, and cut down their groves, and burn their graven images with fire. For thou art an holy people unto the LORD thy God: The LORD thy God hath chosen thee to be a special people unto himself, above all people that are upon the face of the earth. The LORD did not set his love upon you, nor choose you, because ye were more in number than any people; for ye were the fewest of all people: But because the LORD loved you, and because he would keep the oath which he had sworn unto your fathers, hath the LORD brought you out with a mighty hand, and redeemed you out of the house of bondmen, from the hand of Pharaoh king of Egypt. Know therefore that the LORD

thy God, he is God, the faithful God, which keepeth covenant and mercy with them that love him and keep his commandments to a thousand generations;[16]

God keeps His covenant forever with those who enter into a covenant relationship with Him. He invited Israel to do likewise. The directives were clear.

Thou shalt make no covenant with them, nor with their gods. They shall not dwell in thy land, lest they make thee sin against me: for if thou serve their gods, it will surely be a snare unto thee.[17]

Take heed to thyself, lest thou make a covenant with the inhabitants of the land whither thou goest, lest it be a snare in the midst of thee: But destroy their altars, break their images, and cut down their groves: For thou shalt worship no other god: for the LORD, whose name is Jealous, is a jealous God: Lest thou make a covenant with the inhabitants of the land, and they go a whoring after their gods, and do sacrifice unto their gods, and one call thee, and thou eat of his sacrifice; And thou take of their daughters unto thy sons, and their daughters go a whoring after their gods, and make thy sons go a whoring after their gods.[18]

If ambiguities existed, then certainly questions were in order. How could they miss it?

Unto thy seed have I given this land.[19]

And I will set thy bounds from the Red Sea even unto the sea of the Philistines, and from the desert unto the river: for I will deliver the inhabitants of the land into your hand; and thou shalt drive them out before thee.[20]

I will drive out before thee...[21]

...thou shalt smite them, and utterly destroy them; thou shalt make no covenant with them, nor
shew mercy unto them:[22]

...you are not to allow any of them to live... and do not show mercy to them.[23]

Then you must destroy them totally... and show them no mercy.[24]

God's instructions called for the children of Israel to totally an-
nihilate those greater, more powerful, more savage and more warlike
nations. The language of the covenant left no question as to what the
conduct of the people ought to be. God demanded that the people be
completely eradicated from the land they must occupy. It must have
been frightening. Every man, woman, and child—even babies—must
be killed. Destroy everything. If they plead and entreat you, have no
mercy on them. Make your heart like steel and your ears as pitiless brass.
Get ready for the battle. I will be with you. If the heart begins to feel a
sense of compassion, do not yield to its weakening feeling.

Remember, *do not forget*, that when the choice is between anything,
anyone and God, duty demands that God's voice, His covenant, be
obeyed promptly and without reservation, and with exactness. Had
God not made these demands upon Israel they would appear savage and
brutal. But all of the stern interdictions emanated from a heart of love
that had waited and waited for a chance to do otherwise.

Should you take a long look at Genesis 15:16, you will see a God
you've never seen before and your admiration of and for Him will grow
with each passing moment.

But in the fourth generation they shall come hither again: *for the
iniquity of the Amorite is not yet full*.[25]

God waited four hundred years for the people who occupied the
Promised Land to get it together. Before He drove them out they enjoyed the grace everyone is afforded. Had they accepted God, given
their hearts to Him, knowing how compassionate He is, they would
have been saved. He would have found another way and yet maintained
the covenant provisions. But the doors of probation finally closed on
them. Their day of grace had its limits. The land beneath them could
no longer carry the weight of their crimes. The nameless and shameless
wickedness we will view was revolting.

There were a few obstacles that stood in the path of the fulfillment
of the covenant: Abraham and Sarah were childless and beyond child-
bearing years (so they thought); Esau and Jacob had a feud; Jacob was
compelled to take flight from home; and the treacherous act of Joseph's

brothers who sold him into slavery and then lied to conceal their deeds. Joseph was falsely accused and imprisoned in Egypt. Jacob was given prime property in Goshen and encouraged to settle there. Israel had a peaceful existence in Egypt until fear struck Pharaoh's heart because the Israelites multiplied in the land. Then they passed through the furnace of affliction which included hard labor, for they had to make bricks without straw. Then God, true to His covenanted word, brought them out of Egypt with a mighty hand and an outstretched arm. He took them through the Red Sea on dry ground and into the wilderness. They had a pillar of cloud by day and a pillar of fire at night. Mark the rebellion and the ingratitude. Examine the patience of God with a nation so few in number. He shed His love upon them and would not let them go.

While all that was transpiring, the four hundred years from Abraham to the release of Israel out of Egyptian captivity and those forty years of wilderness wanderings, God granted more time to the Canaanites to get right with Him. "For the iniquity of the Amorite is not yet full," He said. In the meantime, God had Israel waiting for the fulfillment of the covenant. During the entire time He worked miracles to demonstrate His love and that He would keep His promise. That is a portrait of a loving God. He was merciful to the Canaanites then, and He is to us today.

THE PROMISED LAND

What was God protecting Israel from when He demanded total destruction? Although the Promised Land was a land flowing with milk and honey, a beautiful land, a fruitful land, God's choosing was far from desirable in other features. A survey of that territory yields some disquieting things.

> The Ugaritic epic literature has helped to reveal the depth of depravity which characterized Canaanite religion. Being a polytheism of an extremely debased type, Canaanite cultic practice was barbarous and thoroughly licentious... The brutality, lust and abandon of Canaanite mythology is far worse than elsewhere in the Near East at the time. And the astounding characteristic of Canaanite deities, that they had no moral character whatever, must have brought out the worst traits in their devotees and entailed many of the most demoralizing

practices of the time, such as sacred prostitution, child sacrifice and snake worship....

So vile had the practice of the Canaanites become that the land was said to "vomit out its inhabitants" (Lev. 18:25) and the Israelites were warned by Yahweh to keep all His statutes and ordinances "that the land," in which He was about to bring them to dwell, "vomit" them not out (Lev. 20:22). In the case of the Canaanites, instead of using the forces of nature to effect His punitive ends, He employed the Israelites as the ministers of His justice.[26]

The land of Canaan comprised the whole country west of the Jordan. Its southern border ran from Gaza to the Dead Sea (Gen. 10:19), and the eastern border was formed by the river Jordan (see Num. 32:32; 33:51; etc.).

It is not known when the Canaanites moved into Palestine, but they formed the indigenous population of that country in Abraham's time (Gen.12:6). They were in possession of the largest and strongest cities in the country until dispossessed by the Israelites toward the end of the second millennium BC.

The idolatrous religious rites were connected with gross immorality, and centered around a worship of the fertility of man, flocks and herds, and the land. The sacrificial system was similar to that of the Hebrews, but besides clean animals, unclean beasts and sometimes human beings, especially children, were offered on altars. Their nature cults seemed to have a great attraction for the Israelites and were therefore widely adopted by both Israel and Judah. For a time the Canaanite Baal rivaled Yahweh."[27]

> It is without sound theological basis to question God's justice in ordering the extermination of such a depraved people or to deny Israel's integrity as God's people in carrying out the divine order...[28]

We have summoned a few facts for us to have a better picture of what we are dealing with in terms of conduct. But God forbid that those facts will be anything less than an endorsement of what God had said. Our faith in God must allow us to accept whatever He does as right, and fair, and just, and good.

God has demonstrated His long-suffering nature repeatedly so that we will never view Him as a vengeful God. For one hundred twenty years He tolerated the antediluvians. In mercy He has delayed His coming to afford as many as possible an opportunity to accept Jesus Christ as Lord. Like our world, the Canaanites' cups of justice deferred were running over. It is apparent from biblical and extra-biblical literature that the Canaanites had stooped so low, had become so debased that God could no longer retain or tolerate them on the earth.

WHY THE PROMISED LAND

Israel's deliverance out of Egyptian bondage and servitude was infinitely about more than to get away from the lash; that boy babies would not be thrown into the River Nile; that they got to execute judgment on the enemies of God; yes, it was that but much more, more than freedom. God wanted them to go and to worship Him. He intended that through His intimate, personal relationship with His people, His gracious dealings, the knowledge of Him, His grace, forbearance and love would have covered the earth as the waters cover the seas.

It was common knowledge throughout the world that the horde of slaves, fresh out of Egypt, delivered by an outstretched arm, had as their principal leader the great I AM. The death of the first born of man and beast in Egypt, and the miraculous crossing of the Red Sea on dry ground were noised around. While they wandered in the wilderness for those forty years, it was not the world's best secret of God's personal intervention. If Rahab on Jericho's wall knew and heard about what happened to Sihon and Og,[29] then surely others were privy to that information. The news should have melted hearts and made converts. They heard that Israel was fed with manna from heaven, God's provision for forty long years. Water came gushing out of rocks to quench their thirst. God opened streams in the desert. A pillar of cloud sheltered them during the day from the sweltering heat of the sun and at night a pillar of fire provided heat and light. They had an organization and management administration without equal to direct the affairs of all the people with equity and justice. The sacrificial system was celebrated morning and evening, and throughout their journey, kept fresh in their minds the redemptive plan of Christ, the Lamb of God who would take away the sin of the world, an act done from earth's foundation.

What a magnificent God! He met their every need. Neither their shoes nor clothes showed signs of wear over a span of forty years. Sickness and disease never invaded the camp. No HMO's, hospitals, or clinics were established within those sacred precincts, for God healed all their diseases. They had the splendor of His glorious presence, the covenants, and His holy, immutable law. They came from a patriarchal lineage, and had the promise not only of land but the Messiah through their seed. Daily, God manifested His sovereignty, His fatherly care, and new mercies.

After forty years beyond the allotted four hundred years, the surrounding nations should have confessed by observation that Israel's God is the true God. God had designed that Israel would be the light of the world. Their strategic positioning and their geographical location were for theological reasons. The nations of earth would see and hear of the character and love of God, the King of kings. Every lamb offered would show the one and only sacrifice for sin.

> Although the Amorites were idolaters, whose lives were justly forfeited by their great wickedness, God spared them four hundred years to give them unmistakable evidence that He was the only true God, the Maker of heaven and earth. All His wonders in bringing Israel from Egypt were known to them. Sufficient evidence was given; they might have known the truth, had they been willing to turn from their idolatry and licentiousness. But they rejected the light, and clung to their idols.[30]

Instead of asking the way to salvation, instead of acting like the Ninevites, instead of humbling their hearts, instead of discarding their idols, instead of seeking ways to accept Him, knowing that the mighty God was leading Israel and that eventually the inhabitants of Canaan would be destroyed, they immersed themselves deeper in their idolatry and sinful practices.

What happened, you ask? Like the antediluvians, the stench of their wickedness rose to the highest heavens. They became despicable and abominable in the sight of God. In mercy to them He would destroy them, for they had well-nigh obliterated every semblance of the divine. Furthermore, their lives would contaminate those with whom they came in contact, and in love He removed them from the face of the earth. God would protect Israel, steer them away, and they should scrupulously avoid any contact as He had commanded. God knew that the evil consequences caused by association would have been inestimable. Therefore, God told Israel to confidently, promptly, unquestioningly obey.

> Victories are not gained by ceremonies or display but by simple obedience to the Highest General, the Lord God of heaven. He who trusts in this Leader will never know defeat. Obedience to God is liberty from the thralldom of sin, deliverance from human passion and impulse.[31]

The covenant made with Abraham over four hundred years previously would be ratified by a simple act of Israel's will to do what God required. They would get to the Promised Land, the goodly land, the land flowing with milk and honey; the Canaanites would be dispossessed as assured by God; life would be peaches and cream; heaven would be pleased and earth would rejoice. I guess the simplicity of that procedure escaped Israel then and the "Israel of God"[32] today. All that God required then and now is obedience. It eluded them then. May it not elude us today.

THE BATTLES AT JAHAZ AND EDREI

In the battles at Jahaz and Edrei we see the operation of God toward those who go beyond His will, and the care and protection afforded His people.

"These nations on the borders of Canaan would have been spared, had they not stood, in defiance of God's word, to oppose the progress of Israel."[33]

They might have become worshippers of the true and living God. Their peoples might have had the joy of being the first converts to Judaism. The record reveals otherwise. The news out of Heshbon and Bashan, although contrary to a story of conversion, had its impact. God was glorified.

Thirty-eight years had passed since Israel left Kadeshbarnea. All who God said would never enter the Promised Land died in the wilderness. God keeps His word as solemnly as this fact is.

> Now rise up, said I, and get you over the brook Zered. And we went over the brook Zered. And the space in which we came from Kadesh-barnea, until we were come over the brook Zered, was thirty and eight years; until all the generation of the men of war were wasted out from among the host, as the LORD sware unto us. For indeed the hand of the LORD was against them, to destroy them from among the host, until they were consumed.[34]

As Israel began their northerly journey to their final destination, travel restrictions were rehearsed. They were instructed to leave the Moabites and the Ammonites alone.

> That the LORD spake unto me, saying, Thou art to pass through Ar, the coast of Moab, this day: and when thou comest nigh over against the children of Ammon, distress them not, nor meddle with them: for I will not give thee of the land of the children of Ammon any possession; because I have given it unto the children of Lot for a possession.[35]

God knows how to chart a course of action, and gave specific details regarding every mission He authorized:

> Rise ye up, take your journey, and pass over the river Arnon: behold, I have given into thine hand Sihon the Amorite, king of Heshbon, and his land: begin to possess it, and contend with him in battle. This day will I begin to put the dread of thee and fear of thee upon the nations that are under the whole heaven, who shall hear report of thee, and shall tremble, and be in anguish of thee.[36]

Israel will be unrivalled. God gave them the opportunity to possess all the land under heaven. The territory over which King Sihon ruled was not in the original promise to Abraham. But watch this. We must remember that Moses' act of striking the rock had barred him from the Promised Land. However, God called upon him to take possession of this piece of real estate. Therefore, this can only be considered as extra domain. Better than that however, since after the conquest of two Amorite kings, two and one half of the tribes of Israel would request that portion as their inheritance, would not go over Jordan with the other tribes, and were granted permission to do so, I like to feel that God permitted Moses to have a foretaste of what awaited the children as they traveled to their final destination. Granted, this might be far-fetched, but when I think of how long-suffering, and good and patient our God is, I conclude that He gave His servant Moses a glimpse of the victories that awaited Israel. He helped him to see that He would fight for them and how the conquest would be carried out.

Rahab's testimony in Joshua 2:8–11, given before the defeat of Jericho, confirmed the fact that "the dread and fear of Israel would be upon the nations."[37] One can readily see from Deuteronomy 2:25 that God had indeed accomplished what He said about Israel's impact upon the people.

Moses made a simple, civil, reasonable request of King Sihon. Nothing would have happened to him and his people had he followed and agreed with the request Moses made. Having ruled in Egypt, I believe that all the courtesies and matters of protocol known to Moses, because he served in high places, accompanied the petition.

When the Amorite king refused this courteous solicitation, and defiantly gathered his hosts for battle, their cup of iniquity was full, and God would now exercise His power for their overthrow.[38]

All Moses wanted was permission to pass through his territory on the way to Canaan. It was the only way they could reach their destination. Moses pledged that in the event anything was disturbed, full and prompt payment would be forthcoming. Intentionality marked their travel pattern. They would not turn to the right or the left. Moses said, "We are on a direct course and I want to assure you we will not bother or destroy anything belonging to you and your people." Sihon said, "NO!" There was not even a window of discussion opened.

It is strange how the human mind can suffer from serious lapses, conveniently:

For Heshbon was the city of Sihon the king of the Amorites, who had fought against the former king of Moab, and taken all his land out of his hand, even unto Arnon.[39]

Sihon and his people lived on land confiscated from the Moabites. If he had forgotten, and he could have, this fact he should have recalled with a certain promptitude. The Israelites and the Moabites were blood relatives. For someone to occupy confiscated land, land that belonged to family members, the least he could have done was to respond fairly and reasonably to a civil request.

Sihon wallowed in his pride. Inebriated with power, he concluded that he was strong enough to wipe out the oncoming Israelites. So arrogant was Sihon, his selfishness blurred his vision. He overlooked the mighty God who would fight for Israel. In a little while God would give him and his people and all they possessed into the hands of the Israelites. He did not even live long enough to see the rights he denied triumph. Sihon and his army came out to fight against Israel. He underestimated Israel's God. His choice became his fate. God stepped in and ended his choice. The line he crossed was it. He was held in tungsten steel shackles of doom. Heshbon's destiny rested in the hands of its king alone, and he was witless, stupid, ignorant, and crazy enough to fight against the almighty, all-powerful God who said, "Vengeance is mine."[40]

> Then Sihon came out against us, he and all his people, to fight at Jahaz. And the LORD our God delivered him before us; and we smote him, and his sons, and all his people. And we took all his cities at that time, and utterly destroyed the men, and the women, and the little ones, of every city, we left none to remain: Only the cattle we took for a prey unto ourselves and the spoil of the cities which we took. From Aroer, which is by the brink of the river of Arnon, and from the city that is by the river, even unto Gilead, there was not one city too strong for us: the LORD our God delivered all unto us.[41]

Not a word of Israel's prowess underlined this battle. God delivered them into their hands. Sihon, his sons, and all his people were killed;

nothing remained. Deuteronomy 2:34 says, "utterly destroyed." From one end of his kingdom to the other there was only rubble. It was a war of complete extermination. In matters that pertain to God, victory will never go to the opposition. Ask King Sihon of Heshbon. He will tell you that he was completely wiped out. He never lived to tell the tale. He was gone, irretrievably gone.

THE BATTLE AT EDREI

You have heard the adage that "discretion is the better part of valor." It seems to me from where I stand, King Og did not exercise good judgment. In doing a background check on him, it is mentioned that he was a remnant of the Rephaims or giants, apparently greater than King Sihon. He had sixty cities in the region of Argob built of blackstone, hard as iron and perched amidst the masses of basaltic rock over which he ruled.[42]

Like Belshazzar in Babylon who felt that the massive walls were impregnable, King Og felt that his sixty cities built of black stones hard as iron could not be taken by force, and especially not by the wandering stragglers called the Israelites. A sense of false security took hold of him. He followed in Sihon's path.

> Then we turned, and went up the way to Bashan: and Og the king of Bashan came out against us, he and all his people, to battle at Edrei.[43]

King Og employed absolutely no strategy in this conflict. Confident of his victory over Israel, everyone came out to do battle. The battle at Edrei was quick, sudden, decisive, complete, overwhelming, and amazing. Like the battle with King Sihon at Jahaz, all the people were destroyed and the cities taken. Those cities became Israel's property. The inhabitants were destroyed. The seemingly impregnable walls and gates of Bashan crumbled and fell. The great God who made the men that made the walls and gates destroyed them both. Not Israel, but Israel's God.

Israel's confidence in God could not now be measured. New courage must have sprung up in their hearts. No song or refrain like the one composed by Miriam, Moses' sister, after Israel crossed the Red Sea is recorded, but something tells me that praise ascended to Yahweh. This song wafted in the air, "And He did it again." Two kings and their peoples were killed and the cities taken. Times of success can turn the eye and heart away from God. Moses would allow no feeling of self-important bearing to rear its ugly head, so he quickly reminded Israel,

> So the LORD our God delivered into our hands Og also, the king of Bashan, and all his people: and we smote them until none was left to him remaining. And we took all his cities at that time, there was not a city that we took not from them, threescore cities, all the region of Argob, the kingdom of Og in Bashan. All these cities were fenced with high walls, gates, and bars; beside unwalled towns a great many. And we utterly destroyed them, as we did unto Sihon king of Heshbon, utterly destroying the men, women, and children, of every city. But all the cattle, and the spoil of the cities, we took for a prey to ourselves.[44]

Moses recalled how his secret failure of faith when he did not thoroughly rely on God's faithfulness and power at the crag in Kadesh had severe consequences. The price he paid for not giving all the glory to God was exclusion from entry into the Promised Land.[45] Self can emerge without a moment's notice. The creature then attempts to upstage the Creator. Moses would have no part in any such reckoning. Listen to his conclusion. "The LORD our God delivered into our hands Og also."[46] He rightly attributed all the glory to God.

As we ponder all the facts surrounding these two battles, we cannot but ask, why would Moses not have a day where everything came up roses? We can understand life in the wilderness wanderings where the children of Israel doubted and complained morning, noon, and night. But here they had gotten rid of the skeptics and doubters. They were homeward bound as God commanded. Why were Israel's travel plans obstructed by Sihon and Og? Why, when God's commands were explicitly followed? Will there ever be smooth sailing?

CONCLUSION

Even when doing good, noble Christian deeds and duties, the life and heart are aggressively opposed and tried,

> Against every subtle influence that seeks entrance by means of flattering inducements from the enemies of truth, God's people must strictly guard. They are pilgrims and strangers in this world, traveling a path beset with danger. To the ingenious subterfuges and alluring inducements held out to tempt from allegiance, they must give no heed.[47]

The Scriptures tell us that Jesus the Christ "went about doing good,"[48] but as long as He sojourned on earth, never a day came in which He was not pressed down by the devil or some of his agents. Even in the house of worship the Jewish leaders plotted to kill Him.[49] Yes, in the church! And if He, God's only begotten Son, were subjected to such trials and abuses, His followers will not escape.

The struggles are varied. As we go or prepare to go to the house of God, there are the subtle temptations, the suggestions and hindrances to a holy life. In the church all sorts of promptings come. They are suggestions of the evil one. "Give only a portion of your tithe and offerings or none at all." "Criticize those of like faith." "Find fault with the worship experience." "Engage in conversations unworthy of the place and time." "Reject God's appeal to a holier life." All kinds of temptations burden the heart and conscience. But God has promised to deliver. The "Sihons and Ogs" are no match for God who will do battle for us, and cause us to be victorious. As long as life lasts, we will be engaged in one battle or another,

> For we wrestle not against flesh and blood, but against principalities, against powers, against the rulers of the darkness of this world, against spiritual wickedness in high places.[50]

We are called upon to:

> Fight the good fight of faith, lay hold on eternal life...[51]

The struggles are evident not only in or on the way to God's house. They are on the job, at home, in the car. Have you ever heard of road rage? Temptations are everywhere. That is precisely why the invitation is to put on not some, *but the whole armor of God.*

Jesus, after fasting and praying for forty days and nights, and when His physical energies waned, confronted and battled the greatest temptations, but He won. Satan's attacks are made on the weakest point of the character. That is when the tempter comes. His fiery darts are aimed at weaknesses not strengths. The trials will come in like the bad news that came to Job, one after the other. They will come from and be inflicted by friends and family, from members of the household of faith; just after baptism and the heart has pledged its allegiance to the Father, Son, and Holy Spirit; immediately after promises to serve God faithfully have been made. They will come after triumphant Red Sea crossing experiences. Then, soon after crossing the Red Sea and there is no water, no obvious escape from a dilemma, faith wilts, courage dims, doubt swallows trust, even while the miracle is still visible. During and after going around in circles for years, and at long last God has blessed, self rears its ugly head to take the credit and eliminates God. It is as if He never existed when life gets good. Some will be skirmishes, some wholesale war as with Sihon and Og. Some we will have fought before and others will be new. The encounters will be with the giants like the sons of Anak, not dwarfs. The giants have to be killed and all that pertains to them. Kill them in the wilderness or wherever they are found. Doubt, fear, self, hate, anger, covetousness—kill them. The instruction from God still is: destroy everything, and make sure it is dead.

The path to Canaan must remain unimpeded. When attempts are made to get out of the wilderness to enter the Promised Land, the walls of your situations, made out of black stones hard as iron, as found in Bashan, will present obstacles that seem impassable. But God will fight to grant deliverance. The orders must be obeyed. Break down every wall. Destroy man and beast. Do not wound them, for who knows if in one unguarded moment, one giant that you presumed dead rises to destroy you. If your right hand, left hand, one or both eyes, ears, or feet—whatever it is that would cause you to deviate from strict obedience to God—surfaces, kill it, cut it off, get rid of it. God's words to the travelers bound for the Promised Land then are still relevant today. Destroy every impediment. Why? Because God knows that all which is needed to forfeit the kingdom of heaven is one giant, one dwarf, one spot, one mistake, one wrinkle, just one thing.

Diligence is recommended:

> Let us lay aside every weight, and the sin which doth so easily beset us, and let us run with patience the race that is set before us, Looking unto Jesus the author and finisher of our faith;...[52]

Victory is promised at the start as well as at the end. The same God who delivered Sihon and Og into Moses' and Israel's hands will ensure safe passage for us into His eternal abode.

The battles at Jahaz and Edrei clarify in part why a loving God sanctioned and even participated in wars that accounted for the terrible destruction of human lives. Apart from the tremendous pastureland territorial acquisition which would be given to Reuben, Gad and the half tribe of Manasseh,[53] the defeat of Heshbon and Bashan created a reservoir from which Israel could draw strength, courage, and faith. It kept faith alive. They saw the fatal error of unbelief exhibited by those who perished in the wilderness. That one mistake had a price tag of forty years of deferred blessings. Moses, when he saw God's deliverance and His direct and personal involvement in the defeat of Sihon and Og, could say to Israel, "I told you so." At the same time he rejoiced, that, while unable to direct the entire conquest, he enjoyed a foretaste.

There are however, spiritual values that transcend the death of the people in Heshbon and Bashan. God had Israel, you, and me, in mind.

"In their conquest of Og and Sihon, the people were brought to the same test beneath which their fathers had so signally failed. But the trial was now far more severe than when God had commanded Israel to go forward. The difficulties in their way had greatly increased since they refused to advance when bidden to do so in the name of the Lord. It is thus that God still tests His people. And if they fail to endure the trial, He brings them again to the same point, and the second time the trial will come closer, and be more severe than the preceding. This is continued until they bear the test, or, if they are still rebellious, God withdraws His light from them, and leaves them in darkness."[54]

There is a God who carries us on His heart. His words of encouragement outweigh every other consideration.

> "This experience has a lesson for us. The mighty God of Israel is our God. In him we may trust, and if we obey his requirements he will work for us in as signal a manner as he did for his ancient people. Every one who seeks to follow the path of duty will be assailed by doubt and unbelief. The way will sometimes be so barred by obstacles, apparently insurmountable, as to dishearten those who will yield to discouragement; but God is saying to such, Go forward. Do your duty at any cost. The difficulties that seem so formidable, that fill your soul with dread, will vanish as you move forward in the path of obedience, humbly trusting in God."[55]

Chapter 2

THE RECIPE FOR VICTORY

(Based on 2 Chronicles 20)

Ticker-tape parades with all the confetti and shredded paper on any city's major thoroughfare, the gold, silver, and bronze medals in the Olympics, and the Oscars in the entertainment world are given or celebrated after an accomplishment or a victory. We have before us an Arabian invasion where a king and over one million soldiers sang a song of victory, like Martin Luther's famous hymn, "A mighty fortress is our God," before the first steps of a ten-mile trek to war were taken.

The mind of Jehoshaphat, Judah's king, was not upon the over one million soldiers in the army, but upon the words communicated to Jahaziel by the Holy Spirit. He told Jehoshaphat, God said, "Be not afraid nor dismayed by reason of this great multitude; for *the battle is not yours, but God's*."[56] "Ye shall not need to fight in this battle: set yourselves, stand ye still, and see the salvation of the Lord with you, O Judah and Jerusalem: fear not, nor be dismayed; to morrow go out against them: for the Lord will be with you."[57] Jehoshaphat believed in God. Immediately the battle became God's. It was His to fight and win. And as the king and his soldiers responded to the attack by the Moabites, Ammonites, and the others,[58] they were undergirded by the sure promises of God's word.

It would be wonderful if we like Judah could always remember that however large the army, however vast the resources, an absolute, unwavering trust must be placed in the marvelous righteousness of God. Jehoshaphat believed and praised God for the glorious victory promised. God told him it would be unnecessary for him to fight in that battle. God claimed it as His fight. Jehoshaphat accepted the declaration by faith, knowing that victory was theirs. His faith laughed at seeming impossibilities of the mission. Then he appointed singers.[59] They should praise the beauty of holiness, and as they joined the army they sang, "Praise the Lord; for His mercy endureth for ever."[60] "And when they began to sing and to praise"[61], God went ahead of them and destroyed their enemies; "none escaped."[62]

Judah went to the battlefield singing, a rather gladsome procession. Call it worship to God. The appointed singers rendered praise to the Lord for His continued mercies. They sang out of personal experiences with God. They created as they journeyed to the battlefield a temple without walls. The soldiers were able to identify with songs sung by the Levities. As a result, the division of soldiers and singers disappeared. It immediately became a worship service. The minds of the singers and soldiers were focused on God, His might, His love, His goodness, His care, His protection, His provision, His promises, His presence, His performance, and His providence. They recalled Asaph's words, "Whoso offereth praise glorifieth me: and to him that ordereth his conversation aright will I shew the salvation of God."[63] The battle, the overwhelming odds, the vicissitudes of life, the oncoming armies, all allowed by God were lost sight of in glorious adoration. They focused on God. He was central. Adoration and thanksgiving ascended. They had none like it in Israel before and God heard every voice. His eyes saw every worshipper and looked at each heart. Can you imagine how transcendent that must have been? Can you hear those voices trained for worship in the temple, in robust harmony, joined by angels, singing, "Praise the Lord; for His mercy endureth forever?" They achieved victory because of their faith and worship.

If every facet of this event could be grasped by all of God's children, we would be supremely blessed and courageous in all our conflicts. Just to stand still and see the salvation of God were the requirements. Armed with the shield of faith, unquestioning trust, and total belief in God, king and people marched to meet the enemy with tuneful lips.

Their faith in His word defeated every foe. Victory promised was victory delivered. And if we will only believe that Christ has already won our battles, we too, if focused on Him, can go forward each day in the strength of that victory, assured that we are more than conquerors, because the battle is His.

Was it the music that stirred the heart of God? God commissioned them to go into battle and then granted victory without a single engagement. Not a single soldier killed anyone. Is that the same operation of God in our lives today? Is our responsibility only to stand still and see, in this the twenty-first century? Has God altered the procedures in any degree? Is the battle still the Lord's?

We will review this battle and its principal characters, Jehoshaphat and Judah, to see God's transactions in the life and work of His children who lived in days gone by. We will seek to ascertain whether His methods have changed and answer the questions posed.

Judah's fourth king, Jehoshaphat, ruled for about twenty-five years (872 BC–848 BC); during which time he and his people were the benefactors of God's blessings. He died at sixty years of age, a glaring proof that the promise of long life is not to be considered a reward for piety, good deeds, great leadership, noble endeavor, or dedicated service. The promised time is three score and ten years.[64] Long life therefore is not a payoff, nor is it intended to be such. There is reason to believe that he was a coregent with his father Asa who reigned for forty-one years. Asa was diseased in his feet and apparently Jehoshaphat performed some of the regal duties in the absence of his incapacitated father. Probably that worked to Jehoshaphat's advantage, for Asa might have trained him to be his successor. Jehoram, Jehoshaphat's son, also reigned with his father, although under different circumstances.[65] Jehoshaphat was the sole ruler for about seventeen years. It is true, in light of the total picture painted of him, that he did have an appreciation for spiritual values. The testimony of Scripture is "He followed the example of his father Asa and did what was right in the eyes of the Lord and didn't deviate from it."[66]

Many Christians fail to find in the Christianity they get from their parents a source of power for their own lives. Jehoshaphat went as far as he could in right doing. However, "Jehu the seer, son of Hanani, went out to meet him and said to the king, 'Should you help the wicked and love those who hate the Lord? Because of this, the wrath of the Lord is upon you. There is, however, some good in you, for you have rid the land of the Asherah poles and have set your heart on seeking God.'"[67] Jehu rendered the criticism because of Jehoshaphat's actions when he supported the wicked king Ahab. The acknowledgment of Jehu that there is some good in the worst of us and some bad in the best of us is a sobering thought. However, God is in search of the good He places within us. There is no question He finds ways of raising that good to another level…

> …Jehoshaphat like Hezekiah did a tremendous amount of good for Judah. He commissioned the Levites, princes and priests to go throughout the land to teach the people the Law of God. He had judges in all the cities in his kingdom. He requested that the judges do justice to their office, take no bribe, be no respecter of persons, love mercy, do justly, and walk humbly with God in that rather exacting duty. The Judge of the whole earth does right always and the call to duty demanded that they should endeavor to be like Him.[68]

It is marvelous to read how the promises of God were fulfilled in the lives of the children of Judah. When the Levites taught the word of God in the communities, and the people understood the demands of God and the relationship He sought, life became a thing of beauty. In the first of seven beatitudes recorded in Revelation, (the others are found in Revelation 14:3; 16:15; 19:9; 20:6; 22:7, 14) there is announced in chapter one and verse three a special blessing for reading, hearing, and doing what the Word of God pronounces. Judah and Judah's king were supremely blessed as a result of adherence to that promise. Among other things, peace existed between Judah and Israel. The surrounding nations were afraid to attack. In fact, many nations contributed to Jehoshaphat's great wealth and power.[69]

If only there were no *buts* in life. If only life had no faults, errors, regrets, and blunders. If only God's words and promises were adhered to as required, life would be an existence of beauty. But we are made of clay. Yes, the entire frame is so fragile, subject to cracks, flaws, and brokenness. God knows how we were formed. He remembers that the

perfection with which He made us at the start is gone. The broken pieces
have to be placed in His hands over and over again. To have complete
restoration, the clay must be placed in the Potter's hands again, on the
wheels, and into the kiln. The Potter refuses to discard the broken vessel until He makes a vessel of His own design. "So we have nothing in
ourselves of which to boast. We have no ground for self-exaltation. Our
only ground of hope is in the righteousness of Christ imputed to us, and
in that wrought by His Spirit working in and through us."[70]

Jehoshaphat, the great king, was not lame in his feet as his father,
Asa, but had "feet of clay."

> When Jehosaphat became wealthy and highly respected, he made
> a marriage alliance between his son Jehoram and Ahab's daughter
> Athaliah.[71]

The union of a lamb and a tigress is ludicrous. The marriage of those
children of two reigning kings sealed the alliance Jehoshaphat made.
The historical records reveal the undoing of Jehoshaphat's spiritual
reformation due to this alliance.

The unprecedented evils of Jehoram and Athaliah almost extin-
guished the light God had lit during Jehoshphat's good reign. Had it
not been for the covenant God made with David regarding a king from
his lineage on the throne, it never would have happened. Jehoram and
Athaliah attempted to overthrow that covenant-promise. They came
close to its accomplishment, "but God." The marriage of Judah's next
king to the daughter of Israel's king, Ahab, resulted in bloodshed and
unprecedented problems in Judah.

Apparently Jehoshaphat wanted the ties disallowed with Israel un-
broken. He joined Ahab in his attack on the Syrians to regain Ramoth
Gilead from Benhadad. Self conquered his better judgment. During
that war which the prophets said they should not embark upon, Ahab
was killed and Jehoshaphat miraculously saved.[72] Jehoshaphat should
have encouraged Ahab not to go since the prophet Micaiah told Ahab
he would not return alive from the war. If obedient, his end might have
been different. But no, he joined Ahab at his insistence. He could have

spared Ahab's life. He had a great responsibility but he failed. "Good men are not always good and wise men are not always wise."[73]

Jehoshaphat was an integral part of the promise made by God to David. The covenant child was rebuked but not rejected, corrected for his actions but not condemned. God would have the royal line pass through Jehoshaphat and his offspring. Ultimately the Christ child would trace His lineage to David and from the tribe of Judah. Because God made a promise and covenant with David, He protected His word and remained faithful to His promise. Athaliah's scheme and murderous act would have wiped out the lineage of David, but for Joash who survived through God's deliberate intervention in human history.[74]

The words of God's prophets ought to be believed. The word of Micaiah came to pass just as he said.[75] Ahab died in battle. This experience alone should be a lesson to all to have full faith in the Word of God. The knowledge of the false prophets Ahab called should teach the lesson never to suppose that what is pleasant and agreeable is worthy of belief before what is true.

Some interesting facts surfaced during Jehoshaphat's reign. As a result of his alliance and collaboration we see intermarriage, consociation, joint ventures for trade—Israel the dominant partner, and the prophetic rebuke to Judah. Jehoshaphat and Ahab even gave the same name to their children, Jehoram and Ahaziah.

The feature most prominent in Jehoshaphat's life happened during the later years of his reign. However, it must be said of him that the way in which he handled prosperity—and prosperous he was—and adversity was remarkable. His punishment came for helping the wicked and loving those who hated the Lord.[76]

The Moabites, Ammonites, and the Edomites joined forces and invaded Judah from the south. Jehoshaphat did not grow up in a climate of political unrest. During Asa his father's reign Judah enjoyed peace. He knew nothing of terrible conflicts as a coregent, and when the Ethiopians came, he saw how God defeated them in answer to prayer. So Jehoshaphat summoned all Judah to prayer as a nation. While they were yet speaking to God, before they said Amen, God communicated His will to Jahaziel. The heart of the message to His people consisted not only in a dissuasive against fear, the duty of standing still, awaiting the salvation of God, but the cardinal fact was that the battle was not theirs, but God's.[77]

Jehoshaphat had just appointed the judges for fairness and righteousness. Then one day, out of a clear blue sky, the Arabian invasion against him and Judah began, entirely unexpected. But isn't that the way life is? There is very little if any of what is called fair play. This is a dog-eat-dog world. Without a moment's warning nations and individuals are at each other's throat. And oftentimes justifiable reasons cannot be given for the hostility that ensues. The same men who promised to be, and who were considered best friends, on whom they could rely, turn into opponents. Life's aims and purposes are thwarted; the brilliant summer morning becomes a dark and foreboding midnight. The one who should have been an ally becomes the enemy. Life which moved forward so graciously and unsuspectingly comes to a sudden stop. Grave situations arise. But that is life. These were not exceptional happenings in Jehoshaphat's life. Into every life a little rain, and sometimes a lot of rain, even torrential showers will fall. For Jehoshaphat, it was only par for the course. Here is the war.

A great army of Arabian soldiers pitched their camp at Engedi, about twenty-five miles south of Jerusalem. It is a town near the middle of the west shore of the Dead Sea. The Moabites and the Ammonites were east of the Dead Sea. The Edomites, descendants of Esau, were south of it. Judah and the Edomites, whom they were ready to fight, and themselves, were blood relatives. Moab and Ammon were first cousins, the product of incestuous relationships between Lot and his daughters.[78] Abraham and Lot were also related Abraham being Lot's uncle. They were on the doorsteps of Jehoshaphat's kingdom, Judah. Family members became fierce enemies.

Long before this altercation, God had given Moses specific instruction regarding those nations. He was not granted the green light to attack and possibly destroy them when they refused passage to the Israelites. The instructions were clear.

> And command thou the people, saying, Ye are to pass through the coast of your brethren the children of Esau, which dwell in Seir; and they shall be afraid of you: take ye good heed unto yourselves therefore: *Meddle not with them*; for I will not give you their land, no, not so

much as a foot breadth; because I have given mount Seir unto Esau for a possession… And the Lord said unto me, Distress not the Moabites, neither contend with them in battle: for I will not give thee of their land for a possession; because I have given Ar unto the children of Lot for a possession *and when thou comest nigh over against the children of Ammon, distress them not, nor meddle with them: for I will not give thee of the land of Ammon any possession; because I have given it unto the children of Lot for a possession.*[79]

Balak was the king of the Moabites. The same Balak who requested the services of Balaam to curse Israel was the very king who denied passage to Israel on their way to the Promised Land.[80]

You will recall the curses were blessings pronounced, but Israel succumbed to the idolatrous and licentious practices observed by the Moabites. In the divers laws and ordinances given to the children of Israel, God told Moses,

An Ammonite or Moabite shall not enter into the congregation of the Lord; even to their tenth generation shall they not enter into the congregation of the Lord forever: Because they met you not with bread and with water in the way, when ye came forth out of Egypt; and because they hired against thee Balaam; the son of Beor of Mesopotamia, to curse thee. Nevertheless the Lord thy God would not hearken unto Balaam; but the Lord thy God turned the curse into a blessing unto thee, because the Lord thy God loved thee.[81]

The Lord was not content with the line drawn by the Ammonites and the Moabites. Their response to Israel in a time of crisis was out of character. It was unacceptable conduct on the part of anyone, but especially family.

Christ's rule of life, by which every one of us must stand or fall in the judgment, is, "Whatsoever ye would that men should do to you, do ye even so to them Matthew 7:12."[82]

It would do us well before we take an action that we would place ourselves in the position as the recipient of the action we are about to take. Wear that very pair of shoes first. Just feel how it fits. The suggestion of Christ guarantees fewer heartaches, if any at all.

But God is long-suffering. His plan of worldwide inclusion was operative even during the period of the judges in Israel, although ten generations had not passed for the Ammonites and the Moabites. It is not that God had changed, but He operates on so many different levels at the same time it is just interesting to see how He gets His will accomplished. Watch this transaction before we continue the activity of Jehoshaphat. It is a crucial insight into God's doings.

During the time of the Judges, a famine raged through Palestine. Elimelech, a citizen of Bethlehem, had moved to Moab to preserve life. *The marriages of his two sons were to Moabite women, Orpah and Ruth.* After taking up residence and getting involved in the culture, in just a short space of time the three men, father and two sons, died. Naomi, Elimelech's wife and Ruth her daughter-in-law returned to Bethlehem. Through a series of providential occurrences, *Ruth a Moabite became the wife of Boaz an Israelite. Ruth is the ancestress of David, and of course, our loving Lord and Savior, Jesus Christ also.*[83] God used the lineage of *Ruth a Moabite* to show He is no respecter of persons. When Jesus came as our Savior and substitute, John said, "But as many as received Him, to them gave He power to become the sons of God even to them that believe on His name."[84] Furthermore, "God so loved the world, that He gave His only begotten Son that whosoever believeth on Him should not perish, but have everlasting life."[85] God is no respecter of persons. Many individuals from all kindred, tongue, and people will be in the kingdom of God. All who enter will be saved as individuals.

However, the fact that *Ruth, a Moabite*, held such a pivotal position in sacred history was no proof that as nations the Moabites, Ammonites, and Edomites were free to attack and plunder Judah. At no time or on any occasion did God retract from His word concerning those nations.

The news of the oncoming Arabian invasion frightened Jehoshaphat. When the Ammonites, Moabites, and Edomites came to do battle against Jehoshaphat, he had one million, one hundred and sixty thousand mighty men of valor in Jerusalem.

With this colossal army of trained soldiers, it would seem like Jehoshaphat would say to the oncoming forces "bring it on." He could not call upon Ahab, king of Israel. He had died in a previous battle. In the conflict where he was called upon to support King Ahab, he had discovered that "the arm of flesh will fail you, ye dare not trust your own."[86] He decided to seek his God. There were no treaties made. He had a number of options opened to him. Jehoshaphat could have utilized his secret service officers to explore the possibilities of fighting the Syrians. The forecast would have been positive. The advice of the Joint Chief of Staff, the Secretary of Defense, the Secretary of National Security, Secretary for Homeland Defense and the Secretary of War was not sought. He did not summon an emergency meeting with his cabinet. The leaders in the various branches of his government did not submit their ideas. Jehoshaphat did not give ear to a single proposal. He made an appeal to his God. The king and subjects' sole reliance will be on their God. The psalmist said: "God is our refuge and strength, a very present help in trouble."[87]

When trouble comes, and it will, the sole solution is to turn to God. It should be stapled on the mind that, as a nation, as a country, a church, as an individual, God has been our help it ages past and will be our only hope for years to come. Better still, the personal conviction in the heart must be, that in dangers and extremities, God has many ways of deliverance. If so, fear would never, ever become man's lot. Instead of fear there would be a growing confidence and an unshaken faith. "Our heavenly Father has a thousand ways to provide for us, of which we know nothing."[88]

Without contradiction it can be affirmed that when the crises of life come and in prayer and supplication hearts turn to God, help will come from Him. Faithful men and women know no other refuge than God. The act was not only one of faith on the king's part when he called for a national day of prayer, but he pronounced a kingly act.

When the pounding feet of the oncoming soldiers are heard, courage, Christian fortitude, and moral stamina are musts. When overrun with situations too formidable, like the oncoming abominable Ammonites, the mean Moabites, and the eager Edomites, do not give up. Look up! Too often the cry is, "What shall I do?" "Where do I turn?" "To whom do I go?" Too often the cry is accompanied by the wringing of the hands as if orphaned or as if the arm of flesh will grant a solution. Be assured of this—it is a great, grand, and glorious fact that the *only* help, the *only* meaningful help, the *only* source of moral courage is to place unwavering faith, complete trust, and total reliance in the God of the universe. If only this great fact that, "*the battle is the Lord's*" were always readily recalled, mountains of worry and unnecessary concern would never afflict the human heart. Jehoshaphat drew from a river of truth. All may draw; that river will never run dry. There are so many tributaries that run into that majestic river of God's boundless love. Jehoshaphat's struggle with the Arabians proved to be an awesome battle, but there are those truths left on the pathway to the victory over the Ammonites, Moabites, and Edomites. A few of those tributaries clamor for exposure.

Here are the cold facts. Jehoshaphat brought the people together in the temple for a day of fasting and prayer. They came from all over the nation to seek God at the request of their king. He called upon God to grant power and strength for victory in the battle against those who had received special exemptions. They were honored.[89] He enlisted the intervention of God to protect the city and to destroy those who were bold enough to come up against it. They occupied the territory granted them as a part of their share of the Promised Land division. Here is a day, an occasion, an event, a moment worth recording. The whole congregation, all the men of Judah, together with their wives and children were in tears before the Lord and in supplication.[90]

Jehoshaphat, unlike Hezekiah, had no letter to spread before the Lord, but he had a great need. God will take whatever we bring and use it. Ultimately, His name will be glorified. The indefensible attack of those nations made prayer a necessity. The promise is,

> And this is the confidence we have in Him, that, if we ask anything according to His will, He heareth us: And if we know that He hears us, whatsoever we ask, we know that we have the petitions that we desired of Him.[91]

Here is further encouragement as it pertains to prayer,

> Make your requests known to your Maker. Never is one repulsed who comes to Him with a contrite heart. Not one sincere prayer is lost.

Amid the anthems of the celestial choir, God hears the cries of the weakest human being.[92]

Then let us never forget that prayer has,

subdued kingdoms, wrought righteousness, obtained promises, stopped the mouths of lions, quenched the violence of fire... turned to flight the armies of the aliens.[93]

It is really interesting to note that God does not need our advice. There is no fair question that can be posed in all His dealings with the children of men. However, to sense one's limitation is a sign of growth. Jehoshaphat made some awesome admissions. They resound with a sense of humility, confidence, and a deepened trust.

O our God, wilt thou not judge them? For we have no might against this great company that cometh against us: neither know we what to do: but our eyes are upon Thee."[94]

"WE HAVE NO MIGHT"

That statement is absolutely true. Indeed, God opens His hands and satisfies the desires of every living thing. Angels, man, birds, beasts, planet, and plants, yes life, everything and anything one can think of, all depend on God. "For in Him we live and move and have our being."[95] When King Jehoshaphat made the pronouncement "we have no might," he spoke for all creation. It asserts total human frailty, total impotence. We have nothing to offer our loving Lord. Augustus M. Toplady said it best:

Nothing in my hand I bring,
Simply to Thy cross I cling;
Naked, come to Thee for dress,
Helpless, look to Thee for grace;
Foul, I to the fountain fly,
Wash me, Saviour, or I die."[96]

Did Jehoshaphat and the people in one chorus speak truthfully? He had at his command one million, one hundred and sixty thousand trained soldiers. A well-trained army awaited his directions, and yet he reported, "We have no might." With all that military brass and ammunition, mighty men of valor ready to attack, and he makes a confession of no might? A deeper look reveals not only a sign of humility, but also an admission of who is in charge of all of life's undertakings. It is comforting to know that there is available power to make the weakest strong. "My strength is made perfect in weakness"[97] said our Lord to the apostle Paul. A draught from this tributary suggests that the same God who heard Jehoshaphat's confession of no might is still attendant to like calls. He is able to assist the church, His people, or an individual in all the conflicts that arise. However, the same admission of trust, humility, His Lordship, obedience, and a consciousness of total dependence must be evident.

"NEITHER KNOW WE WHAT TO DO"

Here is another admission of Judah's fourth king: "Neither know we what to do." Sometimes we run across individuals with answers for every question and solutions for every problem. They have knowledge of the entire universe. Mr. Fixit All. Jehoshaphat was in a quandary. Where will he turn even after he has called for fasting and prayer? There should be a relationship between God and all His children categorized as special. He delights to have them come with all their weaknesses, utter dependence, and lack of know how. We should acknowledge God's power and might. Praise Him for who He is. We should possess a faith that takes Him at His word.

> Jehoshaphat was a man of courage and valor. For years he had been strengthening his armies and his fortified cities. He was well prepared to meet almost any foe; yet in this crisis he put not his trust in the arm of flesh. Not by disciplined armies and fenced cities, but by a living faith in the God of Israel, could he hope to gain the victory

over these heathen who boasted of their power to humble Judah in the eyes of the nations.[98]

"BUT OUR EYES ARE UPON THEE"

It is wonderful to live a focused life. The issues that demand our attention grow with each passing day. Myriad of impulses have to be addressed daily. Who is in charge? A friend related the experience of a down day recently. He said nothing went right. The day was bleak and very cold. The heater in the grade school malfunctioned. The operations in the day care center were suspended and the children sent home. The problems that day seemed to be legion. The entire grade school and day care center came to a screeching halt. Nothing was going right and nothing could be fixed, it appeared. He happened to walk into one of the now-vacant classrooms, and the teacher had a large sign in the window. It read: "RELAX!! GOD IS IN CHARGE." That is the truth, isn't it?

Like my friend, Jehoshaphat was on the horn of a real dilemma. The Moabites, the Ammonites, and the Edomites were on their way to do battle. He and his people confessed "that they had no might", "neither know we what to do", but "their eyes were on the Lord."

Quite often that is the predicament in which an individual, a nation, a church, an organization, a life finds itself. It is confronted by stalwart emergencies, situations too difficult to analyze or resolve. Listen: "Relax! God is in charge." If you, like Jehoshaphat, have had the Word of God throughout the realm by dutiful scribes, the judges have participated in equity, righteousness, fairness, and good judgment, then, "Relax! God is in charge!" The words of David, words of confidence in God, will articulate the next move. That was precisely how Jehoshaphat moved.

Some trust in chariots, and some in horses: But we will remember the name of the Lord our God.[99]

Jehoshaphat remained focused, his eyes fixed on God, his trust in Him riveted with expectations of God's faithful response. Judah had the will of God rehearsed in their hearing. They were knowledgeable of His requirements, His judgments, His hatred of sin and the severe penalties attached thereto.[100] When they came face to face with the overwhelming situation of doing battle with the Ammonites, the Moabites, and the Edomites, they believed God would hear their plea for help.

Jehoshaphat neither overestimated nor underestimated the situation at hand. Although he had a spiritually and militarily prosperous nation, a mighty nation, he would not rely on past blessings. He turned to his God whose mercies are new every morning. Chariots, horses, military might, and walled cities are good protection, but as his support in a time of crisis… a million times, no. God is our only support always and forever. "Our eyes are upon Thee," 2 Chronicles 20:12, Jehoshaphat said. God will be all and in all. No part of Judah, not its militia, not even the spiritual encounters would be offered as capable, substitution, or supportive in warfare. "Our eyes are upon Thee." God would be everything. He will maintain His rightful place as the omnipotent, omniscient, omnipresent, almighty, sovereign, all sustaining, redeeming, and saving God. God will not be considered a shareholder, no, not even with 99.9% interest. He will not be a contributor or a partner in this conflict. Jehoshaphat announced a great truth when he prayed, "our eyes are upon Thee." It was centuries later that Peter remarked,

> Neither is there salvation in any other: for there is none other name under heaven given among men, whereby we must be saved.[101]

These lines add stature to Jehoshaphat's position.

> God was the strength of Judah in this crisis, and He is the strength of His people today. We are not to trust in princes, or to set men in the place of God. We are to remember that human beings are fallible and erring, and that He who has all power is our strong tower of defense. In every emergency we are to feel that the battle is His. His resources are limitless, and apparent impossibilities will make the victory all the greater.[102]

King Jehoshaphat led his people to declare a confidence in God that he himself possessed. His relationship with his God was good for Judah then and a great lesson for us now. He led by example. His eyes and his people's were on the Lord. If he were living today, we would hear him saying, "Turn your eyes upon Jesus, Look full in His wonderful face."[103] Any life that has God as the one and only focus will not be exempt from the daily battles, but will find repose in knowing that *the battle is the Lord's.*"

What a testimony to have when that son or daughter dies, when unemployed, when the car is repossessed, the family ties are broken by divorce, cancer assails, dialysis is required and it is relentless, the electricity is turned off, or when any other battle is raging to be able to say, "our eyes are upon Thee." When extremes of life arise again, and they will, although different in nature, read the words of Jehoshaphat in 2 Chronicles 20:3–3, but especially verse 13: "And all Judah stood before the LORD, with their little ones, their wives and their children."

That was a moment of great spiritual triumph. I fail to recall the last time there was total consent on any issue outside of the day of Pentecost when they were of one accord.[104] The closest I have heard of almost total consent was when Shaquille O'Neal of the Los Angeles Lakers basketball team received all but one vote to make him the unanimous choice as the most valuable player. But that is in sports. It fell one short. In Jehoshaphat's reign, all Judah stood before the Lord, even the little ones. You see, faith in God is not taught, it is caught. Even the babies were endorsers that God would take full responsibility when the gaze was on Him who would bring deliverance to His people. O for a faith that will not bend or break, wilt or weaken, fail or falter, but for one that holds on despite the circumstances, and trusts where it cannot trace. Like Abraham, they believed God and it was counted to them for righteousness.

And this is a victory that overcometh the world, even our faith.[105]

The rhetorical question of Jesus still echoes down the corridor of years,

Nevertheless when the Son of man cometh, will He find faith on the earth?[106]

Faith is our most important spiritual commodity. Jesus posed the question because He wanted to make sure faith is evident in every life, not Jehoshaphat's faith, but a personal faith, a personal trust. Faith is gained by reading God's Word, the Bible. Based upon what is discovered, confidence is achieved in Him, and the individual or nation having knowledge of His dealings can believe that whatever God asks or says is achievable. Trust is what results from faith in God. Each individual must possess a personal, intimate, and unwavering confidence in the Savior and His promises.

Consider some real facts as they relate to the unwavering faith of which we speak. If Noah had parleyed with his thoughts and his direct assignment, the ark would never have been built. In fact, had he not believed, after seven days without a drop of rain, he might have been tempted to leave the ark. But his faith held on to the promises of God.[107]

Reason would never have permitted Abraham to leave Ur of the Chaldees, his home, his family and country to go he knew not where. It was surrendering the known for the unknown. But faith in God held on to the promises and especially the covenant as genuine. He did precisely as God said.[108]

Reason never would have permitted Joshua and his army to march around Jericho for seven days as God had ordered, considering the conditions imposed for success, but faith did.[109]

Reason would never have urged David with his sling and a few stones to go after Goliath with his sword, shield, and spear, but his faith told him that the battle was the Lord's.[110]

Reason never would have let the woman with the issue of blood muster her last ounce of strength, that woman who after all the medical help received had grown worse, to say if she could only touch the hem of Jesus' garment, she would be made well again, but faith did.[111] God delights in rewarding faithfulness.

Jehoshaphat brought the people together in the temple for a day of fasting and prayer. They came from all over the nation to seek God at the request of their king. He called upon God to grant power and strength to be victorious in the battle against those who had received special exemptions, which were honored. He enlisted the intervention of God to protect the city and to destroy those who were bold enough to come up against it. They occupied the territory granted them as a part of their share of the Promised Land division. Here is a moment worth recording. The whole congregation, all of Judah, with their wives and children, were in tears before the Lord and in supplication.[112] God is faithful. He said,

> And it shall come to pass, that before they call, I will answer; and while they are yet speaking, I will hear. [113]

As Jehoshaphat and his people were praying, right at that juncture, out of the vast concourse of people stepped Jahaziel, a Levite, an Asaphite, a prophet upon whom the Spirit of the living God had descended and moved, and he declared,

> Thus saith the Lord unto you, Be not afraid nor dismayed by reason of this great multitude; *for the battle is not yours, but God's.* Tomorrow go ye down against them: behold, they come up by the cliff of Ziz; and ye shall find them at the end of the brook, before the wilderness of Jeruel. *Ye shall not need to fight in this battle:* set yourselves, stand ye still, and see the salvation of the Lord with you, O Judah and Jerusalem: fear not, nor be dismayed; to morrow go out against them: for the Lord will be with you.[114]

When Jahaziel made his immortal pronouncement, no upstaging of the king was intended. God's Spirit gave him a message for His people. His brief, terse, simple-sounding statement, which was directed to the nation of Judah, still applies to the nations of today, the church and the individual. It is not so easily followed, especially the issued dissuasive against fear.

Knowing human nature, one can hear the commanders, captains of thousands, and soldiers saying, if not aloud but in the heart, "What is Jahaziel talking about?" "Has he ever been in a war zone?" "Just stand still and see!" "Ye shall not have to fight in this battle." "That is absolutely the weirdest thing I have ever heard in the face of an impending conflict." "How is a war won by standing still?" "Are the Moabites, the Ammonites, and the Edomites going to withdraw because of Jahaziel's statements?" "Isn't there a passage of Scripture that suggests personal involvement? There is one which says, 'Work out your own salvation.'"[115] "Is God really going to watch us stand by and do nothing?" "Where is the old adage which says, 'God helps those who help themselves'?" "Will God win this one for us?"

And really, that is the crux of the whole matter of salvation and man's relationship with God. All God requires is the activation of the faith He has already implanted in the human heart. Demonstrate trust in Him. Obey His commands. Just stand still and see God's requirements. But in each of us there is that compelling desire to do something to merit God's glorious intervention in our world and in our lives. There is nothing we can do to earn salvation. Eternal life comes by believing in the Son of God and a willingness to trust and obey His will. The simplicity of it perplexes so many. They just want to do something to merit God's grace. They cannot understand that no preparations are necessary. It is come just as you are. No penance, no rituals, no purification, no special procedure, no waiting list; nothing is demanded. All Jesus asks is for us to depend on Him completely. If you believe wholeheartedly, then eternal life is yours. The apostle Paul could not state it any clearer. He said,

> Who hath saved us, and called us with an holy calling, not according to our works, but according to his own purpose and grace, which was given us in Christ before the world began, But is now made manifest by the appearing of our Saviour Jesus Christ, who hath abolished death, and hath brought life and immortality to light through the gospel:[116]

However, it is ingrained in man's nature to be concerned about outcomes. What will eventually happen? Will victory be a reality? Will I be saved or lost? If we could just leave every situation in God's hands, peace would flood our lives. If *the battle is the Lord's*, and it is, then the comfort is that the outcome, the beginning as well as the ending, will also be the Lord's. God never asked anyone to vindicate Him, only to trust Him.

> Trust and obey, for there's on other way
> To be happy in Jesus, But to trust and obey.[117]

If ever God gave a task, trust is it. It is so difficult "to let go, and let God." It is so hard to relinquish one's own ideas, plans, strategies, wealth, whatever, and believe that God will do the rest.

Faith is the first prerequisite to receive divine support. We seem to trust everything, and everyone, but God. We trust the banker every time a deposit is made. We believe the money deposited is there in the bank. The deposit slip says it is. We trust the physician if he recommends an appendectomy. We have never seen it, but he says so, and we willingly go on the operating table. It is *Amazing*. What confidence.

In March 1999, my wife and I boarded a Korean Airlines jumbo jet out of Los Angeles International Airport bound for Seoul, Korea's Kimpo International Airport. We were in the air for thirteen-and-one-half hours. Never once did I go to the cockpit and ask the pilots, "Say, do you know where you are going?" "Is this your first flight?" "Do you have enough fuel for the journey, not to mention food?" We trusted those pilots and flight attendants without reservation. We landed safely at Kimpo International Airport. Having been there before I knew we were in Seoul. If we grant persons we have never met before that amount of faith and confidence, why should we not have the utmost confidence in our Savior? I am sure this conduct or some other could be told several times.

In all His dealings with His children, spiritual growth is God's number one objective. In the conflict with Jehoshaphat and the Arabians, God was concerned about the personal relationship that would develop and grow out of that experience. When the war ended, at the conclusion of the conflict, God wanted to know, are My people closer, more faithful as a result? Outcomes were on the heart of God. He simply waited for them to glorify His name for His wondrous deeds. He knows that whoever offers praise, glorifies God. But like the ten lepers cleansed, He awaits a word of thanks, some show of appreciation.[118]

The role of Jehoshasphat in this conflict was commendable. He listened to and obeyed every word of the prophet Jahaziel. As soon as Jehoshaphat heard God's commands he placed his faith in the Lord, and the battle became God's. Jehoshaphat simply disappeared from of the picture. In like manner God takes full responsibility of those who cast all their cares upon Him. Jehoshaphat assured Judah that God had heard their prayers, and that He would fight for them. They responded by going down from Jerusalem to Tekoa. Their minds were made up. They would not fight against the Ammonites, the Moabites, and the Edomites. They would only stand still. They would stand firm and resolute for battle. They would observe the hands of God in action.[119]

Look, if you please, at the king and his people. They fell down, worshipped, and gave thanks while the Levites sang hymns to God accompanied by all kinds of musical instruments. They praised God with a loud voice. Wasn't that marvelous? The grand and glorious experience lent itself to humility and reverence, adoration, and submission. The inhabitants of Judah and Jerusalem were in an act of worship. The promise of God's saving power resulted in head bowing and heart-hallowing. The attitude of spiritual victors is always one of worship. They are ever aware of their benefactor.

Early in the morning, king, people, Levites and the entire army, girded with faith and courage, afraid of nothing or no one, with Jehovah as captain of the Lord's host, positioned themselves in battle array. They awaited the salvation of their God.

Usually kings do not go on the battlefield. For example, in the battle against terrorism (2001), the United States and the coalition's search for Osama Bin Laden and others, President George Bush of the United States did not join the forces go to Kabul or Kandahar in Afghanistan, or elsewhere. The responsibilities were delegated to others to manage the affairs of war. Not so with Jehoshaphat. He rallied the troops by his presence. He exhorted them as they marched through the city gate one regiment after the other that God was in charge. He reminded them of His promise, "Ye shall not need to fight in this battle."[120] He spoke positively about all the promises God made.

There never was a war like this before. It had some unique features. Victory was assured before the first soldier donned his uniform. Even before seeing the enemy they knew that the war was a done deal. Singers praising the Lord marched ahead of the troops. They sang of God's goodness, His holiness, His majesty, and His beauty. They maintained that as the hills were round about Jerusalem, so He would encircle them. Levites arrayed in their sacred regalia joined the people, and together they sang, "Praise the Lord; for His mercy endureth forever."[121] Blessed is that man, woman, or nation that can praise God for the promise He has made, and moves on, expecting miracles. Remember, if it is seen, it is not faith. But when in faith the individual or nation takes God at His word; it is accounted for righteousness. God kept His share of the promise. He rewarded their faith.

In the battle against Jericho, Joshua's army walked around the walls of that city, and finally the music of their rams' horns, which seemed ridiculous to the Canaanites, brought the walls down after seven days.[122] In this battle, Jehoshaphat's forces walked out of Jerusalem singing right onto the battlefield. While they were in the vicinity of the enemy they praised God for His goodness. They worshipped because they expected a miracle.

The Ammonites, Moabites, and Edomites must have wondered as they heard all kinds of musical instruments in the distance and melodious voices raised in song, and joined by angels. "What in the world is going on?" they asked. "What is an orchestra and choir doing out in the desert?"

Can you imagine the Boston Pops, the Mormon Tabernacle Choir, or the New York Philharmonic Orchestra leading soldiers into war? That must have been one grand sight. The various colors, the pomp and pageantry, the confidence with which each step was taken, an air of triumph, and a sense of expectation characterized Israel. It was spectacular but divine in origin. But isn't that exactly how life ought to be? When under-girded by the Word of God, boldly and fearlessly go forth to stand in Jehovah's name. God kept His word. Without the involvement of one soldier, the conflict ended. It was over, except for collecting the spoils. Here is the biblical account:

> And when they began to sing and to praise, the Lord set ambushments against the children of Ammon, Moab, and mount Seir, which were come against Judah; and they were smitten. For the children of Ammon and Moab stood up against the inhabitants of mount Seir, utterly to slay and destroy them: and when they had made an end of the inhabitants of Seir, every one helped to destroy another. And when Judah came toward the watch tower in the wilderness, they looked unto the multitude, and, behold, they were dead bodies fallen to the earth, and none escaped.[123]

The Moabites, Ammonites, and Edomites annihilated one another. They went after each other's throat and destroyed one another. We need only to trust in God. The enemy will dispose of himself or one another. The Valley of Berachah was full of dead bodies. God, by His power, without Judah's labor or involvement, granted them the victory. This great truth cannot be over-emphasized. The songwriter J. H. Sammis in the hymn, "When We Walk With The Lord," expresses it best in the following verse.

> But we never can prove The delights of His love
> Until all on the altar we lay;
> For the favor He shows, And the joy He bestows,
> Are for those who will trust and obey.

For three long days they gathered together all the spoils, riches, precious jewels, and more than they could carry away. That was a lot of loot. We do not have a head count of how many went down to see this great miracle of God. But irrespective of the count, can you imagine three days spent in gathering all God had provided? More than victory in battle was derived from the encounter. God provided for their needs.

Grateful for God's unspeakable deliverance right before their eyes, just as He said He would, Jehoshaphat on the fourth day gathered all his people on the spot where God's intervention, so real, so unbelievable, had occurred. Berachah was the valley where they evidenced God's control and power. There their lives were spared. It was the site of victory and covenant keeping. It was the valley of spiritual, material and unnumbered blessings. With a grateful heart Jehoshaphat praised and thanked the Lord. The nation offered thanksgiving on the site and at home.

God won a signal victory for Judah. *The battle is the Lord's* and He knows no defeat. We have a God who will fight for us. The same God who was with them will be with us. That is a promise. Jesus said, "Lo, I am with you alway."[124]

Because God is with us always, when the "Ammonites, Moabites, and Edomites" approach, whoever they are, whatever they are, wherever they come from, or with whatever they come, we can walk toward them with hymns of praise and thanksgiving confident that *the battle is the Lord's.*

Because it is God's responsibility to work out the details of the conflict and our involvement is only for our own spiritual growth and maturity, we can sing courageously,

> Calm me my God, and keep me calm,
> Soft resting on Thy breast;
> Soothe me with holy hymn and psalm,
> And bid my spirit rest.[125]

The battle is the Lord's.

Because our ammunition will not be for a carnal warfare, we will arm ourselves with faith and holy trust, and irrespective of the size of the "Ammonite, Moabite, and Edomite" army, we will neither overestimate nor underestimate them. Quantity shall never be a consideration, but the quality of our faith will be. Not numbers, but character must win the day. It should and must be remembered that,

> Not to the strong is the battle,
> Not to the swift is the race,
> Yet to the true and the faithful
> Victory is promised through grace.[126]

The battle is the Lord's.

Because often in the conflicts of life we have girded the wrong armor, sometimes we have even unwittingly tried to win the battle. We have believed that through negotiations, schemes, alliances, and human resources the possibility existed. We have even called upon our own righteousness and good deeds, so called, to conquer indwelling sin and to gain success against the attacks of the evil one, the roaring lion and the enemy of us all. We have found failure to be our lot. But in those moments of sane recollection we are reminded that the sole protection against the forfeiture of our heritage, sons and daughters of the Most High God, soldiers in the Lord's army, is that *the battle is the Lord's.*

The Christian is called to have faith, not to fight; to believe, not to battle; to have confidence, not be called to a conflict; because *the battle is the Lord's.*

We serve a mighty and powerful, yet loving God. He makes every concern of ours His. He makes Himself responsible for all that is thrown on us or at us. He has promised victory. We believe that to be a fact. We have Jesus Christ who fought the greatest battle yet on record, the battle of sin and death on Calvary. He won on our behalf.

What lessons can we take from Jehoshaphat for our lives? Certainly a lesson of faith: the surest guarantee of victory. The trial of our faith is more precious than gold.[127] Without faith it is impossible to please God.[128] Faith laughs at the impossibilities or the seeming impossibilities in life and declares, "It already is." This is the victory that overcomes the world, even our faith.[129] He was a man of tremendous faith. We can certainly take a lesson in obedience: he did what God told him to do, and which is man's greatest need. We can take a lesson in prayer: He prayed for himself and his people. It is from answered prayer that God's highest glory is revealed. And yes, a lesson in learning to wait: He had to wait. "Stand still" was the directive, and observe the salvation of God. So must we, in the darkest hours, anticipate the brightest hope, salvation through our Lord and Savior Jesus Christ. *THE BATTLE IS THE LORD'S.*

Chapter 3

AN OPEN LETTER

(Based on 2 Kings 19; 2 Chronicles 30 & 31 and Isaiah 37)

No war outside of the Civil War, fought in 1861, so fiercely divided the United States as much as did the Viet Nam War in 1968. It was fought on the home front as well as in Viet Nam. In many ways 1968 was one of the most tragic years in American history. According to the Center for Social Studies Education, "The U.S. war in Vietnam was the longest and second most costly in U.S. history. More than two million Americans were sent to fight. More than 58,000 were killed, more than 300,000 wounded, and almost 14,000 completely disabled. According to the U.S. Veteran's Administration, up to 800,000 Vietnam veterans have been diagnosed as having "significant" to "severe" problems of readjustment. The war cost U.S. taxpayers hundreds of billions of dollars and these costs will continue for decades in the form of veterans' benefits and interest on past loans." When my wife and I visited Viet Nam in 1997, from Hanoi to Ho Chi Minh City, we asked ourselves just what was there in that country of extremes that warranted that onslaught. We had no answers.

Biblical history also contains some outrageous figures. Here is an historical record of c. 690 BC. The outcome overwhelms the mind. The facts are more unimaginable and of a greater magnitude. This conflict has success written all over it. One hundred eighty-five thousand soldiers fully clad, armor on, ready for war, sword in hand and poised to do battle with the Israelites. All are dead and not a single bomb had exploded or sword unsheathed. Unlike the 1991 Gulf War with Iraq which took days, a short time as compared with previous wars, this was an overnight job. Israel suffered no loss of property, no mine fields were left to cause subsequent damage, millions of dollars were not wasted, no loss of tanks, helicopters downed, no Scud missiles deployed, and no prisoners of war taken. Add to the unbelievable aspects of the battle one more fantastic element—Israel had not summoned one soldier.

God fought the Assyrians by Himself. He kept His word as always. In fact, word from the prophet Isaiah, brought by a messenger to King Hezekiah, indicated that God had heard his prayer and He would care for the matter at hand. God would reveal His awesome character while dealing in righteousness with sin and the chatter of Sennacherib, king of Assyria.

What an amazing sight! The Assyrian army decimated. They drank no Kool-Aid and potassium cyanide potion as did the people in Jonestown, Guyana in the Jim Jones episode. The record reads that the morning following the day that Hezekiah had gone to speak with God in His house, thousands of soldiers were seen stretched out in ranks near Israel's border. Thousands of bodies were dead in their platoons. Nothing moved. They had had their last meal, drank the last glass of water, and obeyed Sennacherib's last command. They would never see their families and friends again. Who could have predicted this was their last engagement?

There is no record of Hezekiah's reaction upon learning that the entire Assyrian army had died. However, he must have been struck with the rapidity and completeness of God's work, and awed by His faithfulness. Certainly, he drew some conclusions, one of which might have been that the deadly enemy to any country or person is unrighteousness. He must have surveyed the scene where thousands had died overnight. In his deliberations with his cabinet, those who brought the letter, he spoke to the fact that God must be respected and obeyed. Can you not hear him even now admonishing the people to maintain a deeper trust in God? If Israel violated God's commands and needed to be punished and disciplined, it would not be done by an unauthorized nation. He witnessed first-hand the judgment of God on Assyria because of their folly. They refused to reverence the God of heaven and earth. How ignorant it was and is to fight against God! That episode can be described in this way: "Sodom… overthrown in a moment."[130] They, like us, seldom if at all, think of how much can happen in a moment. Solomon said,

> No one knows when he's going to be faced with evil times or even death. It will happen when he least expects it. It's like birds that are hopping along the ground looking for food but unexpectedly become entangled in a snare, or like schools of swimming fish that are suddenly trapped in a net.[131]

The spiritual impact of the open letter to God in His house might have been Hezekiah's greatest consideration. Before we give due attention to this awesome military campaign won by God, who responded to an open letter, there are issues that ought to be settled: the fact that God has great respect for faith… that prayer is the Christian's most potent weapon… that the Scriptures are replete with experiences of answered prayers… and that Hezekiah could have been helped by Jacob's encounter and sagacity. We will observe that when trouble comes, and it will come, prayer must be a first choice and not a last chance.

As Jacob wended his way back to Bethel, house of God, the place he met the Lord when he fled from Esau's anger, he sent messengers to meet his brother Esau. They should tell him how God had blessed his brother Jacob with great wealth. They were to try to conciliate him. Jacob learned that Esau was on his way to meet him. See Genesis 32. That day, as the evening shadows lengthened and night drew on, Jacob sent all that he had over the Jabbok River. His wives, concubines, eleven sons, and all earthly possessions were removed from his presence.[132] "And Jacob was left alone"[133] on the northern bank of the Jabbok, known today as the Wadi Zerqa, "the blue river," an eastern tributary of the Jordan. He was in real trouble. His aloneness granted him the opportunity to open his heart to the God of the universe and to pray. His prayer was not a prayer of praise and thanksgiving, not a prayer of repentance and confession. He was in trouble. He needed deliverance and he sought help, which could only come from God. He left on record what those who know God ought to do when difficulties arise. Jacob was successful in his struggle, and his time of trouble and deliverance is left on the record as a type of the trouble and deliverance promised to God's people. The promise is that everyone will be delivered, but in the process they will be purified and come forth as gold tried in fire.[134]

Jacob on this particular occasion would not rely on his cleverness or schemes. At long last he had come to the full realization that his total trust must be in God and God alone to save him from Esau's anger, and for the salvation of his family. In that nocturnal struggle, God sent Jesus to help him work through his troubles from midnight to the break of dawn. Jacob was victorious and so will we be when we learn to depend, not in our strength and ingenuity, not in our wisdom and might, but to trust wholly upon God.

No one is immune from trouble. It comes when least expected. From Adam to our generation, all can testify to the fact that their journey through life is fraught with problems of one kind or another. It has no respect of persons. Look at Hezekiah, Judah's thirteenth king. He found himself in serious trouble. The vicious Assyrians were ready to destroy Israel. It is my opinion he must have been familiar with God's intervention on behalf of His people on previous occasions, but particularly with Jacob's trouble. It seems he was conversant with Israel's history; he knew of God's readiness to bring deliverance and to answer before they called, even while they were speaking. He employed a rather different approach to war when the powerful, formidable enemy, the Assyrian army under Sennacherib, invaded Judah. He took the Assyrian's letter, filled with threats, one which insulted and derided the God of heaven and earth, one with unwarranted and unnecessary self-exaltation, one with profane and blasphemous remarks, to the house of God, the temple. He went alone. He opened the letter before the Lord in prayer. God rewarded his faith by a miraculous display of His might. It literally boggles the mind. One angel destroyed 185,000 Assyrian soldiers in one night.[135] Like Jacob, faced with a seemingly insurmountable problem, Hezekiah repaired to God and deliverance came.

The circumstances leading up to the demonstration of God's might, His covenant, His opened ears to His children's prayers, the vindication of His person, His ability to enter into combat and to be victorious without man's aid, and yet for man's benefit can be traced to a series of events in King Hezekiah's life.

Hezekiah the King

Hezekiah was the son of King Ahaz.[136] His mother was Abijah, the daughter of Zechariah.[137] He ruled jointly with his father for fourteen years and with his son Manasseh for about ten years, (c. 729–686 BC). He served for about forty-three years, twenty-nine of them alone.[138] His reign was marked by prosperity, spiritually and otherwise. He built store cities and sheepfolds.[139] He fortified the walls of Jerusalem.[140] His rock-cut Siloam tunnel, 1,755 feet long from the spring of Gihon in the Kidron Valley, connecting with a new lower pool inside the city (2 Kings 20:20; 2 Chron. 32:4, 30) was his greatest technical accomplishment.[141] He is best known for his brave fight against the powerful Assyrian army, and for his faith.[142] His father Ahaz had made himself an Assyrian vassal,[143] and he, Hezekiah, was determined to shake off the Assyrian yoke. Regrettably, he made an alliance with Egypt despite Isaiah the prophet's opposition to such an unwise action. His relationship with Ethiopia, Egypt, and Merodach-Baladan, a Chaldean who was king of Babylon, and the one who sent him gifts upon his recuperation from his mortal disease, did not help in his struggle for freedom from the Assyrian yoke. Sennacherib did attack Judah during his reign, took forty-six fortified cities, countless villages, and two hundred thousand one hundred and fifty citizens of Judah. Hezekiah also paid tribute to Sennacherib, amounting to three hundred talents of silver (eleven tons) and thirty talents of gold (approximately one ton).[144] Isaiah, Hosea and Micah were the prophets active during his reign. His greatest spiritual undertaking was to break loose from his father's evil practices. He repaired and cleansed the temple. He reorganized the religious services; he celebrated the Passover to which he had invited the ten northern tribes; destroyed all the idols; even the bronze serpent, that great reminder of the uplifted Christ, which Moses had raised in the wilderness, for Judah now used it in their idolatrous practices.[145]

Hezekiah's Parents and Lifestyle

Hezekiah and his father were as different as night and day. His lifestyle indicated that he condemned the claims of heredity on the side of his father. The closest observable connection between these two kings, father and son, was the co-regency.

We owe so much to Christian mothers who by God's grace avert what would otherwise be disastrous. Be it ever so farfetched, let us give his mother Abi the credit for affording him an opportunity to develop a character to withstand the strain of all the evils of his day. I imagine at various times her good counsel, her parental support, her godly life, and her grasp of God's holiness impacted his life and the lives of those over whom he reigned.

The rainbow overarching his administration can be found in this statement: "And he did that which was right in the sight of the Lord, according to all that David his father did."[146] He did not have two fathers, but this interesting conclusion was drawn because of God's covenant with David, and particularly because of his direct lineage with David, hence a son. "According to all that David his father did" raises an interesting concept of service. A review of his reign shows that success attended every aspect his work. He revived the best traditions of the theocracy.

When you do what is right in the sight of the Lord, it is fundamentally true, unalterably right, that a great blessing will follow. History attests to the fact that God showered His favors upon him and his work. Hezekiah was not a cautious strategist; he was not a theorist; he was not a procrastinator; he simply knew the will of God and did it. He certainly did what was right by cutting across the grain, going in a direction opposite to the lifestyle of the people in his community. He brought an end to the idolatrous practices of Judah. The religious reformation he began was contrary to what his father and previous kings did. It was said of many of them, "they did well in the sight of the Lord," but Hezekiah "did" that which was right. He shunned the example of his renegade father, Ahaz, chose to give God the glory, feared Him, and did what was right in the Lord's sight.

It was impossible to direct the affairs of any portion of the kingdom of Judah or Israel without great and personal faith in God.

> He removed the high places, and brake the images, and cut down the groves, and brake in pieces the brazen serpent that Moses had made: for unto those days the children of Israel did burn incense to it: and he called it Nehushtan.[147]

It was not an easy assignment for Hezekiah to undo all the moral ruin the idolatrous worship and practices Ahaz had condoned and did, yet Hezekiah had the distinction of being closer to God, better than any king in Judah before him or after him.

> He trusted in the Lord God of Israel; so that after him was none like him among all the kings of Judah, nor any that were before him.[148]

Consider men like Jehoshaphat, Uzziah, Asa before, and Josiah after him. That is quite some honor to bestow. They were faithful men too, but God, the final judge of human conduct, could make such a statement. To render an opinion, they might not have served with their whole heart as did Hezekiah, or as some who did well for a while then returned to idolatry, nullifying their reformatory labors. The commendation granted Hezekiah was born out of a trust in God that transcended mere profession. Commendation came to him not because of the title king or being of David's lineage. He possessed a made-up mind and purposed in his heart to do right. He hid self. He made God first and last and rendered total compliance to God's commandments. He had a God who was central. God received his highest praise, best service, and deepest trust. Hezekiah found favor with God and man. His iconoclastic endeavors, his assignment of priests and Levites, the reading and study of God's Word by scribes, the celebration of the Passover and temple services were among the highlights of his reign.

THE PASSOVER CELEBRATION

The Passover and worship celebration that Hezekiah and the priests restored received such acclamation that pulpit and pew wanted seven more days to extol the goodness and mercies of God. Every worshipper, upon hearing the promises and the covenant made by God with Abraham, Isaac, and Jacob, requested seven more days to celebrate. The list included everyone in Judah, the common people, priests and Levites; everyone who responded to the great celebration from the northern kingdom and every proselyte from Israel and Judah. Think about it.

They wanted seven more days away from their normal duties because God had revealed Himself.

And the whole assembly took counsel to keep other seven days: and they kept other seven days with gladness.[149]

Normally, Passover activities lasted seven days. The visitation of God's Spirit at that high and holy convocation, the unequalled joy in worship and fellowship, the re-commitment and re-consecration to God turned into a two-week convocation. The Passover worshippers had to be granted a special dispensation to qualify them to participate.

> For they could not keep it at that time, because the priests had not sanctified themselves sufficiently, neither had the people gathered themselves together to Jerusalem... And the whole assembly took counsel to keep other seven days: and they kept other seven days with gladness... Then the priests and Levites arose and blessed the people: and their voice was heard and their prayer came up to His holy dwelling place, even unto heaven... Now when all this was finished all Israel that were present went out to the cities of Judah, and brake the images in pieces, and cut down the groves, and threw down the high places and the altars out of all Judah and Benjamin, in Ephraim also and Manasseh, until they had utterly destroyed them all. Then all the children of Israel returned, every man to his possession into their own cities... And thus did Hezekiah throughout all Judah, and wrought that which was good and right and truth before the Lord his God. And in every work that he began in the service of the house of God, and in the law, and in the commandments, to seek his God, he did it with all his heart and prospered.[150]

Every now and then circumstances alter cases. The strict adherence to the letter of the law regarding the celebration of the Passover yielded to sound judgment and reason. "The weightier matters of the law, judgment, mercy, and faith"[151] had taken priority. Hezekiah by no means relaxed the claims or laws of God, but the great leader demanded that individuals who for years had not shared in the Passover services should do so before returning to their tribes now scattered. Not since when Solomon reigned as king over Judah and Israel as one nation did God's people congregate in that manner. Never since then in Jerusalem have they openly celebrated their "Fourth of July," their "Independence Day," their release from Egyptian bondage. Nothing meant so much to those people. The command of Hezekiah to permit the priest and scribes to read the Word of God and offer sacrifices to Him rekindled a flame of commitment to their God. Freedom from Egypt was God's act. Hezekiah brought the people to the place where they could say,

The dearest idol I have known,
What-e'er that idol be,
Help me to tear it from Thy throne,
And worship only Thee.[152]

There are high moments in our worship and adoration of God when in retrospect we feel like Peter, James and John on the mount of Transfiguration. At that significant moment, like the disciples our spirits declare, "It is good to be where we are in our walk with God." If Jesus were to come then, we need not exchange that mountaintop experience for another mountain height. To go from one spiritual mountain peak to another would not even be a consideration. If only Hezekiah's record ended at that juncture when the Levites, priests and people's voices were heard in heaven and God had accepted them and their worship, it would have been marvelous. It was a magnificent period in the history of God's people.

In writing the history of the people of God, God leaves on record that which encourages and sustains faith and that which ought to be avoided. You will recall the statement "according to all that David his father did."[153] In the ordering of our lives it must ever be kept in mind that the ultimate standard is Jesus Christ our Lord. David, a man after God's own heart, is certainly not a bad measuring rod, especially when his love for God, His honor, and worship are considered. But Jesus is the example. Paul speaks in Corinthians of not judging ourselves by others. That comparison is flawed. The only standard should be Christ, the perfect pattern:

Be like Jesus, this my song,
In the home and in the throng;
Be like Jesus all day long!
I would be like Jesus.[154]

HEZEKIAH'S SIN

Hezekiah was preeminently a great and good king. There was none like him before or after in Judah. But while the possessor of stellar qualities, exceptionally great, Hezekiah could not, like us, claim perfection. The words of Solomon rang true for him as they do for us.

> For there is not a just man upon the earth, that doeth good, and sinneth not.[155]

He sinned. He failed. His vessel, like ours, was "marred in the Potter's hands."[156] He acted foolishly and in so doing left scars and blemishes upon his service. He transgressed, veered from the path by taking things into his own hands. How squeaky clean his lifework would have been otherwise. Lack of full faith in God muted his testimony. If only he had waited on the Lord. Because of his cringing fear of Sennacherib, he cowardly recanted and his faith in God deserted him. The offence of his independence rather than trust in God, that sin called "self" reared its ugly head. The apostle Paul gave some great advice to the believers in Corinth. It came just too late to be helpful to him. If only Hezekiah had it, it would have been a savior for him in a crucial time. Paul said,

> But don't become overly confident and think of yourselves as standing so firm that you can't fall or that you can do anything you want and it won't affect your salvation.[157]

Hezekiah purchased peace from Sennacherib. What an awesome price! He made a rather humiliating appeal to him, yielded his courage, apologized, and agreed to pay tribute to Assyria, an immoral pledge his ancestors had made. The record is plain.

> Now in the fourteenth year of king Hezekiah did Sennacherib king of Assyria come up against all the fenced cities of Judah, and took them. And Hezekiah king of Judah sent to the king of Assyria to Lachish, saying, I have offended; return from me: *that which thou puttest on me will I bear.* And the king of Assyria appointed unto Hezekiah king of Judah three hundred talents of silver and thirty talents of gold.

And Hezekiah gave him all the silver that was found in the house of the Lord, and in the treasures of the king's house. At that time did Hezekiah cut off the gold from the doors of the temple of the Lord, and from the pillars which Hezekiah king of Judah had overlaid, and gave it unto the king of Assyria.[158]

No excuse will be made for sin or sinning, but it is wonderful to know that, "Jesus knows the circumstances of every soul."[159] He is aware of the frailty of His children, yet He accepts, redeems, reconciles, forgives, and saves us despite our shortcomings, failures, weaknesses, mistakes, even when overpowered by the enemy. That is great salvation, great redemption, by a great Savior, through the work of the Holy Spirit.

Man cannot transform himself by the exercise of his will. He possesses no power by which this change may be effected. The renewing energy must come from God. The change can be made only by the Holy Spirit. He who would be saved, high or low, rich or poor, must submit to the working of this power.[160]

Hezekiah blundered, but God's grace, amazing grace, held him in high esteem despite himself. Despite his situation, he was considered to have done right in God's sight. The Scriptures say that there was no king like him before or after him in Judah.[161] God "will not always chide... for He knoweth our frame; He remembereth that we are dust."[162] Jesus is a wonderful Savior. He looks beyond our faults, failures, and flaws and observes our great need. He reads the heart. It is like God to rescue from folly and sin.

HEZEKIAH'S PROBLEMS

What were Hezekiah's problems? For one, it was seeking an alliance with Egypt, a bruised reed, and Ethiopia. The political measure employed implied a lack of confidence or trust in God. The path followed was one of sight, dealing with armies they could see, rather than with a God who is invisible, omnipotent, and omnipresent. When the demands of Sennacherib had to be met, help from the alliances made did not materialize. The friendships yielded no support in a time of crisis. At that juncture Hezekiah's faith in God dwindled to a flickering candle. He yielded to the pressures of the demand for three hundred talents of silver and thirty talents of gold as tribute. To meet this great debt, the treasury was emptied; the king's treasury likewise, and even the gold on the temple doors, God's house, was scraped off to pay the debt. Just consider the length to which the king had to go to satisfy the rapacious Sennacherib and the greedy Assyrians. Sennacherib would squeeze the sponge dry. His whetted appetite would drain the cup of the last dregs. He would turn the heat up to the last notch.

I have seen out-of-control forest fires in California. Sometimes it seems as if there are insufficient trees and brush to satisfy the angry flames. They just cannot get enough to char. So it was with Sennacherib. The tribute money he received from Hezekiah, taken from God's treasury, seemed inadequate. He demanded more. His appetite would be appeased if he erased God's people from the face of the earth. One writer states, "Only by leading men to feel their own weakness does God train them to rely upon His help."

Hezekiah must have had a rude awakening when Rabshakeh brought the letter of profanity and blasphemy, although Judah had scraped the bottom of the barrel to satisfy the claims presented. This was not Political Science 101. He quickly learned that when full dependence is placed on God, dependence on man is unnecessary. God taught that bitter lesson as a crash course to help oncoming generations. The great army came and the demands were outrageous. Life, liberty, freedom, and the entire nation must be handed over to Assyria. Hezekiah gave Sennacherib an ounce of flesh; he demanded a pound. They gave him an inch; he sought a yard. That's like the devil, cunning and crafty. He wants life and limb. The day cannot come too soon for God to stifle all his plans to harm His children. The devil is never satisfied. Already he had muted Hezekiah's testimony. His attacks were relentless. He returned to create more disaster. Hezekiah had two options: submit to the demands of Sennacherib or submit himself and his people to God. The issues were national liberty or bondage. Judah found itself on the horns of a real dilemma.

Thus saith Hezekiah, This day is a day of trouble, and of rebuke, and blasphemy: for the children are come to the birth, and there is not strength to bring forth.[163]

Sennacherib went too far in his letter. He made light of Hezekiah's faith in God. Due to other conquests, he belittled the great God of the universe. He spoke about Him as if He were another god or one of his gods. He had conquered other nations and their gods and his logic led him to conclude that Jehovah and His people would be dealt a like blow. He was so sure of his military might and genius. As far as he was concerned, victory over Hezekiah and Judah were finished transactions. He gloated, "It already is." In his exultation he forgot that:

1. "Before destruction the heart of man is haughty, and before honour is humility."[164] He was only a mortal man. If only he had some history to lean upon. For example, in his declaration, "Is not this great Babylon, that I have built for the house of the kingdom by the might of my power, and for the honour of my majesty?"[165] Nebuchadnezzar took too much for granted. God humbled him. Napoleon would ever recall Waterloo. The rich farmer in holy writ heard words like, "Thou fool, this night thy soul shall be required of thee: then whose shall those things be, which thou hast provided?"[166] The line between the Creator and the creature was blurred, nonexistent in Sennacherib's eyes. He thought himself invincible. He thought the victories of yesterday guaranteed the conquests of tomorrow. Little did he realize that God puts up and God takes down. Kings and rulers, prime ministers and presidents, governors and leaders of all sorts are only instruments in God's hands to do His biddings. Sennacherib lost reason and became irrational. God had no other alternative but to declare that He is the great I AM, the sovereign Lord.

2. "Pride goeth before destruction, and a haughty spirit before a fall."[167] Sennacherib should have considered that God would be a part of the equation when it affected His people *before* he went spewing off at the mouth.

Hezekiah's Trials

God will correct and straighten Hezekiah's path. Trials come when they are least expected. They will stretch every nerve. Unless they are resolved upon arrival, they return with even greater force. Sin, like Sennacherib, can never be satisfied. It will take the last dime, and when there is no more gold on the temple doors to be had, its founder will take the individual, which was really the goal in the first place. Notice how it operated in the life of Hezekiah. He veered away from God then sin grew into a power that held his soul in its grasp until it enslaved it. Attempts to rise above, to move, to do that for which the soul was created found no response. It was held down, barred. When evils come it is best to resist in the power and strength of Christ. A victory gained through Christ makes the next trial or difficulty less intense. Think how differently Hezekiah's record would have read if at no time he gave in to the temptation of an alliance or trusted his own wisdom. Not until on Mount Moriah, when Abraham raised his hand with the knife to slay Isaac, did the angel of the Lord say,

> ...now I know that thou fearest God saying thou hast not withheld thy son, thine only son from Me.[168]

God will allow the trials of life to perfect character in His children. Hezekiah was wiser now than when he emptied Israel's treasury to appease Sennacherib. He would not yield to popularity or human demands or be cowed by the Assyrians. Like Hezekiah, we must learn the lesson of complete trust in God, however painful. History is replete with stories that demonstrate that when trials, difficulties, and temptations come, the soul must yield to God in all its fullness. God will make a way of escape, and we will be "more than conquerors." His promises have never failed.

HEZEKIAH, SENNACHERIB'S LETTER AND PRAYER

Upon receipt of the letter from Sennacherib, Hezekiah read it and immediately,

> went up into the house of the Lord, and spread it before the Lord.[169]

He did not take pen and paper and frame a reply. **He did not** use the might of spiritual evidence to refute its contents. **He did not**, although he could, champion the honor of God's name. **He did not** spell out Sennacherib's folly of blaspheming the God of heaven and earth. *He went into the house of the Lord.* No question, Hezekiah was in trouble. But he left on record a course of action it does well for all to follow. It is a biblical exhortation.

> And call upon Me in the day of trouble: I will deliver thee, and thou shalt glorify Me.[170]

When we are sick, we seek the aid of the family physician or the hospital. If the automobile will not function, we go to the mechanic. If we need food, the supermarket is the place to find needed supplies. So often when financial crises come, when trouble is our lot, we seek support or assistance from the arm of flesh. Hezekiah made a great move. He took the letter to God's house. Whom have we on earth besides Jesus, whom in heaven but a faithful high priest, sitting at God's right hand? Hezekiah realized, and so must we, that prayer is the mightiest force placed within our reach. The Lord Jesus Christ opens a door through which we should enter and take full advantage of daily.

> Ask, and it shall be given you; seek, and ye shall find; knock, and it shall be opened unto you:[171]
> And all things, whatsoever ye shall ask in prayer, believing, ye shall receive.[172]
> And whatsoever ye shall ask in my name, that will I do, that the Father may be glorified in the Son. If ye shall ask any thing in my name, I will do it.[173]

Whatever the circumstance—the approaching Assyrians, financial reversals, a time of war, a friend proves untrue, an ugly scene, sickness that brings one near death's door, loss of employment, loss of one kind or another, the family circle broken by death, divorce, family issues, a friend breaking with the church, wedding bells, promotion, success in a new venture, reasons to rejoice—take them to the Lord in prayer. It need not be done in the house of God to receive a response.

Prayer can be offered anywhere. The dying thief prayed upon the cross. Prayer can be short—like Peter sinking in the Sea of Galilee, or long like King Solomon at the dedication of the temple. Pray in silence like Hannah in the temple, asking for a child; or aloud like the Phoenician woman. Pray at any time. Jesus prayed early in the morning or all night long. At midnight Paul and Silas prayed in jail. At midday Daniel did with his face turned toward Jerusalem. Pray in old age like Simeon or in sickness like Job. Pray in childhood like Samuel saying, "Speak Lord" or in youthful days like Timothy. It is just wonderful to know that the invisible God has invited us to come. Even more marvelous is the fact that every sincere prayer is heard in heaven and receives an answer.

> Never is one repulsed who comes to him with a contrite heart. Not one sincere prayer is lost… We pour out our hearts' desire in our closets, we breathe a prayer as we walk by the way, and our words reach the throne of the Monarch of the universe… It is God to whom we are speaking, and our prayer is heard.[174]

Hezekiah went to the temple. He opened the letter before the Lord of the universe. Because of His omniscience, He knew the contents. There is nothing hidden from God's eyes.

There's not a place where we can flee but God is present there.[175]

God saw every letter, every word, every sentence, every mile of the journey that Rabshakeh took to Hezekiah. He saw him when he arrived. He was aware of the larger implications of what was transpiring. The Assyrian invasion was really not about Sennacherib, Rabshakeh, Judah, and Assyria. It was a part of the great controversy that has been in progress between Christ and Satan for millennia. The conflict which began in heaven has been transferred to earth. Satan has always desired to berate the God of heaven and earth. Subtle and varied are the means employed. In this instance, he lured Sennacherib to denounce God and to go to war with Judah. During all the intervening transactions, he knew God would avenge His people. He knew God would defend Hezekiah's leadership. What is not immediately recognized is that out of the entire experience, God will establish faith, courage, and loyalty in the hearts of His children and the leadership, and be glorified. *The battle is the Lord's.*

What did God not know? Hezekiah's prayer was not intended to give God an insight into the matters raised in the correspondence. Our prayers can never grant God a vision of our situation. God knows everything. But God delights in our speaking with Him on an intimately personal level regarding issues from the minutest to the greatest. As powerful as God is He cannot answer a prayer that has not been prayed. God's name, His sovereignty, His universal rule, ownership, and majesty were at stake. And Hezekiah prayed.

O Lord God of Israel, which dwellest between the cherubim, thou art the God, even thou alone, of all the kingdoms of the earth; thou hast made heaven and earth. Lord, bow down thine ear, and hear: open, Lord, thine eyes, and see: and hear the words of Sennacherib, which hath sent him to reproach the living God. Of a truth, Lord, the kings of Assyria have destroyed the nations and their lands, And have cast their gods into the fire: for they were no gods, but the work of men's hands, wood and stone: therefore they have destroyed them. Now therefore, O Lord our God, I beseech thee, save thou us out of his hands, that all the kingdoms of the earth may know that thou art the Lord God, even thou only.[176]

God heard Hezekiah's prayer. Isaiah the prophet sent word to Hezekiah confirming that fact.

Then Isaiah the son of Amoz sent to Hezekiah, saying, Thus saith the Lord God of Israel, That which thou hast prayed to me against Sennacherib king of Assyria I have heard.[177]

Earnestly and specifically, he prayed from the heart. He recognized God as the ruler of heaven and earth. He had developed an acquaintance with God prior to that prayer session. That conversation was simply the continuation of spiritual privileges heretofore engaged in. God heard his prayer and will hear your prayer likewise. When one seeks the honor of God, where there is zeal for His name and reverence for his holiness, God responds.

Tennyson, in his *Morte d'Arthur* wrote:

More things are wrought by prayer

Than this world dreams of. Wherefore let thy voice
Rise like a fountain for me night and day.

Like the fire on the altar of sacrifice, there should be in the heart
of each child of God an inextinguishable faith in the efficacy of prayers
directed to Him. A faith that knows God hears and that He answers.

GOD ANSWERED. GOD FOUGHT.

God responded. God acted.

> And it came to pass that night, that the angel of the Lord went out,
> and smote in the camp of the Assyrians an hundred fourscore and
> five thousand.[178]

Israel's deliverance was immediate ("that night") and effective. When
Assyria thought the victory won, a time of peace and safety, then came
sudden destruction. Think on it. One hundred eighty-five thousand
soldiers killed in one night by one angel. Sennacherib learned quickly,
"Ye know not what shall be on the morrow."[179] His ego, his exalted
concepts of his power, had inflated him, but God reduced him in short
order. One angel, just one, did the mission. We ought not to forget the
words of inspiration.

> Angels are sent on missions of mercy to the children of God. To
> Abraham, with promises of blessings; to the gates of Sodom, to rescue
> righteous Lot from the fiery doom; to Elijah, as he was about to perish
> from weariness and hunger in the desert; to Elisha, with chariots of
> fire surrounding the little town where he was shut in by his foes; to
> Daniel, while seeking divine wisdom in the court of a heathen king,
> or abandoned to become the lions' prey; to Peter, Doomed to death
> in Herod's dungeon; to the prisoners at Philippi; to Paul and his
> companions in the night of tempest on the sea; to open the mind of
> Cornelius to receive the gospel; to dispatch Peter with the message of
> salvation to the Gentile stranger—thus holy angels have, in all ages,
> ministered to God's people.[180]

The angel destroyed those 185,000 Assyrians soldiers because God said they would not come into the city.

> By the way that he came, by the same way shall he return, and shall not come into this city, saith the Lord. For I will defend this city, to save it, for mine own sake, and for my servant David's sake.[181]

The death of the 185,000 meant Jerusalem was saved. It is interesting to note that the flood that destroyed the antediluvians floated the ark of Noah and his family. The waters of the Red Sea became walls for Israel but swallowed Pharaoh, his chariots, and his army. The divided path was a dry highway, a plain path for the children of Israel, but the chariots of Pharaoh got stuck in mud and found it an impassable way.

In the destruction of the Assyrian army one can take the position that the judgment of God appears swift and cruel. Let us never forget that one of the attributes of God is that He is long-suffering. Noah and the antediluvian world is a case in point. God bore with their reluctance to do His will for one hundred and twenty years. He demonstrated the same patience with Sennacherib and Assyria. However, oftentimes God's goodness is mistaken for weakness and inaction. Ultimately, our world, seized in the grip of wrong and the rejection of the grace His Son Jesus Christ offers, will one day answer to the just and merciful Judge. The Assyrians answered to God's justice and His mercy and Israel was delivered.

Like the Assyrians swooping down upon Israel, God's children today are aware of the imminence of Jacob's time of trouble. It will be a day of darkness and not light, of great suffering, but everyone will be delivered if reckoned faithful and whose names are in the Lamb's Book of Life.[182] Prayer to God, faith and trust in the shed blood of Christ, will count for everything. Whatever the plan, whichever of a thousand different ways God has in mind to deliver, of which we are oblivious, one thing is certain, He will deliver and save. Victory is promised. God will vindicate His people, fight, and win. The end of the great cosmic conflict will be one of triumph. Jesus has already declared, "It is finished."[183] His chosen people are simply awaiting the crowns of victory and robes of righteousness. Like Sennacherib's army, sin and Satan will be forever destroyed and God's people will live happily ever after.

Can you imagine for a moment the stress and strain that came upon Hezekiah as he pondered his next move while surrounded by the Assyrian army? But oh, the change that came over him on his way home from the temple when he knew that God had taken full responsibility. Isn't that the way it happens in our lives? God thwarted all of Sennacherib's plans and refuted every statement he made while intoxicated with pride. Hezekiah wended his way to the palace overjoyed, not so much over the destruction of so many lives, but over the fact that his confidence in God before whom he opened the mail received immediate attention and a reward. He had said to his men,

> Be strong and courageous, be not afraid nor dismayed for the king of Assyria, nor for all the multitude that is with him: *for there be more with us than with him: With him is an arm of flesh; but with us is the Lord our God to help us, and to fight our battles.* And the people rested themselves upon the word of Hezekiah king of Judah.[184]

The people in Judah believed in Hezekiah and in God. God can be trusted. If only we like them could remember that the arm of flesh will fail us, we dare not trust ourselves. "With us is the Lord our God to help us, and to fight our battles for us." The massive armies that attack us must first contend with that greater power on our side. Judah looked for the Assyrians and they were gone. They celebrated His wondrous deliverance because,

> In Judah is God known: his name is great in Israel. In Salem also is his tabernacle, and his dwelling place in Zion. There brake he the arrows of the bow, the shield, and the sword, and the battle. Selah. Thou art more glorious and excellent than the mountains of prey. The stouthearted are spoiled, they have slept their sleep: and none of the men of might have found their hands.[185]

Have you ever been in the desert of disappointment, with trials and burdens too hard to carry, where difficulties overwhelm the soul, and the only water you have is from the tears dripping off your face? Is the light at the end of the dark tunnel through which you are traveling the headlight of an oncoming train? Take heart, my friend.

> Whatever your anxieties and trials, spread out your case before the Lord. Your spirit will be braced for endurance. The way will be open for you to distance yourself from embarrassment and difficulty. The weaker and more hopeless you know yourself to be, the stronger will you become in His strength. The heavier your burdens, the more blessed the rest in casting them upon your Burden Bearer.[186]

Heaven would be a black, empty place if there were no beam of light to see the Father's face, no opening to the cry of the human heart. How hopeless our lives would be, if in the day of distress, if in our day of jubilation, we had no access to the ear of God. Think of it: this world, blackened by sin, may become for us anywhere we are, the audience chamber with the King of kings. Our closets can be a place gilded with His glory, where His ears alone are opened to our conversations and the contents of those private, secret meetings. Prayer is the breath of the soul. "Men ought always to pray, and not to faint."[187] We must, we ought, because we are always dependent upon Him. In Him we live, and move, and have our being."[188] The Lord has an open ear for our cry, and an open eye for our heart. As A. Procter said in Handfuls on Purpose,

> Pray, though the gift you ask for
> May never comfort your fears,
> May never repay your pleading,
> Yet pray, and with hopeful tears!
> An answer—not that you long for,
> But diviner—will come some day;
> Your eyes are too dim to see it
> Yet trust, and wait, and pray.

Spread it out before the Lord. He will hear. He will see whatever it is. He will assassinate every foe to righteousness. Remember, do remember, that the battle is His to fight, the victory yours to enjoy, the glory His to have, and life eternal the consummate gift bestowed.

Chapter 4

IMPLODED WALLS

(Based on Joshua 6)

Joshua a son of Nun of the tribe of Ephraim,[189] was the successor of Moses. He was the military commander for Moses during Israel's wilderness wanderings. We see him first in that role in the victory over the Amalekites when the children of Israel on their way to Mount Sinai were attacked at Rephidim.[190] Although God had appointed Aaron as Moses' mouthpiece,[191] he had no discussion with Joshua as it pertained to turf, lines of duty, or anything regarding authority. Moses delegated the responsibilities given to him by God for Aaron, and the leadership roles to Joshua. For example, it was Joshua who accompanied Moses when he went up to Mount Sinai, while Aaron was in charge of the people.

> So Moses took Joshua, his assistant, and went back up the mountain to be with God.[192]

When the twelve spies were sent to survey the Promised Land, Joshua represented the tribe of Ephraim.[193] Only he and Caleb assured the people that they were able to take the territory. In their minority report, they called upon Israel to act in faith, to believe that God would fulfill His promise, and urged them not to demonstrate their unfaithfulness. It is recorded in Numbers the 14 chapter verses 6 to 9.

At last the time came for the orderly transfer of Israel's leadership. Ballots did not need to be counted to determine who Israel's leader should be. God in His own appropriate way informed Moses that he would die soon, and spoke to the transfer of his authority and leadership to Joshua, which should happen in the presence of the people. This biblical account lights the pathway of how the business of God ought to be conducted.

> The Lord said, "Go and get Joshua, the son of Nun. He is humble and listens and is someone the Holy Spirit can use. He will be your successor. You need to transfer your authority to him in front of the people, and they'll accept him as their new leader. Take him to Eleazar, the high priest, and in the presence of the people lay your hands on him to indicate the transfer of leadership. Tell the children of Israel that Joshua will receive directions from me through the two stones, the Urim and Thummim, that are on the garments of the high priest. One stone will light up to give a 'Yes' answer or the other one will cloud over to give a 'No' answer. Israel is to move at his command." Moses obeyed and did what the Lord asked him to do. He called for Joshua and had him stand in front of Eleazar, the high priest, in the sight of the children of Israel. Then he laid his hands on Joshua and transferred the responsibilities of leadership and authority to him as the Lord had instructed him.[194]

Joshua assumed full leadership of Israel as ordained. Note that God's plans were laid well in advance of Moses' death. Few men if any step into responsible positions without preparation. There is no ready-made, fully prepared, here I am, God's gift to man leader. God is never caught unaware and then has to provide leadership. Well in advance of the crossing of the Jordan, the invasion of Jericho, forty years prior to those encounters, Joshua was being prepared. One of the admirable features of leadership is vision. God certainly gave him one, and assigned him specific missions.

He provided remarkable leadership as the man who, in the providence of God, would be the channel through whom God would fulfill His promise made four centuries before to Abraham.[195] With Joshua at the helm as leader of Israel's affairs, the promises of God made to Abraham were on the verge of being ratified.

Joshua had a record of faithful service, a strong faith in God's words and promises, voted against the majority report, maintained his ground, served as an intern under Moses, became his personal minister, a great follower, a taker of orders, and had the distinction of being with Moses when God spoke to him face to face. That was no mean attainment for leadership on tiptoe. God buried Aaron and Moses His workmen, in that order, but not His work, for He had a man named Joshua to succeed Moses.

For Joshua it must have been a humbling, but marvelous feeling to go from second in command of God's special people to first, and then be given an infallible prescription for success in the work of God. He never asked God, "What is my first move?" "Where do I go from here?" God defined the tasks and gave the conditions for success. I think I hear the conversation so clearly. God appealed to him not to hold on to the fragments of Moses' leadership. "Moses is dead," God says. "Move on." The past failures, successes, losses, gains are behind. And isn't that the same word to us; to let go of our yesterdays?

> I certainly don't consider myself as having reached the divine standard of complete Christ-likeness. However, there is one thing I have done and will continue to do, and that is to forget things that are in the past and to look ahead toward the spiritual goal held out to us by God who is calling us heavenward through Jesus Christ His Son.[196]

Joshua received the terms and conditions from God to be successful. He would be with him as He was with Moses.

Here are the conditions for success.

1. He must know the will of God.
2. He must demonstrate faith in God.[197]
3. God will be with him, an inexhaustible legacy.[198]
4. He should be strong and courageous.[199]
5. He must turn neither left nor right.[200]
6. He must make God's words first and foremost.[201]
7. There must be obedience to God's revealed will.[202]

Those promises and the demands worked for Joshua, and they will for any child of God who is desirous of being successful. Joshua's primary responsibility, although there were others, was to lead Israel into the land of Canaan.

God had sworn that those who murmured and complained would not enter Canaan because they believed the evil report and demonstrated their unbelief in His word. One of the prerequisites for entrance into the Promised Land then or now remains the same, full faith in God. Some of the Israelites who left Egypt, with every intention of occupying the Promised Land, died in the wilderness because of their unbelief.

Just before Moses died, he took a census of the people. The results of the census taken when they rebelled compared with the one taken before his death indicated that everyone who came out of Egypt of a certain age, died during the forty years of wilderness life. Not one remained. God would be true to His promise. He was explicit regarding the results of Israel's faithlessness.

> …the LORD spake unto Moses and unto Aaron, saying, How long shall I bear with this evil congregation, which murmur against me? I have heard the murmurings of the children of Israel, which they murmur against me. Say unto them, As truly as I live, saith the LORD, as ye have spoken in mine ears, so will I do to you. Your carcasses shall fall in this wilderness; and all that were numbered of you, according to your whole number, from twenty years old and upward, which have murmured against me, Doubtless ye shall not come into the land, concerning which I sware to make you dwell there-in, Save Caleb the son of Jephunneh, and Joshua the son of Nun.[203]

Joshua would lead an entirely new generation into the Promised Land. Long before Israel reached the walls of Jericho, while they were still enslaved in Egypt, God petitioned Pharaoh to release Israel. Their freedom was demanded for one reason and one reason alone—to worship Him, the true and living God.[204] Oftentimes I wonder, almost aloud, asking myself, "Is there ever a time when our concerns and conditions are absent from God's great heart of love?" Israel's entrance into the Promised Land, the land of milk and honey, the "good life," should not eclipse one central fact. God's release from slavery of any kind, such as self and self-seeking, the tyranny of passion, pride, love of self, covetousness, or anything over which one must gain victory is simply to bring the individual or nation into the freedom of adoring worship of Christ the Savior.

The worship Israel offered in the wilderness was in tents. God called it a sanctuary.[205] Whereas God does not need a great cathedral for His children to worship Him, a permanent place should be expected once their wanderings ceased. After crossing Jordan they began the conquest to establish permanency. Jericho was the first such task.

The battle at Jericho possesses a number of factors admired by young and old, Christian and non-Christian, teachers, scholars, and historians. Involved in this campaign are some interesting circumstances and principles worthy of note. The hiding of the spies; Rahab on the wall with her family who accepted the living God; Jericho itself, the giant walls, the spiritually unprotected impenitents behind those massive walls, on and behind the walls Jericho's military; outside the walls a host of Israelites bound for the Land of Promise, the ark of the covenant, priests with trumpets and a fearless leader, Joshua. Each will significantly impact this first major conflict.

Israel will engage in their first major war to conquer Canaan. Joshua had already sent out two spies whose reconnaissance mission yielded confirmation that the citizens of Jericho were afraid of the oncoming forces. Rahab, their only contact, gave a rather informative testimony:

> And she said unto the men, I know that the LORD hath given you the land, and that your terror is fallen upon us, and that all the inhabitants of the land faint because of you. For we have heard how the LORD dried up the water of the Red sea for you, when ye came out of Egypt; and what ye did unto the two kings of the Amorites, that were on the other side Jordan, Sihon and Og, whom ye utterly destroyed. And as soon as we heard these things, our hearts did melt, neither did there remain any more courage in any man because of you: for the LORD your God, he is God in heaven above, and in earth beneath... And they said unto Joshua, Truly the LORD hath delivered into our hands all the land; for even all the inhabitants of the country do faint because of us.[206]

Joshua sending two spies from Israel's camp to survey Jericho simply mimicked his mentor Moses. You see, whether the spies brought back a good or bad report, the covenant that God had made would not have been affected one way or the other. They could not help, improve, change, or simplify the covenant promise of God. "God is not a man, that He should lie."[207] His word would be true, irrespective of the positive or negative testimony.

We ought to walk by faith and not by sight. If only we would take God at His word. God does not need our vision or input to endorse His promises, or to support their fulfillment. While no reprimand from God for sending the spies can be found, their military surveillance did not yield one fact that aided in Jericho's overthrow. God bypassed their gesture to be supportive, led them to Rahab, because in His love He had a trophy there, and would use her testimony to help the spies to see that the sovereign Lord is never left without His own witness. Frequently, God overlooks our attempts to help Him with our salvation, only to grant a wider vision that hopefully we can have a deeper confidence in His promises.

However, some things rise as clear as crystal out of this spy mission.

God is no respecter of persons.

1. The salvation of individuals considered "outside the faith" beyond narrow denominational lines of those who adhere to imposed guidelines, the tradition of men, is important to Him. Those who will crowd the gates of heaven will not be there because of denominational affiliation, but thanks be to God, only because of His Son, our Lord Jesus.
2. Had the spies not gone and searched out Jericho, the personal testimony of Rahab would have been lost, and the bright beam to lighten their pathway missed.
3. God used the spies to show forth His glory, to more fully define how salvation is granted, and to leave on record that Israel alone would not, could not conquer Canaan, neither will we win heaven by our deeds of righteousness, of which there are none.
4. God's power to save in unusual ways would not have been evidenced.
5. The nobler truth that whosoever, rich or poor, black or white, learned or unlearned, educated or uneducated, male or female, boy or girl,

handsome, pretty or ugly, yes, whosoever will may come and be saved. Have you ever stopped and considered that under normal circumstances Rahab and her household would not have become a part of the chosen of God by man's standard of inclusion, into the ranks of the faithful few?

Immediately after Israel crossed the Jordan, the manna ceased. Then Joshua, on his way to his first conflict armed by faith, had a special confrontation:

> And it came to pass, when Joshua was by Jericho, that he lifted up his eyes and looked, and, behold, there stood a man over against him with his sword drawn in his hand: and Joshua went unto him, and said unto him, Art thou for us, or for ouradversaries?[208]

> As Captain of the host of the Lord am I now come... It was Christ, the Exalted One, who stood before the leader of Israel. Awe-stricken, Joshua fell upon his face and worshiped, and heard the assurance, "I have given into thine hand Jericho, and the king thereof, and the mighty men of valor," and he received instruction for the capture of the city.[209]

What a wonderful surprise! God vouchsafed to appear unto him as the Commander-in-Chief. God in Jesus Christ is on our side. We need not fear or be disheartened, irrespective of the magnitude of the responsibility. He is the author and finisher of our faith. He is Alpha and Omega. He is the First and the Last. He is the Beginning and the Ending, and Jesus still leads on. In this initial conflict in the conquest of Canaan, the Lord will show Himself as a warrior, prince of the Lord's host, visible and invisible. The appearances of God to His people have always been in accordance with the project or situation at hand.

Moses needed to be reminded of the indestructibility of the church and to whom it belongs. After four hundred years in Egypt, Israel was still the church of the living God. So God appeared to Moses in a burning bush that would not burn up. That inextinguishable burning bush represented Israel, the church, with God in the midst. Moses, on seeing that unusual sight, went close to get a good view. The ever-present God commanded that he should take off his shoes. His prompt response indicated the obedience, worship, and reverence that ought to flow spontaneously from the heart. Joshua did not have a burning bush, but in his face-to-face confrontation with the Lord, he, like Moses, removed his shoes. Likewise, when in God's presence we appear, we, like Moses and Joshua, would do well while standing on holy ground, receiving instruction from the Commander-in-Chief for present and future tasks, lay aside anything that defiles, take off the "shoes", and respond in obedience and worship. It was most fitting then, and is today. While Jesus bids us "come boldly to the throne of grace,"[210] there should be no rash intrusion into the presence of the almighty God. One ought to be ever so conscious of that line of demarcation between the Creator and the creature created. Moses and Joshua respected the limits. Mankind would do well to follow those footsteps.

God reveals Himself in various forms to meet our needs?

To Jacob fleeing, He was a wrestler.

To Abraham, He was the judge of the whole earth who did right, and Jehovah Jireh, a God who provided.

To those who mourn He is the God of all comfort.

To the lonely and friendless, He is a "friend that sticketh closer than a brother." What a friend we have in Jesus!

To the widow, He is a husband.

To the storm tossed, He is a shelter in the time of storm, yea even more a haven of rest. When the billows roar and the waves would inundate the soul, He is the mighty rock.

When the burdens press, when the heart is weighed down with the cares of life, He is the God of hope.

To all of His children who like Joshua must get to the Promised Land, where conquests must be made, battles fought and won, He is the captain of the Lord's host.

If ever any transaction could be called a "done deal," here is one that holds that distinction:

And the LORD said unto Joshua, See, I have given into thine hand Jericho, and the king thereof, and the mighty men of valour.[211]

Before the military assignments or the strategy were given or rehearsed, the battle was won. When the perfect will of God is done, success is assured. Victory is promised through faith and obedience.

> The secret of success is the union of divine power with human effort. Those who achieve the greatest results are those who rely most implicitly upon the Almighty Arm.[212]

THE MILITARY STRATEGY

The military strategy was simple and uncomplicated. Like the plan of redemption, anyone can attain unto it. It involved an army and priests with the ark, shofars, trumpets, making one trip each day, in silence, for six days around the seeming impregnable walls of Jericho. They were to circle the walls seven times on the seventh day, shofars should blare, the people should shout at the blast of the ram's horns, and the walls would topple. They did.[213] The demands of God as they relate to the matter of salvation are simple yet profound, uncomplicated and right.

> But God hath chosen the foolish things of the world to confound the wise; and God hath chosen the weak things of the world to confound the things which are mighty; And base things of the world, and things which are despised, hath God chosen, yea, and things which are not, to bring to nought things that are: That no flesh should glory in his presence.[214]

God only tests faith. Jericho's walls were not theirs to crumble. God, you will recall, had assured Joshua victory before the engagement commenced. However, God watched to see whether the Israelites possessed and demonstrated a like faith as did Joshua in His leadership. Could they hold out for seven days without complaints? Joshua will take God at His word, but each Israelite must demonstrate his personal trust in God. It is impossible to live off the spiritual capital of others.

God arranged the strategy for the defeat of Jericho, and based upon the results we can only say that if all things were done God's way, life would be one spectacular, triumphant song. God's ways are certainly beyond our ken. But God employs some of the strangest ways to accomplish His ends. Could it be that this, the simplest procedure, had another benefit? If victory was already discussed and settled, then God could not have been using Israel's circling of the walls to flatten them. Walking around the walls each day was God's testing procedure, exclusively done for Israel. He tested and elicited faith in the people. Israel passed the test.

> But the very plan of continuing this ceremony through so long a time prior to the final overthrow of the walls afforded opportunity for the increase of faith among the Israelites. They were to become thoroughly impressed with the idea that their strength was not in the wisdom of man, nor in his might, but only in the God of their salvation. They were thus to become accustomed to putting themselves out of the question and relying wholly upon their divine Leader.[215]

As the legend goes, one of the men of Jericho, living on the wall, saw the Israelites as they walked around Jericho for two days. He was so impressed by the orderly conduct of the seven priests well dressed in their lavish robes, with their trumpets, the ark of God with its gold glittering from God's glory and the brilliant sunshine, the battalion in its beautiful regalia, and not a sound heard except for footsteps. He became concerned and asked, "What are all of you doing walking around the walls every day in total silence? An Israelite replied, "If you know what I know, and if I were you, I'd get off of that wall as soon as I can."

The instructions were followed exactly. They did their part and God did His. For those six days Israel engaged in the process. There seems to have been solidarity of purpose. There is no record of a dissenting voice. There were those in the community who recalled that Noah was locked up in the ark for seven days before the first drop of rain fell, and who breathed a sigh of relief when the sixth trip ended. The last trip around Jericho was made on the seventh day. Then the trumpets blared, Israel shouted, and those massive walls came crashing to the ground. Israel's first victory in the conquest of Canaan was achieved.

Available to us are all the promises God has made, which if embraced will make us more than conquerors. If we would simply obey without doubt or question, God would work for us in a fashion we have not experienced before. The walls of our circumstances would come down.

It is indeed that simple. The questions have been raised, "Are we to believe that just walking, shofars sounding, and Israel shouting "victory" brought the walls down?" A million times no.

> If the eyes of Joshua had been opened as were the eyes of the servant of Elisha at Dothan, and he could have endured the sight, he would have seen the angels of the Lord encamped about the children of Israel; for the trained army of heaven had come to fight for the people of God, and the Captain of the Lord's host was there to command. When Jericho fell, no human hand touched the walls of the city, for the angels of the Lord overthrew the fortifications, and entered the fortress of the enemy. **It was not Israel, but the Captain of the Lord's host that took Jericho.** But Israel had their part to act to show their faith in the Captain of their salvation.[216]

And then this is how battles are won:

> The Majesty of heaven, with His army of angels, leveled the walls of Jericho without human aid. The armed warriors of Israel had no cause to glory in their achievements. All was done through the power of God... Suddenly the vast army halts. The trumpets break forth into a blast that shakes the very earth. The united voices of all Israel rend the air with a mighty shout. The walls of solid stone, with their massive towers and battlements, totter and heave from their foundations and, with a crash like a thousand thunders, fall in shapeless ruin to the earth. The inhabitants and the army of the enemy, paralyzed with terror and amazement, offer no resistance, and Israel marches in and takes captive the mighty city of Jericho. How easily the armies of heaven brought down the walls that had seemed so formidable to the spies who brought the false report![217]

Angels, ministering servants, pressed into action, took Jericho without human support or intervention.

When one enlists in God's great army as a soldier, victory number one will give courage for battle number two, and each succeeding conflict. In "fighting the good fight of faith,"[218] the Christian should go from strength to strength. Paul did say, "I can do all things through Christ who strengthens me."[219] But sometimes the Christian goes from difficulty to difficulty. The tests change. We are not as unquestioning as we should be. Had Israel taken God at His word, they would have walked out of the Red Sea directly into their inheritance. Blanketed by distrust and hesitation, clinging tenaciously to sight, they forfeited forty years of bliss and happiness. Their failure simply added difficulty.

There are times when we seem to believe that we have just as novel an idea as the Creator, only to discover shipwreck and a voice calling for help in our failures. We have not like Joshua walked away and done exactly what God said. We have even tried to improve on the method of our salvation by giving things to God in the place of our worship. God in love appeals to us to "buy wine and milk without money and without price."[220] Yet mankind has not fully learned the word *trust* despite unnumbered "how to" examples. It seems we just have not learned that whatever our problems, difficulties, fightings within and without, needs, and situations; nothing, that's right, nothing is beyond the ability of God to help us resolve them and make life beautiful. He can pick up the pieces of shattered dreams, restore disintegrating marriages, prevent divorce or separation, find lost children and bring them back into the fold of safety, reconstruct failed lives, put a song back into a broken heart, and make you a winner not a loser. I recently read a story that occurred during the German blitz against London during World War 11. Someone asked an elderly woman how she kept so calm from day to day. She said, "Every night I say my prayers, and when I begin to worry about what Hitler is going to do, I remember how the parson said that Jesus is watching. So then I go to sleep. After all, there is no use for two of us to lie awake." That's awesome. We need an attitude like that, to place our trust in God and trust Him to take care of the outcomes whatever they might be.

The lives of the following persons grant us an opportunity to observe God's methods. It is sometimes from test to test, and sometimes from difficulty to difficulty until He says well done.

Abraham went from a covenant agreement with God,[221] father of the faithful, to lying about Sarah being his sister,[222] to a rendezvous with God on Mount Moriah. The "father of the faithful" would be tested. Only when all the directives were observed as given by a loving Savior did Abraham win God's nod of approval. He told his servants that he and Isaac were going up the mountain to worship. When worship yielded to loving, faithful obedience, God cried out, "Now I know."[223] When our worship yields to total surrender to His will, we too will find our Jehovah Jireh.

Naaman should dip in the Jordan seven times, six would not do. Not until he complied fully did restoration come.[224]

The ten lepers cleansed must go and show themselves to the priest. As they responded by faith, healing came.[225]

Peter must go down to the sea and catch a fish. In the mouth of the first one caught will be tax money for his Master and himself. The miracle happened because Peter did precisely as he was told.[226]

> God will do marvelous things for those who trust in Him. It is because His professed people trust so much to their own wisdom, and do not give the Lord an opportunity to reveal His power in their behalf, that they have no more strength. He will help His believing children in every emergency if they will place their entire confidence in Him and implicitly obey Him.[227]

We can and should learn some great lessons from the first strategic mission in the conquest of Canaan, the destruction and capture of Jericho. They will and should assist us in having a closer relationship with God. The public acts and the private encounters with "the captain of the Lord's host," the gallant achievement of settling the nomadic slaves out of Egypt, and the recognition of the Hebrews as God's peculiar treasure by Joshua, speak volumes.

LESSONS WE CAN LEARN

1. God is a covenant keeper.

His promises are sure. As the sovereign King, His word is His bond. Years will never erode the pledges made. The promises made over four hundred years to transport them to Canaan, God's choosing, came to fruition. They arrived in Jericho just as He said. God keeps His covenant.

And I am come down to deliver them out of the hands of the Egyptians, and to bring them up out of that land unto a good land and a large, unto a land flowing with milk and honey; unto the place of the Canaanites, and the Hittites, and the Amorites, and the Perizzites, and the Hivites and the Jebusites.[228]

God can be trusted. The Lord's plans will succeed. He is a destroyer, but more so a deliverer of His promises. He delivers from slavery to freedom, from sin to righteousness, from sorrow to joy, from sickness to health, from Egypt to Canaan, and ultimately from earth to heaven. God's promises to Abraham, Isaac, and Jacob were not kept due to Israel's virtues, goodness, or values possessed. The goodly land could not render them good. His promises, His covenants, remained intact even when his people were under Pharaoh's lash, in the brick kilns, there in Goshen, abused and scorned. The sovereign, omnipotent God, the omniscient One, the omnipresent God, the deliverer, their redeemer and our savior saw them and knew they would say, "Because there were no graves in Egypt?"[229] Yet out of a covenant-keeping heart, knowing the end from the beginning, their proclivity to murmur and gripe, knowing when and where the variety of obstacles would come across their path, He never relinquished the covenant agreement. No human circumstance could make God change a single word of what He and Abraham discussed, not even alter His pledged word. So it is with us. His promises cannot fail. Our God is trustworthy. We ought to be like Him, a covenant keeper.

Our faith is bolstered when we are assured, even confident, that the God of the universe, the God and Father of Abraham, Isaac and Jacob, yes the Father of our Lord and Savior Jesus Christ is also our covenant- and promise-keeping God and Father. God's promises are true and unfailing.

Thus saith the LORD; …If ye can break my covenant of the day and my covenant of the night, and that there should not be day and night in their season; Then may also my covenant be broken with David my servant, that he should not have a son to reign upon his throne; and with the Levites the priests, my ministers.[230]

The covenant of God is as permanent and binding as natural law and order, and irreversible.

2. God's ways are strange and different.

God employs some of the strangest ways to give us victory over our "Jericho experiences." In the process we develop a faith built on total trust in Him. For example, victory over the Amalekites came by Moses' hands being held up toward heaven supported by Aaron and Hur.[231] Pharaoh and his host were destroyed by water when Moses stretched his rod over the Red Sea.[232] Dipping in the muddy Jordan River seven times healed Naaman's leprosy.[233] By the preaching of the gospel the strongholds of sin and Satan are conquered. The entrance of God's words obliterates the darkness, and benighted souls are lighted.[234] Victory over Jericho came as a result of no talking and just walking. Irrespective of how unachievable the task may appear, pure faith in God, no questions asked, will make it attainable. As strange as it seemed, however long the walk, the instructions were directives from God to be obeyed, and success followed.

Ofttimes we want to *scale* the walls of our circumstances, but the command is to *walk*.

We *decide* to bulldoze the wall; *no, walk.*

We *choose* to dynamite the wall; *no, walk.*

We try to *bomb* or *burn* down the wall; *no, walk.*

Walk children, once per day, and seven times on the seventh day.

When we elect to look away from all our personal preparations, our ingenuity, our know-how, our wisdom and our plans and do God's biddings precisely, exactly as outlined, we discover God's omniscience and omnipotence, and our ignorance and weakness. In our Christian experience, strength, approval, and being fortified come from doing the simple, achievable acts of a loving God. Just walk the walk, and talk the talk. God employs strange, unusual, different, and incredible methods to accomplish His will, and without duplication.

The impregnable, irreducible walls of Jericho came down by walking, shouting, and the blowing of priestly trumpets.[235] That boggles the imagination, but that is what happened. Stranger still, bordering on the bizarre is the fact that the portion of the wall where Rahab and her family resided remained standing for the rescue mission. Those children of God, Rahab and her family, were redeemed from off the wall.[236] God's family outside the wall, the Israelites were saved by the same God, at the same time, only by different procedures. Salvation is never granted in the same fashion to any of His children. Some through the fire, some through great trials, some on the wall, some outside the wall, but all are saved through the blood—Israel with blood on the lintel and doorposts,[237] through the Red Sea and the River Jordan,[238] and Rahab had her scarlet thread in her window as covenanted.[239] The conquest of Jericho was not war in progress but faith in action.

We should forever settle the matter to do things God's way, however unfamiliar they seem. The lessons of complete trust yet to be learned are legion. We must walk by faith and not by sight. Although the requirements are simple, Israel and all of God's children have more often than necessary yielded to sight instead of complete trust in Him. Knowing human nature, Israel must have thought of the process long and hard before they embarked upon the first day's walk.

They debated among themselves, "Just walk, have no conversation, and finally after seven days, shout and blow some trumpets?" "Why do this for seven days?" "Why should it not happen on the first day?" "What will be the essential difference between day one and day seven?" "Will length of days make the walls collapse easier?" "If God had already considered this a 'done deal,' declared He was captain of the Lord's host, why not just go ahead and get it over?" Good questions. We need to remember that God always seeks human involvement however limited. And as stated, the lessons of faith and trust derived by the walk would augment the dwindling faith they displayed. The apostle Paul said, "And let us not be weary in well doing."[240]

Strange as it seems, God's way is the best way. God's way is the right way. Seven days would not have been a long wait. In their unbelief Canaan was deferred forty years. It is not too late to learn to just wait on the Lord—be it 7 days, 70, 700, or 7000 days. God waited on them to get it together for four hundred years first, and then another forty in the wilderness wanderings. He never relinquished His grasp or considered it a waste of His time. He was never burdened by the multiplicity of indecisiveness and problems, neither is He with ours. Those loving hands bore them up despite His wait for them to get it together. And that fact is true of us also.

3. God is no respecter of persons but He has great respect for faith.

> But Joshua said unto the two men that had spied out the country, Go into the harlot's house, and bring out thence the woman, and all that she hath, as ye sware unto her. And the young men that were spies went in, and brought out Rahab, and her father, and her mother, and her brethren, and all that she had; and they brought out all her kindred, and left them without the camp of Israel. And they burnt the city with fire, and all that was therein: only the silver, and the gold, and the vessels of brass and of iron, they put into the treasury of the house of the LORD. And Joshua saved Rahab the harlot alive, and her father's household, and all that she had; and she dwelleth in Israel even unto this day; because she hid the messengers, which Joshua sent to spy out Jericho.[241]

And then,

> Rahab was left for some time without the camp, no doubt to prepare herself for admission as a proselyte. In due time she was admitted into the congregation of Israel, presumably after she and her kindred had been instructed in the religion of Jehovah and had purified themselves from their heathen ways and beliefs. She probably became the wife of Salmon, prince of Judah, and the mother of Boaz, and thus one of the ancestors of our Saviour (see Matt. 1:5). What a blessed privilege awaits those who by faith join themselves to the people of God! How wonderful to know that the gospel of Jesus Christ transcends even the most unfavorable heredity and environment! "Whosoever will," of any color or race, or station in life, may partake of the glorious privileges of sonship.[242]

This is one awesome transaction on the part of God. God was attracted to her faith, which He Himself had implanted. Rahab told the spies, "We have heard how the Lord dried up the water of the Red Sea for you."[243] The testimony of Israel's journey through the Red Sea on dry ground fanned a flame of fragrant faith in her soul. It was manifested long before she made her oath of allegiance to Israel's God, and the agreement with the two spies.

> And before they were laid down, she came up unto them upon the roof; And she said unto the men, I know that the LORD hath given you the land, and that your terror is fallen upon us, and that all the inhabitants of the land faint because of you. For we have heard how the LORD dried up the water of the Red sea for you, when ye came out of Egypt; and what ye did unto the two kings of the Amorites, that were on the other side Jordan, Sihon and Og, whom ye utterly destroyed. And as soon as we had heard these things, our hearts did melt, neither did there remain any more courage in any man, because of you: for the LORD your God, he is God in heaven above, and in earth beneath. Now therefore, I pray you, swear unto me by the LORD, since I have shewed you kindness, that ye will also shew kindness unto my father's house, and give me a true token: And that ye will save alive my father, and my mother, and my brethren, and my sisters, and all that they have, and deliver our lives from death. And the men answered her, Our life for yours, if ye utter not this our business. And it shall be, when the LORD hath given us the land, that we will deal kindly and truly with thee. Then she let them down by a cord through the window: for her house was on the town wall, and she dwelt upon the wall...And the men said unto her,... Behold, when we come into the land, Thou shalt bind this line of scarlet thread in the window which thou didst let us down by: and thou shalt bring thy father, and thy mother, and thy brethren, and all thy father's household, home unto thee.[244]

"And before they were laid down."[245] Her testimony preceded all the covenant agreements made. Her faith and concepts of God dated back to the time when Moses and Israel encountered the Amorite kings. She received word of how God had delivered Sihon and Og into Israel's hands.

One can only imagine the sacred joy, the sense of pride and holy destiny that welled up in her heart as she saw the Israelites day after day going around the walls of Jericho. She knew that she would be delivered soon, and that she belonged among God's chosen people. She had done her share of witnessing. The scarlet cord remained in the window as arranged. Something remarkable about that experience which we ought not to lose is that Rahab's faith was placed in mortal men's promises. The agreement stated that all who remained in the house with the scarlet cord would be saved. She believed in God and in the two men who were His representatives. If only we could have a like trust in God. Even when everything around us seems to be crumbling or is about to crumble, a faith that asserts that God is faithful, that He will save, should be ours. It would silence our doubts and calm our fears.

Apart from her great statements of faith, when she told the spies she hid that it was common knowledge that Jericho would be overthrown, and that God is the one and only true God, not much is heard from or of Rahab in the ensuing years. Yet we cannot forget the pivotal role she had in the life of Israel. Her faith showed a deeper trust in God than the spies' mission had exhibited. She had faith in her family that they would come into her house. God in His rescue mission of Rahab opened an avenue of blessing for the Gentiles (those outside the economy of Israel), which can only be defined as His respect for faith, the faith of Jew or Gentile.

"A heart of faith and love is dearer to God than the most costly gift."[246]

After the purification rites were performed Rahab and her family became members of the Jewish faith. They were no longer outside the camp of Israel. Their changed lifestyles made them God's peculiar people, and the covenants and promises to Abraham, Isaac, and Jacob became theirs. In her, God found a rare, precious pearl. She was His trophy of what happened on the way to the Promised Land. We likewise through Jesus Christ, our scarlet thread, become heirs of the same promises, and are considered "the Israel of God." God will absorb into His church, persons of all nations, kindred, languages, and people. The gospel commission is to preach the gospel in all the world and baptize those who have experienced the new birth. Those individuals become citizens of God's coming kingdom, no longer strangers from the commonwealth.

There is neither Jew nor Greek, there is neither bond or free, there is neither male nor female: for ye are all one in Christ Jesus. And if ye be Christ's, then are ye Abraham's seed, and heirs according to the promise.[247]

For in Christ Jesus neither circumcision availeth anything, nor uncircumcision, but a new creature. And as many as walk according to this rule, peace be on them, and mercy, and upon the *Israel of God.*[248]

That is it. God will search and find persons like Rahab, who although outside of the "camp of Israel," the "community of saints," will confess their faith in the Lord Jesus Christ. The quality and quantity of faith is measured and known only by Him who is no respecter of persons, but has great respect for faith. Through faith in Christ they become "the Israel of God."

You will observe I'm sure, that the two spies who searched out the land had to run and hide for their lives. Upon their return they gave no cogent, strategic, military, or geographic statement, supportive in any manner to assist in Jericho's overthrow. Consider also where they went for information. It showed a lack of good judgment. It is my opinion that God wanted to save Rahab, knew her heart, her faith, had great spiritual reasons; therefore, He allowed these men to cross her path. In like manner, God knows our testimony of faith in Him, and rewards us in this life and the one to come for He respects faith wherever it is found.

4. *God alone threw down Jericho's walls.*

The walls of Jericho came down by God's power. No human hand assisted. But like the Berlin Wall that separated East Berlin from West Berlin, there are spiritual walls that divide and prevent entrance into the Promised Land or in taking possession of it. The walls of Jericho had to come down for Israel to take possession. In like manner all "walls" must be demolished if full and free experience in the things of God is to be enjoyed.

Walls block the entrance and possession. There must be a frank admission that all kinds of walls exist. Walls of prejudice, hate, racism, cherished sins, unwholesome relationships, worldliness, walls of indiscretion, doubt, fear. You can fill in the walls not mentioned here that block entrance and ownership of the Promised Land. Jesus spoke to those walls that ought to be torn down:

> For He is our peace, who hath made both one, and hath broken down the middle wall of partition between us.[249]

His services are free of charge. The six-day walk must come to an end. The seventh with the seven circles must be completed. All that remains to be done is the shout of joy, the sound of the trumpets, and to take possession.

> What a day that will be
> When my Saviour I shall see,
> When He takes me by the hand
> And leads me to the Promised Land,
> What a day, glorious day, that will be.

On that day faith will yield to sight. There will be no walls between.

A boy with a mechanical mind made a toy motorboat to sail up a stream that flowed near his home. On taking it to the stream, he found it was defective, and it sailed far beyond his reach. After many efforts to recover it, he was at last compelled to return home without it. To him, it was lost. Not long after, he was surprised to see his little boat in a store with a card attached, saying, "This motorboat for sale. Price, five shillings." He made his loss known to the owner of the store, but it was futile. He was separated from his boat by the glass. He could only have it for the price asked.

He went home and told his father of his predicament. After hearing the story, the father said, "Here's the money; go and buy your own boat."

When at last he had the boat back in his possession, he said, "You are mine twice. I made you, and I bought you. And now there is no glass between us."

The saved also belong twice to the Lord Jesus. He made them and He has redeemed them. The walls that divide will come crashing down soon, and the shouts of victory will resound throughout the courts of glory forever. The saints will be exultant when they see their Savior, Jesus Christ, face to face with no walls between. They will worship, praise, and adore God, and live in His presence forever with no walls between. Praise God that day is not far away. All who trust Christ's power completely will have Jesus, not Joshua, lead them into the Promised Land, their eternal home. The battle will be won. The Lord Jesus Christ will be the captain of the Lord's host then. The victory celebration will last through all eternity. Plan to be there.

Chapter 5

HORSES AND CHARIOTS OF FIRE

(Based on 2 Kings 6:8–23)

Before the first shot was fired, before the first sword speared a heart, before the invasion strategy unfolded, Israel had won the battle with Syria hands down. Benhadad, king of Syria, was in constant conflict with Israel. War against Israel by any nation meant that they were in conflict against God. Benhadad's ignorance of that fact made it no less true. Strange as it may seem, this was the same Benhadad, king of Syria, who only a few years before sent ambassadors to the king of Israel, Jehoram, living in Samaria on behalf of his trusted servant Naaman.[250]

The little maid in Naaman's employ said, "If only my master were with the prophet who is in Samaria!"[251] She did not say the king in Samaria. But lofty, arrogant King Benhadad was too haughty to correspond or associate with persons beneath his rank or class or with anyone he deemed of lesser status. And on the other hand, give him the benefit of the doubt. It could have been a matter of protocol whereby men of equal status communicate with each other. Prompted by the maid's words, Benhadad did not consult Elisha the prophet, but Jehoram the king. There was nothing complicated about what the little girl said. She said Elisha the prophet.

The need of help for Naaman normalized relations between Israel and Syria temporarily. Naaman's restoration, cleansing from leprosy,[252] those sacred recollections around that miraculous event would not be blurred by the passage of time. However, Benhadad would soon suffer from amnesia. His gratitude died early. Israel and Syria were again at war as usual. The failure of previous attempts by Benhadad taught him nothing. He could not, did not, learn from his mistakes. In each invasion by the Syrians, God demonstrated His power to save in ways never thought of by Israel. The chronic hostilities of the Syrians were unsuccessful. Jehoram foiled all of Benhadad's carefully laid plans.[253] When Benhadad, the Syrian despot, summoned within his blasphemous heart plans to do Israel wrong, God saw them. He laid his ambushes, his sudden attacks, his surprise missions, his border raids in the secret chambers of his darkened heart and bedroom. But God who reads the heart, He who knows all things, gave his plans to Elisha who informed Jehoram. Consequently, all those plans did not materialize.

Before dealing with the fact that all things are naked and open to the eyes of God,[254] however crafty, cunning, or well laid, it is necessary to observe that Benhadad wanted to muzzle Elisha who was only God's mouthpiece.[255] He should first outwit God; then Elisha, and King Je-horam would be secondary considerations. Benhadad was of the opinion that a traitor, an informer, a spy was among the couriers.[256] Unable to detect the informer within his ranks, how will he find Elisha? Benhadad, in his bedchamber, under the tightest security was not dealing with Elisha or King Jehoram. If he could outsmart God he would have had a clear, unhindered pathway. Benhadad dealt with intelligence beyond the secret service of his day, more powerful than the FBI, CIA, KGB, or the Scotland Yard detectives. His men had nothing to do with his chambers being bugged or a breakdown in strategic maneuvers. The entire situation had nothing to do with human beings. Their wisdom, know-how, and well-conceived plans did not share or participate in this undertaking. It was all about God, a God who sees, knows, and hears everything.

In Eliphaz's dialogue with Job, he remarked, "Doesn't God live above the stars? Just look at how high they are! He sees everything going on down here. And yet you ask, 'What does God know?' Do you think He judges people out of ignorance? Do you think that distance or darkness keeps Him from seeing you as He goes back and forth throughout the universe?'"[257] Our God sees everything. God, "telleth the number of the stars; He calleth them all by their names."[258] God knew the number of exiles who escaped Egyptian bondage, and knew every name just as the stars, for He promised Abraham that his seed would be as numerous as the stars of heaven.[259] Nothing in the whole wide world escapes His knowledge. Marvelous is the God we serve. It would do us well every now and then to escape from the mundane petty interests and pursuits of this life on this "mud ball" of ours, and turn our eyes heavenward at night in contemplation of the arithmetician God, who numbers every star. Then observe the glorious canopy overhead. Truly, this would be most engaging. He is a mighty God. "He maketh Arcturus, Orion, and Pleiades, and the chambers of the soul. Which doeth great things past finding out; yea, and wonders without number."[260] God knows everything. He knows your name, where you live, work, bank, and with whom you associate. It certainly should deepen our sense of God's condescending love when we see the heavenly hosts in their ordered march and realize that the God who addresses all those celestial things deigns to know, love, and save. He considers us His children on a personal, intimate basis. His ears; so keenly sensitive to the publican's plea and sigh of contrition,[261] yet so compassionate that nothing, absolutely nothing, escapes His watchful eye.

Benhadad sat upon his conscience. Somewhere inside his soul he must have known that he contended not with Elisha the prophet and King Jehoram. If under the most tightened security of his inaccessible bedroom all the facts, figures, and features are detailed, then it must have been a higher power. Could it be that Benhadad did not want to recognize the sovereign God?

In the first book of the Bible, just after creation, there is compelling evidence that others like Benhadad did not want to recognize God's sovereignty. After the Flood, men decided to build a structure whose top would reach to heaven. "And the Lord came down to see the city and the tower, which the children of men builded."[262] God had commanded those who came out of the ark to replenish, to repopulate the earth.[263] This would be accomplished by going over the habitable places of the earth. But men decided otherwise; they would congregate and build a tower. God's plan was unacceptable. They concluded that even the rainbow in the sky, indicating that there would never be another flood of that magnitude was insufficient. What did God do? He frustrated the builders of Babel by confounding their language.[264] The project which had disobedience written all over it came to a screeching halt. God had already hung a rainbow in the sky and promised no more destruction of the world by a flood.[265] The unbelievers, despite His word, planned this structure. It is my opinion that they did that, that in the event another flood came heaven would have been involved as the waters rose. God disrupted the construction, and they aborted their plans. God's inexhaustible knowledge and power was shown to those who contrived to build the Tower of Babel.

In another instance, God planned for Jacob to receive the birthright with all its privileges and responsibilities, even though he was the second son born to Isaac and Rebekah.[266] In time, Esau sold the birthright to his brother Jacob. The amazing story of how Jacob received the blessing from his blind father, Isaac, based upon Rebekah's preference and favoritism, demonstrates God's intervention in human lives and His plan for each son and daughter of His.[267] If Isaac's eyesight were intact, Jacob would never have been blessed instead of Esau. In every situation God has a plan. He knows everything, He is everywhere, and His objectives will never be thwarted. "I am the Lord, the God who is everywhere, the God who is nearby and far away. I see everything and everyone. No one can hide from me. I am everywhere in heaven and on earth."[268] Isaac gave the blessing to Jacob although that was not his preference. God simply intervened in human concerns.

God had a time schedule for Israel's march out of Egyptian captivity. Speaking to Abraham, God said, "Know of a surety that thy seed shall be a stranger in a land that is not theirs, and shall serve them; and they shall afflict them four hundred years."[269] "And it came to pass at the end of the four hundred and thirty years, even the selfsame day it came to pass, that all of the hosts of the LORD went out from the land of Egypt."[270] We serve an on-time God whose words are dependable and true. Pharaoh placed every possible roadblock in Israel's pathway, but God would intervene and Israel would be delivered on schedule. God's honor was at stake and puny Pharaoh would not frustrate them. Neither would Benhadad disrupt Israel's peace and God's plans.

"All things are naked and opened unto the eyes of Him with whom we have to do."[271] Benhadad ought to have taken notice. The fact is he didn't. We find ourselves in a like predicament. We ought to take notice and be reminded that God is in control. We would all lead such a wonderful life if at the break of each day our opening thoughts were placed on the loving God we serve, the One who is in charge of our world. But oh how often, like Benhadad, we forget that He hears, sees, knows, feels, and understands everything. And yet, despite our ineptitude, He loves, keeps, watches, forgives, and pardons for Christ's sake. It is a sobering thought, one of which all should be constantly aware and adopt. If that were done, there would be a reduction of evil and a surplus of good. Our world would be in possession of God's visible grace. Just stop and think of it. If every thought, every human encounter, every business transaction, in every crisis, in all that we do with family, friends, money, work, whatever, even in dying, if we were ever so conscious that all is naked and opened to God, we would be supremely blessed. Life would be lived in God's holy presence. There would be no sham, no artificiality, no hypocrisy, no façade, no counterfeiting of the real religious walk. Everyone would be "true blue." It would mean that our first encounter in all our dealings would be with the all-knowing, all-seeing God. Then peace, rest, hope, joy, success, and an orderly life would be our earthly lot. Always our consciousness would be of Him over us, around us, beside us, and beneath us. That kind of intimate, personal communion would grant a walk with God such as Enoch had. Like Hagar, "Thou God seest me,"[272] would be our guiding light.

Benhadad learned that Elisha maintained constant communion with the God who told him of His plans, hence the failures in all of the border raids against Israel. Benhadad decided to capture Elisha. His spies told him that Elisha lived in Dothan. However, what Benhadad failed to reason out carefully was that the same God who told Jehoram about his raids on Israel through Elisha could and would have informed Elisha about his oncoming spies. God permitted that situation to occur without the slightest alteration due to His overall plan.

> Dothan, "A town on the regular caravan route between Gilead and Egypt, near the plain of Esdraelon and a pass leading to the highlands of Samaria. It was 15 miles north of Shechem, and 11 miles northeast of Samaria. It was here that a band of Ishmaelites on their way from Gilead to Egypt purchased Joseph (Genesis 37:17–28). This site is now known as Tell Dotha."[273]

Its location on the caravan route made it approachable by whatever military might Benhadad chose to deploy.

When Elisha's servant dusted the cobwebs of slumber from his eyes the following morning, fear and fright overwhelmed him.

> And when the servant of the man of God was risen early, and gone forth, behold, an host compassed the city both with horses and chariots. And his servant said unto him, Alas, my master! how shall we do?[274]

Worry and trepidation took hold of Elisha's servant. The horses and chariots and a large army around Dothan was an unusual sight, to say the least. Many questions flooded his mind. Will they take Elisha captive? Will the city fathers yield to the pressure and deliver Elisha over to the Syrian army? Would Dothan, that little town, become the object of a surprise attack? They were unprepared to do battle with that large army which now surrounded the city. Please be kind to the servant. He had not yet arrived at Elisha's spiritual maturity. Elisha had seen Elijah's flaming chariot transporting him from earth to glory. His servant's eyes must be adjusted from the material to the invisible. His faith must grow out of this experience. Note if you please, Elisha's cool, calm, and collected attitude. "And he answered, Fear not: for they that be with us are more than they that be with them."[275]

Elisha knew, saw, and understood some things his servant must learn. He was therefore rather patient and understanding about the young man's dilemma. His response to the servant's anguish was swift, kind, deliberate, saving, and assuring: "Fear thou not."[276]

The Lord often speaks these reassuring words to His children. In the sojourn of life, the people of God often find themselves in situations that would cause them to be uncertain and afraid. But God makes His presence known. He speaks words of encouragement and hope. Listen.

> *Fear not,* Abraham: I am thy shield, and thy exceeding great reward.[277]

> And God spake unto Israel in the visions of the night, and said, Jacob, Jacob. And he said, Here am I.

And he said, I am God, the God of thy father: *fear not* to go down to Egypt; for I will there make of thee a great nation:[278]

And Moses said unto the people, *Fear ye not*, stand still, and see the salvation of the Lord, which he will shew to you today: for the Egyptians whom ye have seen today, ye shall see them again no more forever.[279]

Only rebel not ye against the Lord, *neither fear* ye the people of the land; for they are bread for us: their defense is departed from them, and the Lord is with us: *fear them not*.[280]

Fear not, neither be discouraged.[281]

Fear not: for I have redeemed thee, I have called thee by thy name; thou art mine.[282]

Fear not, little flock; for it is your Father's good pleasure to give you the kingdom.[283]

As long as God's people are on the earth difficulties will arise and dangers need to be met. Satan will do his utmost to cause the righteous to give way to doubt and fear, but through the mist of uncertainty and doubt the voice of the Lord still comes clear and assuring, "Let not your heart be troubled, neither let it be afraid."[284] You see,

The weakest child of God, seemingly alone and forsaken on earth, need never be afraid of all the forces the enemy may send against him. With God on his side he is more than a match for the mightiest hosts of evil.[285]

Had the servant realized that the battle was always the Lord's, then like Elisha he too would have been reliant, trusting, fearless, brave, and assured.

Elisha was a man of prayer. He prayed,

Lord, I pray thee, open his eyes, that he may see. And the Lord opened the eyes of the young man; and he saw: and, behold, the mountain was full of horses and chariots of fire round about Elisha.[286]

God responded immediately and quickly exchanged the servant's fear, timidity, and uncertainty with hope and a sign of His presence and deliverance.

What *would* life be like if our eyes were always opened? We *would* fear no ill. We *would* never fret nor repine. We *would* see that God's grace is always available. If our eyes were opened always we *would* never exchange the crown of eternal life for earth's tinsel. We *would* never dread the unknown. We *would* ever be conscious of the voice saying, "Lo, I am with you alway."[287] And when situations get bleak and dark, when ominous clouds seem to shut out every ray of light, the eyes of faith would take over and deport the darkness with the declaration that, "the Lord is my light and my salvation; whom shall I fear?"[288]

Courage and strength must be drawn from this awesome experience. When the hills and walls and streets of your "Dothan" are covered with the chariots and horses of fear, tough times financially and spiritually, when the trials of life inundate the soul, "fear not." When there is sickness, death visits the family, the prescription drugs cannot be procured, the heart aches until it nearly breaks and when overwhelmed by doubt, sing a song.

> Then my soul shall fear no ill,
> Let Him lead me where He will,
> I will go without a murmur,
> And His footsteps follow still.[289]

Quote a text of Scripture, "God is our refuge and strength, a very present help in trouble."[290] Or, "The name of the Lord is a strong tower: the righteous runneth into it, and is safe."[291]

Are you discouraged? Is your life without a song? Are you cast down, depressed, stressed? Then lift up your eyes unto the Lord. Your help will come from God. Wherever your "Dothan," whoever is your "Dothan," whenever your "Dothan" comes, rest assured that however relentless the force, however impassable the obstacles seem, however tedious the journey, however strong the gale winds, however overwhelming the sight of the chariots, horses, and the army, a loving God has promised never to disappear, never to forsake, and never to leave. In fact, He invites

His children to call upon Him when troubles come. Another promise is that He will deliver.

Unless very careful, a great spiritual fact will be missed. Elisha's prayer for open eyes was certainly not to observe the natural world. He and his servant had seen already the horses and chariots in Dothan. Elisha prayed for his servant to see the unseen. This is an amazing, illuminating, and spiritually edifying account in the Bible. When the servant's eyes were opened afterwards, he saw,

> the mountain was full of horses and chariots of fire round about Elisha."[292]

God grant us opened eyes to see the heavenly host ready to protect us. This is not the same as the television series *Touched by an Angel*. Our concerns are about redemption.

Again, unless watchful, another great aspect of God's care for His people can be lost. God employed the identical measures of Benhadad to comfort, assure, and protect His servants. Benhadad came with horses, chariots, and an army to scare off, terrify, and capture Elisha. God demonstrated that He too had horses, chariots of fire, and an army that outmatched Benhadad's.

> Fear not: for they that be with us are more than they that be with them.[293]

Whatever evils are conjured up, God will, in defense of His children, outwit the enemy on every occasion. His inexhaustible resources are at our demand and disposal. And the promise is:

> When thou goest out to battle against thine enemies, and seest horses, and chariots, and a people more than thou, be not afraid of them: for the Lord thy God is with thee.[294]

Did God place at Elisha's disposal, yea so many, even an innumerable amount of white, gleaming, saddled stallions from glory? Was this really about horses and chariots? It is true that, "they that be with us are more than they that be with them."[295] But exactly who are "they"? The "they" must have been an innumerable company of angels dispatched by God to care for His children. The subject of angels is so fascinating. The encounter of them in Elisha's conflict should prompt a brief personal review of the work and character of angels; the reality of angels; their presence in Israel's confrontation with the Syrians and humankind down the ages, and ultimately in eternity.

The psalmist David queried,

> What is man, that thou art mindful of him? And the son of man, that thou visitest him? For thou hast made him a little lower than the angels, and hast crowned him with glory and honour.[296]

Man shares with angels, although superior in creation, a common fatherhood. They are not in the same category as Adam and Eve. They have no successive generation.[297] "The chariots of God are tens of thousands and thousands of thousands."[298] "The chariots of God are made up of millions of angels."[299] That innumerable company of created beings, which came into existence by the word of God, do not float out in space on pink clouds with harps. Their role is full-time employment on behalf of those who are, according to the apostle Paul, "heirs of salvation."[300] God's creative ingenuity did not come to a screeching halt when He formed man out of the dust of the earth. Angels, His creation, our relatives, more enduring, are a part of His glorious creation. Just the thought of it awakens in the heart transcendent feelings. God created these bright, higher-than-man beings, members of the family of God, to assist man on his pilgrimage.

You will recall that Jacob, fresh out of his sin, was ministered to by angels whom he saw in his dream ascending and descending upon the ladder from earth to heaven, with a loving God at the topmost rung.[301] In the account under discussion, the moment Benhadad in his wicked designs posted evil men to attack Elisha and Israel, God Almighty posted His sentinels. Angels, majestic beings, always encompass the children of God, their brothers and sisters. Like Elisha's servant they are not always seen or their presence acknowledged, but nonetheless they are present. "The angel of the Lord encampeth round about them that fear Him, and delivereth them."[302]

Sight is wonderful. But there are lots of things we cannot see with the naked eye. The Hubble telescope has penetrated the outer reaches of space. It has given man a view of some of God's glorious creation, and still men cannot count all the stars and galaxies. It, the Hubble telescope, has not seen everything that exists in the universe. Yet they exist. Likewise around man, close to him, is an innumerable company of angels serving and working for God. Whether we see them or not, angels do exist and are deputized to be supportive of us in the matter of salvation. Long before our world was created, God arranged for the creation of these beings to assist in the plan of redemption. He had us on His mind and on His heart.

If God had confided in Elisha the things that Benhadad planned for Israel's destruction, it is logical to feel that God told Elisha that Benhadad's army had surrounded Dothan. And although Elisha might have requested God's intervention, he was humbled by the fact that he did not have to rustle up an army. God's providence had already been deployed. Angels were standing guard. All of God's children on earth have at least one guardian angel.[303] That angel stands nearby to sustain and support. We shall never know what dangers we have been delivered from because of the direct interposition of angels. In our travels, while we sleep at night, in the common walk of life, angels are watching over us. They are bodyguards for the righteous. If Satan had his way he would snuff out our lives at night while we sleep. But all day and all night angels are watching over us. God will not leave His children to be the sport of Satan and his angels. One-third of the angels God created were thrown out of heaven. Therefore, in every conflict, there are two good angels for every one evil angel. The ratio is always two to one. If a situation warrants more than one angel, God is not hesitant to send as many as needed. There are ten thousand times ten thousand and thousands of thousands of angels ready to minister to every need of God's children. They cannot forgive sin, but in the struggle against it, in moments of temptation they stand by the tempted. They take no pleasure in writing down the deeds for a day that reflect defection from the path of duty. Their joys are multiplied when they observe victories gained and battles won. How comforting to know that angels come daily in God's stead to provide heaven's ministry to each person.

God does everything orderly. As Jesus finalized the plan of redemption, God commissioned angels and they had a significant role in the closing moments of His life.

> But God suffered with His Son. *Angels* beheld the Saviour's agony. They saw their Lord enclosed by legions of satanic forces, His nature weighed down with a shuddering mysterious dread. There was silence in heaven. No harp was touched. Could mortals have viewed the amazement of the angelic host as in silent grief they watched the Father separating His beams of light, love, and glory from His beloved Son, they would better understand how offensive in His sight is sin... The world's unfallen and the heavenly *angels* had watched with intense interest as the conflict drew to its close. Satan and his confederacy of evil, the legions of apostasy, watched intently this great crisis in the work of redemption. The powers of good and evil waited to see what answer would come to Christ's thrice-repeated prayer. *Angels* had longed to bring relief to the divine sufferer, But this might not be. No way of escape was found for the Son of God. In this awful crisis, when everything was at stake, when the mysterious cup trembled in the hand of the sufferer, the heavens opened, a light shone forth amid the stormy darkness of the crisis hour, and *the mighty angel* who stands in God's presence, occupying the position from which Satan fell, came to the side of Christ. *The angel* came not to take the cup from Christ's hand, but to strengthen Him to drink it... He pointed Him to the open heavens... He assured Him that His Father is greater and more powerful than Satan... He told Him that He would see the travail of His soul, and be satisfied.[304]

On the resurrection morning God did not just send an angel to roll the stone away from the mouth of the tomb where Jesus lay:

> The great stone was in its place; the Roman seal was unbroken; the Roman guards were keeping their watch. And there were unseen watchers. Hosts of evil angels were gathered about the place. Had it been possible, the prince of darkness with his apostate army would have kept forever sealed the tomb that held the Son of God. But a heavenly host surrounded the sepulcher. Angels that excel in strength were guarding the tomb, and waiting to welcome the Prince of life... Clothed with the panoply of God, this angel left the heavenly courts.

The bright beams of God's glory went before him, and illuminated his pathway… The face they look upon is not the face of mortal warrior; it is the face of the mightiest of the Lord's host. This messenger is he who fills the position from which Satan fell.[305]

God's business has structure and organization. Different classifications of angels ministered to Jesus while He was on earth. He elects the employee for the assignment. In the matters concerning our salvation, it is safe to believe that God has assigned special angels to minister.

When Benhadad's chariots and horses and an army surrounded Dothan, God provided an army also. Benhadad's army's arrival by night, so reflective of Satan's operations, dark and dangerous, but did not prevent good from overcoming evil. Hezekiah's letter from Sennacherib meant nothing. One angel in one night destroyed 185,000 enemies bent on wrong.

Two battalions of guardian angels protected Jacob as he left Laban's home for his own.[306] That was not a dream of the night as when his head rested on a pillar of stone. That was in the clear, calm view of a sunlit day. They were not coming and going. It was not an occasional visit. Jacob, on his perilous path, had angels before him and behind him. That was the work of a matchless God.

Peter was imprisoned and condemned to die. They chained him to and between two soldiers. God's angels appeared on the scene. Armed guards were on duty at the doors. I am of the opinion that the massive prison doors were made of iron with its bars and bolts, closed and protected by soldiers. An angel touched Peter and told him to get up. The chains fell off Peter's hands. He dressed himself with his clothes and sandals as instructed by the angel. Peter thought he was having a vision. He and the angel passed two set of soldiers and finally came to the iron gate which led into the city. That prison gates acted like an electronic door. It opened on its own accord. Peter was led to safety, still thinking that he must be dreaming or in vision. We are left in awe and wonder.[307]

Due to a number of political maneuvers, King Darius placed Daniel in the lion's den. Then he inquired on the following morning, "O Daniel, servant of the living God, is that God, whom thou servest continually, able to deliver thee from the lions?"[308] Daniel replied, "My God hath sent his angel, and hath shut the lions' mouths, that they have not hurt me."[309] God delivered by His angel "out of the den" not "from the den."

That was then, but God is still actively engaged in the lives of His people today. However, it must be understood that God does not act in every situation. Jesus sent no angels to assist His cousin, John the Baptist when he was imprisoned. Matthew 11.

My wife and I were on a vacation in Europe after a meeting in Utrecht in 1995. We rented a car in Frankfurt, Germany and decided to travel in Europe for three weeks. We went to a hotel east of Nuremburg, checked in, parked the car, and boarded a train for Prague. When we arrived, the language barrier was a formidable foe. It took us about two hours to find a hotel. We exchanged U.S. dollars for their currency and decided to visit various places of interest. Our first move presented a snag. We did not have the proper change to ride the bus downtown. Taking a taxi with communication problems and strangers in the city presented its own set of challenges. While we attempted to get the proper change and could not, and pondering our next move, a lady saw our dilemma, and identified herself in fluent English as Irene. She took the money from me and received the needed change. Just then, the bus passed. This gave us the opportunity to engage in conversation. After all of the identifications and greetings were over, Irene, who spoke five languages fluently, and had worked for various embassies, decided to be our tour guide in Prague for the entire day. She had worked as a tour guide before. It seemed stranger than fiction. She told us she came outside to buy some ice cream, which she really should not be eating, and that this was her day off. Throughout the day she protected us like a mother hen with her chicks. We ate together, took the buses and taxis together. Because of her support we saw as much as was noteworthy and possible of Prague for a day. She really knew the city and where excellent gifts and prices could be found. It was minutes to 11 p.m. when we arrived at our hotel that night. Irene refused all that we wanted to pay her for the day's activity as our tour guide. We could not get her to accept it. We told her that if this was something she did for living, working as a tour guide, she should be recompensed. She walked us inside to the lobby of the hotel. I insisted that we would see her to the bus stop. She refused the offer and assured us that she was comfortable going alone although it was late, and night. Reluctantly, we allowed her to go but went after her immediately as soon as she went through the door. We wanted to be sure that Irene got home safely. To our surprise Irene could not be found. She was nowhere. We looked in all directions and knew for certain that she could not have escaped out of sight that quickly. Our search yielded no trace of Irene. The day's review brought us to one conclusion. Irene was an angel. Better still, the fact is that God still sends His angels to the aid of His children in different ways.

In the final crisis angels will place the seal of the living God upon His faithful children. They will accompany Christ on His second return. They will gather the redeemed from the four corners of the earth. They will join the Trinity in welcoming God's children in heaven. They will explain in heaven the pilgrimage of each one who enters the city of God, and the songwriters says, "they will fold their wings" when the redeemed sing the song of Moses and the Lamb.

God opened the eyes of Elisha's servant. He saw the vast company of angels. He also saw the plan of redemption. God's full-time employees came to their rescue.

> Not one soul who in penitence and faith has claimed His protection, will Christ permit to pass under the enemy's power... Angels of God will walk on either side of them, even in this world, and they will stand at last among the angels that surround the throne of God.[310]

Elisha possessed a tremendous personal faith in God and had a close and intimate experience with Him. He prayed that God would open his servant's eyes, and God did. Then he prayed that God would blind the Syrians, and God did. Afterwards, he prayed that God would open their eyes, and God did. Prayer is a mighty weapon in the Christian's arsenal.

God's response in smiting the Syrian soldiers with immediate blindness, according to Elisha's word, should serve to implant in every child of God greater faith. The act of Elisha demonstrates that God's words are true. Jesus said, "If you believe, you will receive whatever you ask for in prayer."[311]

In quick succession, within one day, three mighty answers to the prayer of Elisha, "a man subject to like passions as we are"[312] happened. The first, his servant's eyes were opened,[313] The second, "Smite this people, I pray thee, with blindness."[314] And the third, "Lord, open the eyes of these men, that they may see."[315]

If only we would exercise explicit faith in God, miracles would happen in our lives every day, and the name of Jesus would be glorified. For example, God will not turn down a prayer request for a closer walk with Him, healing for a friend or family member, the release of one bound by drugs, or alcohol, or pride, or covetousness, for someone incarcerated, a wayward son or daughter, one without Christ, or anything that will advance the kingdom's cause. Elisha just prayed. If we do not ask we do not get. God cannot answer a prayer that has not been prayed. Elisha trusted in God. He believed. He accepted God's promises. He knew God would never fail him. He simply believed. That we can emulate. God is on our side. He awaits our cry for help.

Elisha prayed that God would smite the people with blindness, and He did. They followed him to Samaria. They followed Elisha; therefore, it was blindness that they could not identify the man they sought and as soldiers did not even recognize the territory in which they were. Elisha said,

> "This is not the way, neither is this the city: follow me, and I will bring you to the man whom ye seek. But he led them to Samaria."[316]

Another version of the Bible would be needed to attempt any fanciful interpretation of this truth-suppressed statement. There is absolutely no position that can be taken to avoid a declaration that what Elisha said was laced with deception. Candor can be dodged to justify Elisha's statement. For example, it can be said that the morality of the time afforded that latitude. If that is not good enough, we could trade places, and say, if an enemy seeks to destroy and his plans are known, it is defensible to suppress the truth under extenuating circumstances. Benhadad's men wanted Elisha dead or alive. The fact that they went to Samaria proved that not even blindness deterred their mission. Bent on evil, an army with chariots and horses sought the life of the lone prophet. They would travel an additional eleven miles to Samaria through mountainous terrain to apprehend him. They wanted him badly. They did not ask for directions to Samaria, they followed a guide to arrest him. The entire army went as a search party. They were sure they would seize him without a struggle. Look at them. Men schooled in military expeditions and maneuvers. They knew where Dothan was. That was where Elisha lived. Did they lose their sense of geography? In the search for Elisha they could not differentiate between the city of Dothan and the city of Samaria. They did not even request a second opinion. Off they went with the man they sought, their guide, Elisha, seeing but not really seeing. The blind men finally arrived in Samaria. The blindness and decoy had worked.

Before applauding Elisha, take another look. God's miraculous intervention in human history registers a love that is incomprehensible. God had some greater good He intended to achieve. His will *will* be done, irrespective of the conditions. Benhadad's army stood within the walls of the city of Samaria. Israel's King, Jehoram was decked out in his kingly regalia. Israel's army was at attention on the walls, around the walls and inside the walls. They had at their disposal all the military hardware necessary for combat. In their battle gear, the Syrians were positioned to arrest Elisha, the prophet of God. Look closer at the scene. Decoyed, the angels and horses and chariots of fire of the Lord hovered overhead ready to do battle. Jehoram, king of Israel, was commander-in-chief of the army in Israel on earth. Jesus Christ, commander-in-chief of the host of heaven, stood ready to defend His child, Elisha. Amazing isn't it? God has sufficient time to marshal His host to defend His child, against the fiery darts of the devil. In whatever form they masquerade their perilous causes, Jesus will open the eyes and grant victory.

Then Elisha offered a fourth prayer.

> And it came to pass, when they were come into Samaria, that Elisha said, Lord, open the eyes of these men, that they may see. And the Lord opened their eyes, and they saw; and, behold, they were in the midst of Samaria.[317]

Throughout the entire proceedings, the long journey of maybe eleven miles, not one word was exchanged between the Syrians and

Elisha their guide. Now with their eyes wide opened and discovering that the Israelite army surrounded them, they panicked. Undoubtedly awe-stricken, fearful, outwitted, taken, feeling foolish, they just wanted to surrender. They were captured without a single shot fired or sword drawn. The entire army had been taken captive that easily.

When the king of Israel saw the Syrian army he wanted blood. He could taste it. In his mind's eye he saw it flowing all over the streets in Samaria. The king did not even engage in some sort of conversation as to the capture of the army or what would be considered the most appropriate measures to be taken. Here are his first words to Elisha: "My father, shall I smite them? Shall I smite them?[318] Such indecent haste to shed blood poured from the king. But Elisha would not exult over their helplessness. He never mentioned the part he played in the capture of those men. He forbade the king to even think in that vein. He had no articles from the Geneva Convention to consult as to how prisoners of war should be treated, but he had the love of God in his heart. His position was, if they were captured, they could not be slaughtered. King Jehoram did not know that the Syrian army stood within the walls of Samaria in answer to prayer. Should these men be slaughtered after the divine, miraculous activities, it would seem to be acting at cross-purposes with God. Rather than kill those men, Elisha's proposition was to heap coals of fire on their heads. That is called a magnanimous heart, a benevolent act of kindness. The apostle Paul said it better than any tongue could say it.

> Don't function from the premise of getting even with someone who does you wrong. Do everything openly and honestly for anyone to see. As far as is humanly possible, try to get along with everyone.

> Dear friends, never take revenge but turn your hostility over to God. The Scriptures make it clear. "I will see that justice is done. I will take care of it," says the Lord. "If your enemy is hungry, feed him; if he's thirsty, give him something to drink." By doing this, you're placing him in the hands of God for judgment. So don't let wicked people get to you; counteract the bad things they do to you by doing good things to them.[319]

That was Elisha's approach. That spiritual attitude is like an oasis in the Sahara Desert. It is like a moral Kilamanjaro peak in the lowlands of Georgetown, Guyana which is below sea level. Anyone who suffers from a lack of love, who thirsts or hungers for a more noble way of life should pause here in contemplation until the thirst is assuaged and the hunger fed, before moving on. Consider it authentic Christian conduct. Elisha's conduct must be replicated in the lives of all who seek to see God face to face. There must be more than opened eyes. The fragrance of the prophet's behavior covers the stench of this "dog eat dog," "let's kill him before he kills me," and "get even" world in which we live. May those who know us take note that we have been with Jesus. May they observe that the deeds we perform are atypical, that they are a carbon copy of what Christ expects. Turn the other cheek.[320] Go the second mile.[321] Heap coals of fire on the head of the enemy.[322] Cause a mental meltdown by responding to evil in a loving way. If everyone followed the "eye for an eye" principle of justice, observed Ghandi, eventually the whole world would go blind. Elisha was so munificent, so forgiving, so gracious, so charitable, so Christ-like.

It is an established fact that had the Syrian soldiers laid their hands on Elisha, he would have been history. Therefore, he had a just cause. But he refused to participate in even the suggestion of the king. His spirit recoiled beneath the mention of the king's hideous act. On the contrary, he showed love.

> And he answered, Thou shalt not smite them: wouldest thou smite those whom thou hast taken captive with thy sword and with thy bow? set bread and water before them, that they may eat and drink, and go to their master.[323]

Jehoram the king asked, "Shall I smite them?"[324] That showed no imagination, no heart and soul, no diplomacy, and no God-like response. Granted, what King Jehoram sought to do or would have done is replicated daily. It is the base human desire. That is so easy. Anyone could do that. The better question would have been, shall I love them? That demanded courage, Christian fortitude. Elisha chose the highest road. Set bread and water before them was the only option he would exercise. Jehoram thought of several things he could have done. He remonstrated:

> We can make them our servants. No, said Elisha. Set bread and water before them.
> We could starve them to death. No, said Elisha. Set bread and water before them.
> We could chastise them and send them back. No, said Elisha. Set bread and water before them.
> We could lecture them on the ills of war, on goodness, the consequences of sin, and how improperly they acted. No, said Elisha. Set bread and water before them.

We have no idea how many soldiers there were, or how many horses and chariots. This we do know: the king called in his best chefs. They prepared a meal fit for a king. Israel's best spread was laid out for the banquet. The king's hospitality was remarkable after Elisha's suggestion. The Syrians sensed no hostility. The air was congenial, the atmosphere pleasant. They laid down their weapons of war and ate and drank in a friendly climate. After the Syrians had feasted sumptuously, remarked about the friendly and remarkable manner and treatment, they had a few parting words and wended their way home to report to Benhadad.

When Benhadad heard what happened, he levied no blame; he had only one wish, I think, that he could have been present to see firsthand God's intervention on behalf of Israel. He undoubtedly felt embarrassed about some aspects of what had transpired, but it finally dawned on him that his real war was not against Israel but against the Lord of hosts. He realized he had not a fighting chance. He could not outwit or hoodwink God. He heard firsthand that God fights and God wins.

In the acts of kindness shown, the deeds of mercy displayed, in the brotherhood of man exemplified, and the excellence of love demonstrated, Benhadad's proud heart melted. This episode in Israel's history began well and ended well.

And he prepared great provision for them: and when they had eaten and drunk, he sent them away, and they went to their master. *So the bands of Syria came no more into the land of Israel.*[325]

King Jehoram's kindness to Benhadad's men, that magnanimous act, all non-retaliation, snuffed out the flames, created a friendly spirit, and paralyzed the attitude of revenge. Syria did not come back into the land of Israel. Jehoram overcame evil by good. As long as we seek revenge, and demonstrate in our lives the attitude of getting even, then God's place is superseded. He says that the responsibility of caring for injustices is His prerogative. We are safe to leave everything in His hands, even revenge.

All it took was just a little love. What an example. What a pattern. What a generous deed. What a Christ! He won the battle without one soldier from either camp slain. He left ingrained upon the heart that the battle is His. He showed the effectiveness of effectual, fervent prayer from any one of His children. He taught the lesson of human relations with the enemy long before the Beatitudes. He demonstrated that every person in the world belongs to Him. He will work in and through them that His glory might be revealed. Syria ceased the border raids on Israel without negotiations. When Jesus wins the final battle, all raids will cease, and men, all men will live in peace.

Chapter 6

THE FIGHTING FARMER

(Based on Judges 6–8)

There are thirteen judges listed after the death of Joshua, Moses' successor, to the time of Samuel, the first of the great prophets and the herald of the kingdom of Israel. That period of Israel's existence was one of adjustments and transitions. The transition was from a migratory, nomadic, pastoral people into a settled agricultural community or nation. Adjustments had to be made to the peoples of the land who ought not to have been there. God had instructed Israel to destroy the inhabitants before settling in Palestine.

We discover the period of the judges to be one of anarchy. Everyone did what was right is his own eyes. Whatever satisfied their fancy, they did. They became a stench in God's nostrils as they committed atrocious, idolatrous practices. The people were uncouth, rude, disobedient, brazen, and crude.

Israel did not perform the clear directions of Moses and Joshua. They settled down before the completion of the conquest. The period of the judges can best be described as a confused state of affairs. Israel surrendered her faith in God and worshipped the idols of the heathen, Baal and Ashtoreths. The sure and certain result of forsaking God was slavery to other nations and utter humiliation. In fact, God left heathen nations to be conquered to test their obedience regarding the instructions left by Moses.

Now these are the nations which the Lord left, to prove Israel by them, even as many as had not known all the wars of Canaan; Only that the generations of the children of Israel might know, to teach them war, at the least such as before knew nothing thereof; Namely, five lords of the Philistines, and all the Canaanites, and the Sidonians, and the Hivites that dwelt in mount Lebanon, from mount Baalhermon unto the entering in of Hamath. And they were to prove Israel by them, to know whether they would hearken unto the commandments of the Lord, which he commanded their fathers by the hand of Moses.[326]

Constant recurring invasions of marauding, nomadic peoples brought strife and bondage to the Israelites. Israel became like the surrounding nations. Apostasy and idolatry had weakened national unity that loyalty to their God, their religion, and covenant relationship had wrought.

Their broken relationship made it impossible to resist the mission and onslaught of these nations. For 450 years, from about 1400 BC to 1050 BC the records reveal that Israel fell into sin, then cried out to God and He provided a judge. The oppression, servitude, and bondage brought about repentance, and Israel turned to the worship of the true and living God. It was the responsibility of the judge to break the yoke of bondage and to lead his people. As soon as he died however, Israel went back almost immediately to where they were only a short while before. It was a vicious cycle of defection, punishment, restoration, and defection. It lasted for different periods of time, sometimes forty years and sometimes eight years. And yet, the defeat and triumph that occurred repeatedly did not lead them to choose, or to come close to doing right permanently.

That experience of Israel sounds so much like this modern civilization's relationship with God. The God we serve employs different ways to bring consolation and encouragement as modern people struggle against the same odds. Life does not need to be an endless roller coaster ride. We will look at the judgeship, rule and response of Gideon in the hope of extracting from his life and work examples of how to live, work, and resolve our spiritual problems. Gideon considered himself weak and non-influential, but the presence and peace of Jehovah was within him, and he became what God saw he ought to be, "a mighty man of valor."

These lines of the poet speak to Gideon's life from God's perspective.

> For as we see the eclipsed sun
> By mortals is more gazed upon
> Than when adorn'd with all his light,
> He shines in serene sky most bright;
> So valour in a low estate
> Is more admired and wondered at.[327]

When God delivered Israel out of Egyptian bondage by an outstretched and mighty arm, Israel complained and doubted God's promise to take them into the Promised Land. Doubt, lack of faith, complaints, and distrust had a hefty price tag. They would wander for forty years in the wilderness as punishment for their unbelief. On another occasion when they elected idolatry over the worship of the one and only true God, the Babylonians would subject them to cruel chastisement and bondage for seventy years.

In this account we will give consideration to Judge Gideon. The Midianites oppressed Israel for seven years. It was exceedingly devastating and humiliating. The Israelites were forced to live in dens and caves. The mountains became home. The desert peoples caused them to abandon the plains and the good country living they had heretofore experienced. Some went underground to survive and to escape their formidable foes. They were robbed of all their food supply just at the time of harvest. The Midianites timed harvest time and then made their expedition. They confiscated all that Israel had planted. It created a famine; to add insult to injury and as if plundering were not sufficient, the Midianites had the Amalekites and other desert tribes join them.

> And the children of Israel did evil in the sight of the LORD: and the LORD delivered them into the hand of Midian seven years. And the hand of Midian prevailed against Israel: and because of the Midianites the children of Israel made them the dens which are in the mountains, and caves, and strong holds.

And so it was, when Israel had sown, that the Midianites came up, and the Amalekites, and the children of the East, even they came up against them; And they encamped against them, and destroyed the increase of the earth, till thou come unto Gaza, and left no substance for Israel, neither sheep, nor ox, nor ass. For they came up with their cattle and their tents, and they came as grasshoppers for multitude; for both they and their camels were without number: and they entered into the land to destroy it. And Israel was greatly impoverished because of the Midianites; and the children of Israel cried unto the LORD.[328]

Our God is a compassionate God. The seven bitter years, the trouncing they received at the hands of the Midianites, Amalekites, and desert people was not that God had changed, but because Israel had violated the covenant agreement. As always, God maintains whatever agreement He enters into with His children. In verse ten of Judges 6, He reminded them, "but ye have not obeyed my voice." The time of the Judges was marked by some infraction of God's will from time to time. His voice speaking loud and clear can still be heard now as then, "Ye have not obeyed My voice." [329]

God was not rubbing salt into an open wound. He remained the same kind and sympathetic God. He simply wanted to remind them that their poor conditions of life came about due to their rejection of His leadership in their lives. He knew that only repentance and confession would bring the healing they sought. God waited for their acknowledgement. In time they appealed to Him, God, and before long mercy's doors opened. God would respond, not because of some right that they possessed; they had forfeited it by disobedience to the covenant agreement. God's response should not be deemed a reward or something they earned, or wages due and payable. Just because they sought Him, He rewarded their faith. It was a provision of His grace. "His compassions fail not... they are new every morning."[330] His heart of love responded to their predicament.

When we pray for earthly blessings, the answer to our prayer may be delayed, or God may give us something other than we ask, but not so when we ask for deliverance from sin. It is His will to cleanse us from sin, to make us His children, to enable us to live a holy life.[331]

Despite their failure, our failure, God is a very present help in trouble. Sometimes we are prone to feel that when one sins or neglects to maintain the covenant relationship that God is no longer anywhere to be found.

> If I take the wings of the morning, and dwell in to the uttermost parts of the sea; even there shall thy hand lead me, and thy right hand shall hold me.[332]

God never runs off and leaves His children. Their prayers do not bounce off of heaven's windows. God is not a wonderful Savior when we are good and disappears out of our lives when we are not attaining His ideal. Whenever God's children face a need, they have the precious privilege of calling upon Him. Irrespective of the place or circumstance, a call, a cry, an appeal can be made and He hears. Nowhere on earth can be darker than a fish's belly in the bottom of the ocean. It was from there that Jonah cried to His God, our Father, and He heard. When tough times come and the clouds seem to blot out the sunshine of God's love, this quotation is worth memorizing:

> At all times and in all places, in all sorrows and in all afflictions, when the outlook seems dark and the future perplexing, and we feel helpless and alone, the Comforter will be sent in answer to the prayer of faith. Circumstance may separate us from every earthly friend; but no circumstance, no distance, can separate us from the heavenly Comforter. Wherever we are, wherever we may go, He is always at our right hand to support, sustain, uphold, and cheer.[333]

Or,

> Every sincere prayer is heard in heaven. It may not be fluently expressed; but if the heart is in it, it will ascend to the sanctuary where Jesus ministers, and He will present it to the Father without one awkward, stammering word, beautiful and fragrant with the incense of His own perfection.[334]

God is not a mere man. He is not some fickle personality. You will not find Him hiding behind some clump of bushes, like a highway patrolman with a radar gun, simply waiting to apprehend for some violation of a rule or law. Israel was instructed and knew, and so do we, that sin separates. Sin builds chasms between man and God. Sin erects gulfs. It is a pit into which God's children fall. God hates sin, but oh, how He loves the sinner. "God is love."[335] That relationship never changes. He asks, "How can I give thee up?"[336] "I have loved thee with an everlasting love."[337] It is characteristic of Jesus, the loving shepherd, to search *until* He finds the one lost sheep.[338] That is love. He searches relentlessly until He finds that one lost sheep. Mankind means much to God. God wants us. He sent His Son on a rescue mission with enormous consequences to bring about restoration, redemption, and the unification of the family on earth with the family in heaven.

God heard the cry of His children, the Israelites, as indicated in Judges 6:6. God was always there. Before they called He saw their need. He knew they had violated the covenant agreements. In spite of their situation it was not Israel looking for God, but rather God in search of them to provide the help they so desperately needed. The record indicates that God heard, delivered, and helped.

He sent a deliverer—Gideon. Gideon was called to be a judge and a deliverer in a war which was already won. Success was stamped all over this engagement. Knowing that God controlled this battle, He commanded Gideon "to be strong in the Lord," and "be not afraid." He should be courageous, steadfast, immovable, and have fixity of purpose. It is comforting to know that when God calls a person there is absolutely nothing to fear.

Here was a strange conclusion. Gideon, like all of Israel, was in hiding. Yet God stated and addressed him in the following manner. "The Lord is with thee, thou mighty man of valor."[339] Thou mighty man of valor?

Gideon the draftee declared,

1. "My family is poor in Manasseh, and I am the least of my father's house."[340] Is valor compatible with caution?
2. He was hiding, threshing wheat by the winepress under decoy.

3. He was afraid the Midianites would steal his threshed wheat.
4. He had not heretofore led any army in battle.
5. For seven years the Midianites had dominated his turf and he like the rest of Israel repeatedly ran for cover.

The indications here are that Gideon was not a conceited person. He stood ready to undertake a God-given assignment. The angel called him, "thou mighty man of valor." The angel brought to Gideon a remembrance of the high privileges as a child of God. We may and must pause here to thank God that what He sees in us, and thinks of us, no one else does. A look at Gideon's activities would never qualify him as a "mighty man of valor."[341] He was modest, self-distrusting, without political or military training. He also worshipped idols. But God's inventory, His evaluation done from the inside, from His perspective should cause individuals to be fearful of their judgments, and be thankful that He chooses the leaders and equips them. He reaches over and beyond man's self-evaluations. Rank, riches, honor, poverty, family lineage, and societal badges do not impress God.

I believe that in the kingdom of God there will be many thousands of blood-washed, white-robed, palm-branch-waving, hallelujah-singing saints, whose records are in the safe keeping of God and angels only. All along they were considered present and accounted for, but given no responsibility or duty to declare their strength, nobility, genius, or valor. Some might even have been disqualified by earthly standards. Nevertheless, God's records of them and us are faithfully kept.

God will call no indolent, misdirected, lazy, flippant person to fulfill His assigned tasks. He will seek those with a sense of mission, filled with His Holy Spirit, competent, courageous, thoughtful, reasonable, and flexible enough to follow where He leads. Gideon had a great task ahead of him, but behind him an Almighty God.

To take the nation of Israel out of servitude, slavery, cringing fear, dens, and caves, and into strongholds of freedom and victory was no mean assignment. But God told him to go and deliver Israel. It was a direct command. Furthermore, to accomplish that horrendous task without military hardware or know-how posed a serious problem. Gideon recognized his inability to cope with the Midianite coalition. He, like other faithful leaders, felt inadequate for the task. He forgot, "If God be for us, who can be against us?"[342]

When Moses received God's call to take Israel out of Egypt, his reaction was,

> And Moses said unto God, Who am I, that I should go unto Pharaoh, and that I should bring forth the children of Israel out of Egypt?[343]

And Saul said,

> Am not I a Benjamite, of the smallest of the tribes of Israel? And my family the least of all the families of the tribe of Benjamin? Wherefore then speakest thou so to me?[344]

They urged upon God their helplessness, emptiness, poverty, and family lineage, while standing before a full fountain and the source of every blessing. That reaction in the face of His all-sufficient promise only demonstrated a lack of faith in His word and surrender to His will. He delights in fulfilling man's needs so His name might be glorified. Never should anything like self-confidence take the place of humility. It is the sense of inherent weakness that qualifies anyone for the work of God. No one spoke to that fact better than the apostle Paul.

> But God hath chosen the foolish things of the world to confound the wise; and God hath chosen the weak things of the world to confound the things which are mighty;[345]

> Therefore I take pleasure in infirmities, in reproaches, in necessities, in persecutions, in distresses for Christ's sake: for when I am weak, then am I strong.[346]

In all the conflicts of this life with God beside, one should fear no evil. God does not send anyone into warfare without a support system in place. God, sensing Gideon's reliance on Him, immediately promised His support and victory. He asked him, "Have I not sent thee?"[347] His assignment would make great demands. To be absolutely sure it was not a dream, that indeed an angel of the Lord had appeared unto him, Gideon will run some tests. He wants to say like Isaiah, "Here am I Lord, send me,"[348] but he questioned himself if it could be real. Gideon immediately extended hospitality. He provided a meal for his unknown heavenly visitor. Really, it had nothing to do with hospitality. Gideon wanted to test the validity of God's promise to deliver Israel through him.

It is most interesting to see how God had all the time necessary to wait on Gideon while he slipped inside, prepared a kid, unleavened bread and broth, displaying hospitality, while all the time He knows the objective. God will wait for us while we deliberately do everything and make every attempt to bolster faith. Should God be kept waiting? I do not think so. But God waited. Faith should lay hold of His will fully and promptly the first time. While Gideon got ready for a sign, he could have spent the time more profitably, learning to lean on His promises, taking Him at His word, particularly knowing that God had proven Himself faithful.

At his visitor's instruction, Gideon placed the kid, the unleavened bread and the broth, the entire meal on a rock. The place is Ophrah, the high place, the house of Baal-Berith at Shechem.[349] The man who sat beneath the oak tree was an angel in the form of a man. The angel did not ask God to accept the sacrifice and consume it as did Elijah on Mount Carmel or Solomon at the dedication of the temple. The angel lit the sacrifice placed on the altar. What a magnificent transaction. Oh, how we need to learn that God will not send His Spirit until we, like Gideon's offering, are laid on the altar of sacrifice.

There is a great lesson here. Do not pass over it. Gideon asked God for a sign and time to prepare a meal. The angel waited. God knew Gideon's heart. The thin line between full faith and doubt He recognized. In loving, patient response to Gideon's need for a sign, there was an immediate response. Watch this: when we make our sacrifices of praise and adoration; when we commit wholly to God; while we are yet praying; before the notes of praise escape our lips; while acknowledging His great power and might; before we say Amen; God acknowledges our cry, or like Daniel while still in prayer He answers. Unlike the human heart that procrastinates, that waits for a convenient season, is torn between opinions before acceptance or a response, God responds immediately and with exactitude.

The angel knew that Gideon would be afraid. As the column of smoke ascended from the sacrifice, he disappeared while Gideon contemplated his fate. Seeing an angel face to face could have brought severe consequences. God did not destroy him any more than He did not destroy Moses at the burning bush, Joshua with the captain of the Lord's host challenging him, nor Isaiah in the temple in the year that King Uzziah died. Allowing Gideon to live after the face-to-face experience could have been God's note of assurance that would sustain him during the upcoming conflict. It was a way of helping him to burn the bridges of doubt, answering his questions, and leaving behind his idolatry, so there would be no retreat. Over and beyond that was God's assurance of peace that he would not die and words of comfort not to be afraid. He called the name of the place where he met God Jehovah-Shalom. God is Peace.

Reverence for God ought not be a fear-filled experience demanding one's life. When there is a dread that overcomes anyone because of God's outshining, His glorious appearance, His absolute holiness revealed, it is result of man's sinfulness. Adam said, "I was afraid, because I was naked; and I hid myself."[350] Had Adam and Eve been obedient to God's will, life would have been as before, holding sweet communion, awaiting His daily visits and unafraid of His glory. Whereas we have not seen God, have not had a face-to-face experience, yet… it should be our delightsome experience to interface with Him daily at the blessed hour of prayer.

As stated, the Midianites occupied Israel's territory, pilfered their harvest, and had them living in dens and caves because of one simple fact: Israel would not worship God aright and failed to reject the worship of Baal. While Baal worship was an integral part of Israel's life, Gideon, mighty man of valor, could not proceed. There would be for Gideon no going on in the sin of idolatry while at the same time expecting God to bring them victory. So during the night watch, Gideon demolished the altar to Baal and the grove as demanded by God. Gideon destroyed *all* the idols. He recognized that every God-usurping thing around and within them must be overturned and dethroned. It was true then and still is today. Prompted by the Spirit of God, there was a holy boldness that can never be attributed to genius or human power.

When the people awoke the following day Baal was gone. An altar with God's sacrifice burning had taken its place. It almost cost Gideon his life. Note, *almost*. He was prompt to obey God's directives. The people demanded that Gideon be assassinated for destroying the idols. A wise father insisted that Baal ought to defend himself.

> …And when they enquired and asked, they said, Gideon the son of Joash hath done this thing…Bring out thy son, that he may die:..And Joash said unto all that stood against him, will ye plead for Baal?...if he be a god, let him plead for himself.[351]

When a city, town, church, country, family, or individual is cleared of complicity with sin, God will bless beyond one's imaginings. The order of God was instructive. First, the destruction of the altar to Baal and the grove; and second, the altar with its sacrifice to the God of heaven should be built where the angel met him. Before anticipated victory and success over the Midianites, destruction of Baal and the grove, and construction of the altar of sacrifice must be a reality. Reformation must precede deliverance from the Midianites. Release from captivity by the Midianites will come when Israel repents of her sin. God and Baal cannot be worshipped simultaneously. "No man can serve two masters."[352] Israel cannot halt between two opinions. God promised Gideon deliverance from the Midianites, but the worship of Baal, Israel's deepest problem, must be completely omitted.

That which caused God to withdraw His protection must therefore cease to be a part of Israel's lifestyle. To find relief and release from the tyranny of oppression of the Midianites they had to surrender all. God would not tolerate a divided heart. He will be Lord of all or not Lord at all. God would accommodate no compromise. No corridor of the heart could have a pet sin, even though great and expensive sacrifices were made with what remained. God is a jealous God. Lest there be reminders of sin, they used the wood from the grove to fuel the sacrifice made to God, thus obliterating every recollection possible. Every occasion to sin against the God of heaven must be shunned. Everything that would influence the heart to go contrary must be discarded. Sin had to be resisted and overthrown. However, that was only a part of the activity. The heart purified by Christ should be filled with His virtues. To tear down the altars of Baal was an achievement, but it would be greater to replace it with obedience and faith.

It is easier to tear down than to build. Construction is hard labor. It does not take much brain to be a wrecking crew. The world is full of wreckers, criticizers, demolition crews, harsh critics, condemners, and over throwers, because that does not demand brain. It takes vision, initiative, and hard work to build. Reformation that leaves the earth singed, leaves empty spaces, a life darker, an empty but colder heart, leaves a soul bare, bereft of love, a hope, and a future means absolutely nothing. Gideon tore down but he erected on the Rock, Christ Jesus, an altar for a sacrifice.

Gideon was now ready to do battle. The obstacle of idolatry was removed. He blew his trumpet and the hills and valleys of Abiezer reverberated with the certain sound. The clarion call drew out the men of Manasseh, Asher, Zebulun, and Naphtali, thirty-two thousand strong, who responded to the messengers.[353] Gideon, under-girded by God's Spirit, became bold and daring, and did not shirk in the face of danger. His spirit inspired the timid and fearful. They were attracted to his enthusiasm and untamable spirit of commitment to a righteous cause.

- 32,000 men responded to Gideon's call. God had already promised deliverance.
- God's intervention when the men wanted to kill him for destroying Baal and the grove should have been sufficient evidence that God was with him.
- The angel said, "The Lord is with thee, thou mighty man of valour."
- The sacrifice placed on the rock was consumed.

What more did Gideon need? He ought to have accepted God's invitation to service and said, "Lord I believe, help thou mine unbelief," and moved forward. Not so with Gideon. He wanted still another sign from the Lord.

We are often prone to consider Gideon's seeming faithlessness, and what he said to God was just a bit much for someone called of God.

And Gideon said unto God, If thou wilt save Israel by mine hand, as thou hast said, Behold, I will put a fleece of wool in the floor; and if the dew be on the fleece only, and it be dry upon all the earth beside, then shall I know that thou wilt save Israel by mine hand, as thou hast said. And it was so: for he rose up early on the morrow, and thrust the fleece together, and wringed the dew out of the fleece, a bowl full of water. And Gideon said unto God, Let not thine anger be hot against me, and I will speak but this once: let me prove, I pray thee, but this once with the fleece; let it now be dry only upon the fleece, and upon all the ground let there be dew. And God did so that night: for it was dry upon the fleece only, and there was dew on all the ground.[354]

But let us look at the bigger picture. What a precious, loving, long-suffering, compassionate, understanding, and touched with the feelings of our infirmities God we have. God will stay with us until there is confirmation on our part, that the mission on which we are about to embark has His total sanction; we are comfortable; and we can move forward in faith knowing that God has indeed ratified His promises. We ought to walk by faith and not by sight. In no part of the dialog did God upbraid him for his being slow of heart. This is a further declaration of the ways of God, which are past finding out. In His marvelous dealings with us His children, God expends every effort with our frailty. For "He knoweth our frame; He remembereth that we are dust."[355] God did precisely as requested; with the kind of exactness that only our God can do, thus Gideon could trustingly move on with the assignment.

Now that God had his attention He looked at the thirty-two thousand fighting men and told Gideon that this particular conflict did not need that many soldiers. Gideon already had the assurance of victory. If God allowed that many men to go and they were victorious, they would vaunt themselves in feeling they had won the battle. Ten thousand were still too many. Finally, the thirty-two thousand was reduced to a small band of three hundred, less than one percent of the original number. That was enough, God said.

Apart from the difficulty that would arise that they would take credit for the victory that God promised before the engagement, some other issues had to be dealt with immediately. The presence of the fearful, the self-interested, and the timid is always a hindrance to the work of

God. God can get along just fine without the doubting Thomases and fearful professed followers. In battle God will employ our strength and wisdom, but He is not dependent on them to be successful. Our own strength and wisdom would be considered as too many soldiers. It is to the faint that He gives power, and to them who have no might He increases strength.[356] Man looks on the outward appearance, and so much of what we would pass as wheat, when it gets against the fan of God, it proves to be just useless chaff. God has His own selective service. The greater the victory to be gained, the hotter the furnace of trial through which one must pass. Abraham, Joseph, Moses, the three Hebrew boys, Daniel, Job, Paul, and a host of others can testify to this. It is one thing to search ourselves and see if we qualify: it will help to turn us away from much of the tinsel of earth, but when God places His searchlight of truth on us, all we can do is cry out, Lord, search me and try me, and let me know my real condition.[357] This battle, like all of God's, demanded more than a large head count. God's interest lies in the content of the soul. Character will receive God's greatest scrutiny for heaven-bound persons. That happens to be the greatest conflict in which mankind is engaged, the battle against self, the fight to overcome.

Three hundred well-trained, well-disciplined, and well-ordered men will fight against the Midianites, the Amalekites, and the desert people who came "like grasshoppers for multitude; and their camels were without number, as the sand by the sea side for multitude."[358] Three hundred valiant, committed, willing-to- do-and-dare men were all God needed. Could it be that God is still in search, not of large numbers but of tested, tried, true, faithful, and committed-to-the-cross soldiers? They planned a surprise attack, which alone would accomplish the task. Their military hardware consisted of the empty pitchers and lamps within the pitchers, the trumpets, and voices loud and clear that would bellow from three vantage points.

They would surround the enemy before blowing their trumpets. The plan of attack was magnificent. God said He had already delivered the Midianites into Gideon's hands.[359] To affirm Gideon's faith even more, God told him and Phurah to go down to the Midianites' tent and he would hear a testimony of deliverance. The whole scene was a divinely planned coincidence, and another proof of that unerring providence that constrains the faithful servant of God to bow again and again in silent worship. Let us never forget that whereas God delights to give us providential assurances of the truth of His Word, His promises are enough without them.

> And when Gideon was come, behold, there was a man that told a dream unto his fellow, and said, Behold, I dreamed a dream, and, lo, a cake of barley bread tumbled into the host of Midian, and came unto a tent, and smote it that it fell, and overturned it, that the tent lay along. And his fellow answered and said, This is nothing else save the sword of Gideon the son of Joash, a man of Israel: for into his hand hath God delivered Midian, and all the host. And it was so, when Gideon heard the telling of the dream, and the interpretation thereof, that he worshipped, and returned into the host of Israel, and said, Arise; for the Lord hath delivered into your hand the host of Midian.[360]

When Gideon and Phurah heard the amazing dream, faith in God increased, hope and courage re-ignited, and Gideon commanded his soldiers and said, "It is a done deal." If we are not careful we will miss the heart of the divine-human connection. The record states that when Gideon heard the dream and the confirmation from the Midinanites that God had already delivered them into his hands, he worshipped. It was no longer about the Midianites and the Israelites. It was about worship between Gideon and his awesome, covenant-keeping God. We ought not to downplay the battle, but an inquisitive mind will survey all the faithful relations between doubting Gideon; requesting for affirmation Gideon; and a God who looked beyond his doubts and requested affirmation because He was anxious to develop faith in His child. Then Gideon glorified God. The Midianites had confirmed that God had delivered them into their hands and that was final. The young Jewish generalissimo's strategy worked. The strategy with the lamp, the empty pitcher, the trumpet, and shouting worked.

> And he divided the three hundred men into three companies, and he put a trumpet in every man's hand, with empty pitchers, and lamps within the pitchers. And he said unto them, Look on me, and do likewise: and, behold, when I come to the outside of the camp,

it shall be that, as I do, so shall ye do. When I blow with a trumpet, I and all that are with me, then blow ye the trumpets also on every side of all the camp, and say, The sword of the Lord, and of Gideon. So Gideon, and the hundred men that were with him, came unto the outside of the camp in the beginning of the middle watch; and they had but newly set the watch: and they blew the trumpets, and brake the pitchers that were in their hands. And the three companies blew the trumpets, and brake the pitchers, and held the lamps in their left hands, and the trumpets in their right hands to blow withal: and they cried, The sword of the Lord, and of Gideon. And they stood every man in his place round about the camp: and all the host ran, and cried, and fled. And the three hundred blew the trumpets and the Lord set every man's sword against his fellow, even throughout all the host: and the host fled to Bethshittah in Zererath, and to the border of Abelmeholah, unto Tabbath.[361]

At the shouts of, "The sword of the Lord and of Gideon!" the Midianites woke up in panic. The flaming lamps, the blaring trumpets and shout of "The sword of the Lord and of Gideon" gave the impression that thousands were attacking. They were in total disarray. God had ordered a night raid, sometime before midnight. So many decisive things are ordered and done by God in the dead of night. Some enemy soldiers were asleep others not quite asleep; the commotion, the fright, and the noise from the blaring trumpets threw them into confusion.[362] The enemy count and composition we have.

And the Midianites and the Amalekites and all the children of the east lay along the valley like grasshoppers for multitude; and their camels were without number, as the sand of the sea side for multitude.[363]

Gideon and his soldiers killed a few. God needed Gideon and his men to emphasize the divine-human relationship and to declare emphatically that the battle was His. The diverse cultures and languages present did not help the enemy. There were Midianites, Amalekites, and all the children of the east. They were distinguishable by day but could not be identified at night. Each man killed all he saw for he did not know whether the person he encountered was friend or foe. The slaughter was incredible as God allowed the enemy to kill each other. Those who escaped, Oreb and Zeeb, princes of Midian[364], Gideon pursued and did not relinquish his responsibility until every foe was vanquished, and all the praise due Jehovah's name given. The final count was one hundred thirty-five thousand slain.[365] The battle was over and the victory won. The Midianites, the Amalikites, and the desert peoples they had enlisted, Israel destroyed. For years they brought suffering and hurt. The scriptural inclusion of this conflict during the time of the judges declares that at all times, in all periods of Israel's existence, even when they were not all that God wanted or intended them to be, He never abandoned them.

The valor of Gideon and his men fades into insignificance when we review the phenomenal success of three hundred soldiers. The defeat of the enemy when placed in perspective will show that the battle was the Lord's. It was "the sword of the Lord, and of Gideon."[366] Israel cooperated with their divine leader. That was pivotal to the victory. Always the divine-human relationship guarantees success. Before Gideon broke the first lamp, before the first trumpet blared, before the first shout was made, the Midianites and their cohorts were defeated. Isn't this marvelous? Three hundred men under Gideon with a promise from God, and the Midianites and the enlistees who were like grasshoppers were destroyed. It emphasizes again that a few with the Lord is better than thousands without Him. In retrospect, Gideon must have been dumbfounded. Yet, the army reduced from thirty-two thousand to three hundred men demonstrated that God could save with many or by few.

We are told in the book of Acts that the apostles of Christ turned the world upside down.[367] In the twenty-first century, when the church of the living God shall proclaim the gospel of the Lord Jesus Christ with clarity, certainty, and commitment, although they are few in number, the world shall be won. Whether it is Gideon against the Midianites, the apostles against the world, or Christians seeking to complete the mission of Christ, it should always be recalled that "it is not by might or by power."[368] It was not how long, how loud, or how clearly Gideon's men blew their trumpets or shouted. "The horse is made ready for the day of battle, but victory rests with the Lord."[369]

Before we leave this great adventure we need to take another look at a significant feature of conduct in the lives of Gideon's men. Those three hundred soldiers were together as one man. Not a single dissenting voice was heard.

And he said to them, Look on me, and do likewise: and, behold, when I come to the outside of the camp, it shall be that, *as I do, so shall ye do.* When I blow with a trumpet, I and all that are with me, then blow ye the trumpets also on every side of all the camp, and say, The sword of the Lord, and of Gideon.[370]

God can do marvelous things when His people get together, when they are of one accord. Pentecost is our greatest example. Read Acts 2. There is absolutely no question that they knew how to follow instructions precisely. There was no struggle for leadership from another quarter, or any other method suggested. If only the blueprints of the church as given were followed, life would show greater success. Mary said to the attendants at the wedding, "Whatsoever He saith unto you, do it."[371] God taught how beautiful life can be when His will and wishes are followed obediently. "It was the sword of the Lord, and of Gideon."[372]

In review, it is marvelous to see three hundred brothers faithful to Gideon's directions. We can agree that there could have been some other way to gain the victory besides trumpets, lamps, and pitchers. The fact is they were loyal to God first, for Gideon was only speaking for Him. God honored their loyalty, willingness to follow instructions, and their togetherness by a signal victory over their enemies.

The victory struck such a note of concord and unity that they wanted Gideon to rule over them.[373] Their admiration of Gideon's valor evoked a call for him and his descendants to be their ruler. Gideon knew the real captain, the commander-in-chief, the real general. Without a moment's hesitation, he rejected the offer. He knew that if he accepted, he would have assigned divine prerogatives to himself. Strange, isn't it? We gain one victory and all of a sudden we forget our benefactor and quickly attribute success to our own hands, ingenuity, whatever. Gideon would not suffer spiritual amnesia, or any kind of amnesia. The flaming sacrifice was still fresh in his memory. The fleece, wet one night and the ground the next, the ratio of 300 to 32,000 men and God's spirit inside and outside will not disappear from his consciousness like morning dew. We shouldn't forget the great transactions of a loving God in our lives either. When tempted—and the temptation will come to forget all his benefits—then sing,

King of my life I crown thee now, Thine shall the glory be
Lest I forget thy thorn-crowned brow, Lead me to Calvary.[374]

Then crown Jesus Christ our deliverer, as ruler, Lord of all and King of kings.

Chapter 7

BETWEEN THE ROCK AND A HARD PLACE

(Based on Exodus 13–14)

Stephen's unfinished sermon before his martyrdom traced portions of Israel's history. He highlighted their deliverance out of bondage in Egypt by God's outstretched and mighty hand.[375] Israel's constant reminder of that signal act indicated the pivotal place it had in all of God's dealings with them. Many writers of the Bible allude to some aspect of that significant demonstration of God's power and might. Such an outstanding part of God's intervention in human history demands review. Israel became a nation when they departed out of Egypt. Israel's passage through the Red Sea remains as one of God's great miracles. That demonstration of God's might and majesty declared loudly and clearly to the Israelites that their greatness in subsequent engagements must not be dependent upon chariots and horses, any mighty trained army, but upon the help of the living God. The secret of their success as a people, in all places, at all times, must be a direct, personal, unwavering trust in Almighty God. A serious contemplation of Israel's emancipation out of Pharaoh's hands, but particularly their passage through the Red Sea, should have built in the Israelites a deeper faith and trust in God.

Israel went out of Egypt on the night they celebrated the Passover. Pharaoh called Moses that fateful night and demanded that Israel and all they possessed should leave immediately. They were actually forced out. Pharaoh's urgency was probably prompted by imminent or future danger.[376] Within hours after Israel's departure, Pharaoh thought about the economic problems Egypt might face due to the loss of the enforced labor they enjoyed. The slave labor contributed significantly to Egypt's wealth. Even under cruel and inhumane conditions and planned infanticide, God's blessings and grace attended His people.[377] Exodus 1:15,16. Just as "the Lord blessed the Egyptian's house for Joseph's sake"[378], so did Israel Egypt. Egypt prospered because Israel proved to be the salt of the earth. God's multidirectional blessings affected domestic life, agriculture, commerce, politics, and everything they did. The splendid architecture, bales of merchandise, and open markets with piles of fruit did not just exist. Israel's contribution to all aspects of life cannot be denied. As residents and worshippers of God they caused Egypt to enjoy success and prosperity. Israel left hastily under God's direction for the Promised Land.[379] Like Egypt, they would face some new and unique problems. However, leaving Egypt at His command, God would chart the course Israel should take, and the place of worship.[380]

As the Egyptians surveyed Israel's absence, and realized the positive impact they had on their society, they decided to overtake them and carry them back to Egypt.[381] Shut in between inaccessible precipices and the sea, mountains on both sides and a path that terminated in the Red Sea obstructing their flight, with no ship to cross the waters, the Israelites panicked.[382] One cannot but hear the commotion, frustration, and agony of a people who had not yet come to learn to put their trust in God. Imagine the despair, distrust, distress, and fear that possessed the hearts of these people unaccustomed to war and ill prepared to fight. The thought of being captured and re-enslaved carried its own set of frustrations. Their knowledge of God did not afford them the joy of knowing He would provide. They had not the slightest clue that man's extremity is God's opportunity. Although God had demonstrated His power and outstretched arm several times before, they were still leaning on the arm of flesh rather than the Rock of Ages. The Egyptians, the mountains, the sea, and all the seemingly insurmountable obstacles should have deepened their faith. They had yet to learn to rest patiently in the circumstances into which His providence had carried them. God would be greater than all the hindrances they faced.

There will be days when dark clouds come. They seem to block sight of God's presence; human nature is prone to repine. If only we would wait on God. If only we would remember that whatever God has brought us into He will take us out of. He will not need human help. To walk by faith and not by sight is no easy assignment. At one moment of the day the Israelites were full of faith. They prepared the Passover and left for a land they did not know. That demonstrated raw, uncut, undiluted faith. Give Israel some credit. But faith has a way of coming and going. Would we have reacted differently? We must learn to trust God's leading even in the darkest hour. God's ways that are beyond the farthest stretch of the imagination, and His love is fathomless.

In reading Jahaziel's message in 2 Chronicles 20:15–17, I am convinced that this prophet had steeped himself in the Exodus account. The Spirit of God gave him an open declaration as He had given Moses. Although two different sets of circumstances, centuries apart, the statements sound identical. That speaks to the unity of the Spirit, and reemphasizes the fact that, "whatsoever things were written aforetime were written for our learning."[383]

We will examine in passing both passages of Scripture from the Israel-Egypt under Moses confrontation at the Red Sea and Jehosaphat-Moab-Ammon war with God speaking to Jahaziel. The similarities are most interesting.

> And Moses said unto the people, Fear ye not, stand still, and see the salvation of the LORD, which he will shew to you to day: for the Egyptians whom ye have seen to day ye shall see them again no more for ever. The LORD shall fight for you, and ye shall hold your peace.[384]

> And he said, Hearken ye, all Judah, and ye inhabitants of Jerusalem, and thou king Jehoshaphat, Thus saith the LORD unto you, Be not afraid nor dismayed by reason of this great multitude; for the battle is not yours, but God's. To morrow go ye down against them: behold, they come up by the cliff of Ziz; and ye shall find them at the end of the brook, before the wilderness of Jeruel. Ye shall not need to fight in this battle: set yourselves, stand ye still, and see the salvation of the LORD with you, O Judah and Jerusalem: fear not, nor be dismayed; to morrow go out against them: for the LORD will be with you.[385]

Let us look at the parallels.

- Stand still and see the salvation of the Lord.[386]
- Stand ye still, and see the salvation of the Lord.[387]
- The Lord shall fight for you.[388]
- For the battle is not yours, but God's. Ye shall not need to fight in this battle… for the Lord will be with you.[389]
- Fear ye not, for the Egyptians whom ye have seen to day, ye shall see… no more.[390]
- Be not afraid nor dismayed by reason of this great multitude.[391]

Moses and Jahaziel did not collaborate. The time each wrote disallowed any verbal communication. Yet there is a common thread in both experiences. That thread in both battles transcends the human element and can be seen only as a divine achievement. It is obvious from this vantage point that God had much more than another conquest, another miracle in mind. God had a real objective.

> And I will harden Pharaoh's heart, that he shall follow after them; and I will be honoured upon Pharaoh, and upon all his host; *that the Egyptians may know that I am the Lord.*[392]

God had already employed a variety of engagements—a display of His power that the most skeptical mind should have seen and acknowledged as divine. However, Pharaoh resorted to a stubborn and unyielding spirit. The gracious, long-suffering God tried and tried and tried again to get Pharaoh's attention, but he turned a deaf ear to God's freedom cry for His children. Instead of freeing the Hebrews, they were balked, refused, ignored, and rejected. Apparently Pharaoh concluded that ultimately God would succumb to his denials, be intimidated and relinquish His pleas. He should have learned from the ten plagues that God sustains His activities until at long last a cry of surrender is heard.

Pharaoh, Sennacherib, Nebuchadnezzar, the Ammonites, the Moabites, Herod, and Agrippa could have been graciously dealt with by the King of kings, even given lighter sentences if only they had recognized His sovereignty. Their actions and stubborn defiance announced that God in time would not react as He said He would. But let no one ever forget, not Nebuchadnezzar or Pharaoh or anyone else the grand objective God had in mind. "That the Egyptians may know that I am the Lord."[393] That statement ought not to be lost in obscurity. Ultimately, that fact looms larger. The greater the defiance, the brighter the glory of God is seen and adored. The greater the submission, the greater the blessing received.

According to the Exodus census approximately three million Hebrew children lived in Egypt.[394] Within the confines of that country, God's children, who served as slaves, waited for the fulfillment of the promise made to Abraham, Isaac, and Jacob. While captives, they should have demonstrated God's love and salvation. But shut away from worship, not having religious liberty, or at best, the worship experience somewhat altered, the reflection of the character of God, like gold, dimmed. It blurred. Therefore, God assumed divine prerogatives, the right to declare who He was and is. The ten plagues became the defining moment.

> For I will at this time send all my plagues upon thine heart, and upon thy servants, and upon thy people; *that thou mayest know that there is none like me in all the earth.*[395]

God sought a personal affirmation of the great truth announced from Pharaoh. It was not enough that Pharaoh would have observed the Hebrew children, not enough a testimony that, "The earth is the Lord's.[396] There is no God like the sovereign God.

> I am the Lord, and there is none else, there is no God beside me:... I am the Lord, and there is none else... I am the Lord; and there is none else.[397]

> Is there a God beside me? Yea, there is no God; I know not any.[398]

> Ye are my witnesses, saith the Lord, and my servant whom I have chosen: that ye may know and believe me, and understand that I am he: before me there was no God formed, neither shall there be after me. I, even I, am the Lord: and beside me there is no Saviour.[399]

Pharaoh must testify for himself, of his own volition, whether Israel laid an example or not. He must confess Christ as Lord. And not Pharaoh alone, but eventually every tongue will confess that Jesus Christ is Lord. God brought him to the place that eventually he acknowledged Him as the ruler of heaven and earth.

> And he called for Moses and Aaron by night, and said, Rise up, and get you forth from among my people, both ye and the children of Israel; and go, serve the Lord, as ye have said. Also take your flocks and your herds, as ye have said, and be gone; and bless me also. And the Egyptians were urgent upon the people, that they might send them out of the land in haste; for they said, we be all dead men.[400]

God need not have gone that far had Pharaoh just humbled himself and done precisely what God had requested in the first place. The question Pharaoh had posed was not a good one. He asked, "Who is the Lord, that I should obey Him and let Israel go?"[401] God can define Himself. He is the sovereign Lord. He has ownership and exclusive right to everyone and everything. Pharaoh should have known. When we pause and take a critical look, we observe that God could have killed Pharaoh on his king-size bed that night. He could have wreaked havoc over the entire country of Egypt. One swift decisive blow and Egypt would have been history. But He is such a compassionate God. He would await Pharaoh's confession. I read a most interesting story the other day and thought of Pharaoh.

> A number of years ago an atheist declared to passersby, "If there is a God in heaven, I challenge Him to strike me dead in five minutes."
> Five minutes passed, and he said with a sneer, "You see? There is no God, or by this time He would have struck me dead."
> A woman standing by asked: "Do you have any children?"
> The man replied, "Yes, one son."
> "If your son gave you a knife to kill him, would you do it?"
> "Of course not," he promptly answered.
> "Well," she asked, "why not?"
> "Simply because I love him too much."

Before she turned away, the woman explained: "Mister, it's because God loves you too much, even though you are an atheist, that He refuses to accept your foolish challenge. He wants you saved, not lost!"

God heard Pharaoh's question as to who He was. He heard his impudence and challenge, the fact that he remained unprepared to let Israel go. There were so many options opened to the great God and Father of us all; His choice was one of love. He would wait to see whether Pharaoh would get it together. He awaited his admission of His sovereignty, but it never came. Difficult times should not be reserved to acknowledge God. God expects His children to make declarations of His sovereignty. "Whoso offereth praise, glorifieth me."[402] It is wonderful to speak of God's goodness, His mercies, and tender watch-care. Praise and prayer must rise like sweet incense to God, wafted on angels' wings. God delights in hearing His children acknowledge His love and goodness—not a challenge of His love and forbearance.

The test to Pharaoh gave him an opportunity to spontaneously recognize God's leading hand. Israel likewise would be tested on their way to the land flowing with milk and honey. Each would receive a different trial, but nonetheless a test. God knows how to measure out every trial to gain full recognition and our attention.

On the night of the Exodus, the Passover lamb was slain. The blood was splashed on doorposts and lintels. The sacrificial lamb slain had been roasted and eaten with bitter herbs. Israel borrowed from the Egyptians large quantities of silver, gold, clothes, and whatever they could place their hands on. The reparation strategy had been worked out. The owners would be among the deceased. The Israelites remained behind closed doors, no one was allowed outside. The twelve tribes were positioned for swift and immediate departure. At midnight the death angel smote the firstborn of every family with a single stroke; there was not a house in which there was not one dead. Since man began his pilgrimage of pain and sorrow to the grave, no such sudden, wild, frantic, national cry of loss on this earth like that had ever been heard. In one awful moment the angel of death had killed someone in every family in the whole nation with just one stroke. It caused the most crushing sorrow and deepest pain. Pharaoh's house was not exempt, for the heir to the throne had died. Young mothers awakened from slumber by the weeping and wailing found their babies dead in their cradles or at their bosoms. Old parents turned to their sons, but those strong arms were lifeless. Frightened neighbors rushed to each other's houses to find comfort and consolation, only to discover they too had suffered losses. For four hundred years Israel had suffered in varied and sundry ways, but at last He whose business knows no haste or delay came to the rescue. Pharaoh requested a swift exit of all Israel and their possessions. Hurry! Be gone!! Leave!! Now!! Be on your way. Make it out of here before daybreak.[403]

When morning came, the Israelites were a free people, emancipated, safe, beyond the Egyptian borders and destined for their own land. In the illimitable desert before them, only rising clouds obscure the view of their final destination, the Promised Land, a goodly land, God's gift, God's act of love in exchange for the years of toil, the lash, making bricks without straw and all the injustices heaped upon them. Yes, God's compensatory gift from which we draw our deepest and wisest philosophy of His providential leading in human history can be traced to that memorable night. It declares that God is the divine force in all that transpires. Devastated for years, humiliated by servitude, God granted total freedom overnight, a path, a life, a country. All that was required on their part for the undeserved, unearned gift: acceptance.

The incredible deliverance did not prompt the question, "How far is it to Canaan's land?" The Israelites made no inquiry regarding provision of food for the journey or housing. God had taken care of every eventuality. He validated their faith. Even today God, in His matchless goodness, rescues men out of bondage into gracious liberty through Jesus Christ with the promise of eternal life. Without question the objective on His part remains the same: "that the Egyptians may know that I am the Lord."[404]

> And the Lord spake unto Moses, saying, Speak unto the children of Israel, that they turn and encamp before Pihahiroth, between Migdol and the sea, over against Baalzephon: before it shall ye encamp by the sea. For Pharaoh will say of the children of Israel, They are entangled in the land, the wilderness hath shut them in.[405]

Members of the mixed multitude and the Israelites who were up on their geography recognized that what God did could be classified only as unfathomable. To illustrate the point, it would be like being a prisoner in Sing Sing Prison or like a sinner without hope, "shut up between the impassable crags of a broken law and the sinking swamps of human inability."[406] Fresh out of Egypt a mammoth trial came. Were they ready for this great examination of faith? How could they get to the Promised Land if their backs are turned to it? The examination demanded a faith they did not yet possess. One only needs to listen to the wrenching intestinal feelings openly expressed.

> And when Pharaoh drew nigh, the children of Israel lifted up their eyes, and, behold, the Egyptians marched after them; and they were sore afraid: and the children of Israel cried out unto the Lord. And they said unto Moses, Because there were no graves in Egypt, hast thou taken us away to die in the wilderness? Wherefore hast now dealt thus with us, to carry us forth out of Egypt? Is not this the word that we did tell thee in Egypt, saying, Let us alone, that we may serve the Egyptians? For it had been better for us to serve the Egyptians, than that we should die in the wilderness.[407]

If only they had the same faith as when they marched out of Egypt, that midnight hour, then that conversation would have been totally unnecessary and never etched in the Holy Bible. Even an evaluation of their thought patterns would not grant a better feeling of what transpired at this point in their experience. God stated His concern as clearly as He could. "That the Egyptians might know that I am the Lord."[408] Israel must also come to a full recognition of that fact. They needed the faith to just follow. Children of Israel follow God's leading. If only they would go unquestioningly where God instructed.

For His glory to be revealed, God at all times, under varying circumstances sometimes allows His chosen children, even servants, to pass through severe trials, difficulties, dangers, temptations, disappointments, and perplexities to purge dross and expose the pure gold. Call it character building. My favorite Christian author, Mrs. E.G. White wrote,

Our sorrows do not spring out of the ground. God "doth not afflict willingly nor grieve the children of men." When He permits trials and afflictions, it is "for our profit, that we might be partakers of His holiness" Heb.12:10. If received in the faith, the trial that seems so bitter and hard to bear will prove a blessing. The cruel blow that blights the joys of earth will be the means of turning our eyes to heaven. How many there are who would never have known Jesus had not sorrow led them to seek comfort in Him! The trials of life are God's workmen, to remove the impurities and roughness from our character. Their hewing, squaring, and chiseling, their burnishing and polishing, is a painful process; it is hard to be pressed down to the grinding wheel. But the stone is brought forth prepared to fill its place in the heavenly temple. Upon no useless material does the Master bestow such careful, thorough work. Only His precious stones are polished after the similitude of a palace." ..."He who is the King, the Lord of hosts, sitteth between the cherubim, and amid the strife and tumult of nations He guards His children still. He who ruleth in the heavens is our Saviour. He measures every trial, He watches the furnace fire that must test every soul."[409]

Bear in mind God's objective for Pharaoh. The same measuring rod is employed for all His children "that they might know Him..."

Strange and ingenious are the avenues employed by God in receiving glory and praise:

For the last time, Huss was brought before the council. It was a vast assembly—the emperor, the princes of the Empire, the royal deputies, the Cardinals, bishops, and priests, and an immense crowd who had come as spectators of the events of the day. From all parts of Christendom had been gathered the witnesses of this first great sacrifice in the long struggle by which liberty of conscience was to be secured... The vestments were removed one by one, each bishop pronouncing a curse as he performed his part of the ceremony... When the flames rose, they began to sing hymns; and scarce could the vehemence of the fire stop their singing... Huss was no more, but the truths for which he died could never perish...The enemies of truth, though they knew it not, had been furthering the cause which they vainly sought to destroy.[410]

When the trials, disappointments, dangers, perplexities, and losses come, if they are faithfully borne, the fascinating thing is that as a result of life's bitter experiences, individuals are made better. They possess a greater faith, a greater courage, and gain a higher spiritual achievement. The carrier is blessed, the onlooker receives a blessing, and God's truth, His love, and His name are praised and glorified.

Can you hear Israel's despairing cry? "Because there were no graves in Egypt, hast thou taken us away to die in the wilderness?"[411] They were not ready at first to leave Egypt when Moses unfolded God's plan of deliverance. They enjoyed some creature comforts even while enslaved. Now that they found themselves in an awkward position, they simply regressed. We have the record of Israel's cry and their marvelous deliverance. But have we heard our own cry? Why Lord? Why? Why? We have a million and one questions for God when we face our Red Sea experiences with no way out. Like Israel, we too must learn to wait on the Lord, to trust in God. God is always on time. Just as He intervened in their lives, with the same rapidity He will honor our cry, although mingled with questions. Four hundred years before achieving entrance to the Promised Land does seem like an inordinate amount of time, but He did predict that would be the waiting time and then in Exodus 12:41 it says, "at the end of four hundred years, even the selfsame day it came to pass." Whatever comes, whatever He sends, we must rest assured that everything will be right. We must come to the place in our spiritual walk where we can testify like Moses, David, Paul, or Job who said, "…though He slay me, yet will I trust in Him."[412]

It is so easy to possess an air of calmness and serenity, to ripple off a series of conjectures, theories, or even a sound philosophy as to how Israel ought to have reacted in their gut-wrenching plight. We can summon all the resources possible to address life when faced with like situations. However, crossing the Red Sea was the miraculous part. What transpired prior to the passage through the sea is the place we find ourselves most often. Our situation and Israel's can be likened to the description of a painting. The painting depicts a little boy in a predicament. He is holding on by his fingertips from the top of the wall with a bag of stolen apples. On one side is the owner, while on the other side is a bulldog chained to his kennel. He can not go up the wall for fear of the owner, nor drop down for fear of the dog. The painting is titled *In a Fix*. So was Israel. Without telling the Israelites *Do not worry*—because you have already read the conclusion—examine their predicament.

Their journey brought them to the place where they were walled in by mountain ranges on the right and left, the sea in front of them and behind a straight route to Pharaoh's capital. They are weary from the long day's travel. Families, friends, and neighbors have lost track of each other, and every effort has been expended to locate one another. Old and young, men and women, boys and girls, cows and sheep, and all other animals are mingled, crowded, passing to and fro: the journey thus far does not seem to make sense. The homes forsaken in Goshen are now replaced by life in the desert with lowing cows, bleating sheep, and the cries of weary children and babies. Painted on the faces of these weary travelers is a picture of discouragement and fear. Three million people are retracing their steps taken yesterday. Instead of heading for the Promised Land their steps will end in the sea. They had a very sad experience, to say the least. A morning of glad hope and exultant joy, exchanged for an evening of wailing and despair. The voices of the Israelites grew wild and frantic, lifted up in the reproach against the leadership of Moses. The desolation of the area gave the appearance of grave sites. They could neither fight nor flee. They possessed no rifles, no hand grenades, no guns, and had no militia. For over four hundred years they had never been in a battle with anyone; Pharaoh and his indomitable army in chariots drove almost on their doorsteps. They had no ships to cross the Red Sea. Three million fearful people with all their earthly possessions lying about them in the sand was not an easy assignment for Moses. So soon they had forgotten how God had turned the Nile River into blood, and all the other miracles wrought on their behalf. Although they denounced and condemned the leadership of God, in particular Moses whom they could see, God in majesty and splendor stood overhead. The pillar of cloud by day and the pillar of fire by night showed God's presence. Oh children of God, those whom He just passed over, look up!! Turn your eyes on Jesus. There's life in a look.

God's providence sometimes brings us into strange places. The mystery that enshrouds it arises from our partial and imperfect understanding of His plan. If God's plan had been to get Israel to the Promised Land the quickest and easiest way possible, with the least amount of pain and suffering, the reason for the new difficulty they faced would indeed have been inexplicable. God was not merely interested in deliverance from Pharaoh, but that they should be delivered in such a way, and with such a display of His power and His judgments on Pharaoh, that would make him an example to succeeding generations of the stupidity of resisting the Almighty. God would be glorified, and at the same time He would so stamp the memory of His goodness and protection upon the hearts of the Israelites that it would last a lifetime and be passed from generation to generation. Haven't you observed that God usually removes all earthly support and hope to demonstrate heaven's intervention? When earthly friends and supports are snapped, it is amazing how quickly the knees bend, how God appears out of nowhere; how quickly the voice exclaims, "What a friend we have in Jesus, All our sins and griefs to bear! What a privilege to carry *Ev'ry-thing* to God in prayer!"[413]

By the way, have you ever gone down one of life's cul-de-sacs? Ever been hemmed in by the mountains with only the Red Sea ahead? Your great business enterprise failed, investments turned into losses, divorce, repossession of house or car or land or truck, a life-work shattered, engagement broken, or a career failure? Do not repine. Get down on your knees. Today as well as tomorrow is in His care. You will never be able to escape your "between Migdol and the sea"[414] experience. As long as you worship the true and living God, heading for the Promised Land, climbing up the King's highway, you are vulnerable, will be tested, will be in a predicament, but you need not fear. The God who takes you down the seemingly endless highway that terminates in a cul-de-sac will bring you out as long as you serve Him, and refuse to relinquish your grasp on faith in Him. Let us never forget that God told Moses where to take them. If in the process they became faithless and complaining, God's grace will rectify the situation, for God never breaks a promise He makes. The sovereign God will be glorified. God knows how to deliver. He makes it His business to extricate His children when they go down cul-de-sacs. Ask Joseph in prison, the three Hebrew boys in the fiery furnace, Daniel in the lion's den; ask your own testimony. Has He not delivered? He delights in delivering His children from whatever binds, enslaves, or restrains and always in His own time and at His own pace.

Because Israel was delivered after hundreds of years of slavery and deferred blessings, it did not mean there would be a cessation of tests and trials. God had taken up their cause, but their trials and sorrows were not at an end. The first step on the road to the Promised Land had plunged them into a worse plight than before. The winds of sweet liberty had just caressed their cheeks, when suddenly their hopes were dashed. The oncoming army and a darkened situation became nearly unendurable. God's providence to the godliest of His children is often a perplexing mystery. It seems as if God acts contrary to His promises, to His own perfection, purpose, to His character and revealed will on which He encouraged us to trust. The wicked prosper and the righteous are afflicted.[415] Prayers seem to go unanswered and the expectations we have built upon His Word are bitterly disappointed. The race seems to the swift, the battle to the strong. There is a mystery in God's providence. He uses the trials and sorrows to test and discipline character. They bring to light our weaknesses, sift the chaff from the wheat, educate us to trust Him more fully, disenchant us of elusive hopes, refine the gold, lead to a better and more structured prayer life, and ultimately we see things more clearly as the veil is opened and the scales removed from our eyes.

Conversion, baptism, name on the church roll, church attendance with Bible and hymnal in hand, morning and evening worship punctiliously performed, do not preempt renewed daily temptations. Everyone has a Pharaoh who will pursue long after the individual—the former slave—has left his servitude in exchange for duty to a loving commander. This is especially true when the journey leads to the Promised Land. "Between Migdol and the sea," "Between the rocks and a hard place" is oftentimes where the pursuit is most dangerous. It occurs when there is no way out. Old habits, thought broken forever with the idea that they would never be seen again, return. However, the destruction of Pharaoh and his army is the established note of confidence that God will be victorious. God's children will in this life, and ultimately in the life to come, see Pharaoh no more.

The tyrannical cruelty in the depths of Pharaoh's heart drove him to seek recovery of the Hebrews for slave labor, the treasures they carried away from Egypt, but most of all to balk God's command "let my people go."[416] Fear of Pharaoh intimidated Israel, but God would be glorified despite the loss of faith on Israel's part, their murmuring, and reproaches. Moses stood firm, trusting, hopeful.

> And Moses said unto the people, Fear ye not, stand still, and see the salvation of the Lord, which he will shew to you to day: for the Egyptians whom ye have seen to day, ye shall see them again no more for ever. The Lord shall fight for you, and ye shall hold your peace. And the Lord said unto Moses, Wherefore criest thou unto me? Speak unto the children of Israel, that they go forward.[417]

In the face of danger the commands were appropriate and defined Israel's conduct. *Fear not. Stand still. The Lord shall fight. Go forward.*

Let us bear in mind the central fact in this battle. "That the Egyptians may know that I am the Lord."[418]

Had God permitted Pharaoh and his army to capture Israel and re-enslave them, the knowledge of the one and only true God might have been obliterated from the earth. This is not to say that God could not have raised up a new generation to broadcast His will. But God had many reasons for Israel's freedom and salvation. He wanted succeeding generations to worship the one and only true God. In His dealings with them He wanted to leave an account He intended they should rehearse to the generations following. God would not allow that rich part of history—from creation to the leadership of Moses—to rust and waste in the silt of the Nile River. It would not be like the bones of Joseph which were buried and exhumed, only for another graveyard.

Moses seized another opportunity to glorify God. He said to the three million Israelites, "Don't be afraid of Pharaoh's six hundred best chariots, the others and his military might. Just stand still and see the salvation of God."[419] Can you imagine panic-stricken, excited, terrified Israelites being asked to just stand still? Not everyone had a slave mentality. But although weary, discouraged, depressed, and disheartened, a breath of excitement swept over that vast concourse of people. Some expected to fall into the hands of Egypt's taskmasters again who would assign them to the brick kilns and slime pits under the lash. God hung two pictures on their minds, the past in Egypt and the present where

He led. They were told to follow the pillar of cloud over their heads. We can only imagine what a majestic sight that must have been, as God moved majestically in the cloud at a pace that all could follow. As the evening shadows lengthened, it no longer provided shade but light and direction. A toothache when the dentist's office is closed at night seems more severe, more unbearable, than during the daylight hours when his services are available. So with Israel as the Egyptians pressed down upon them. They could not help but think that the Egyptians died in large numbers that midnight hour when they left, and could it be that a like fate would be theirs in this midnight hour? But God quieted their fears with His presence overhead. Not a host of shining angels as He hung over the Bethlehem manger when Christ was born, but God Himself descended upon His people in the cloud.[420] What an awesome God! What an awesome spectacle! Moses reminded them, that the Lord God had promised to fight for them. God knew that the Israelites had no military capabilities which could be called upon to provide Him needed support. At one point Moses told Israel, "stand still." At a later time "go forward." Then God fought for Israel, by Himself and without their aid. The battle remained His to fight and win.

At His divine command Moses stretched the same wonder-working rod he had when God called him at the burning bush at Horeb over the Red Sea and the waters immediately parted at the shoreline. God made a superhighway, the Red Sea Highway, for the millions and all their possessions. The command "go forward" was passed on from the front line to the last group bringing up the rear. It was night, but all Israel pressed forward. They were crossing over on dry ground, walking in the depths of the sea. For their protection God had made walls of water, standing like marble columns. The two walls of water replaced the mountains that had deterred their escape plans before they entered the sea. They tried to understand the miracle that seemed like a nightmare. I am sure they did not understand God's inscrutable ways. They followed each other as they pressed on, knowing that the enemy trailed not far behind. But the outcome resided with God. We too must learn to only trust and obey Him, and reverence Him, and love Him, and know that our salvation is secure even when we find ourselves in deep waters. But God's deeds must be experienced, for no one can fathom the things of God.

The Egyptians discovered that the Israelites were gone from the spot where they had been hemmed in. In the distance they saw the light guiding them and heard voices. Not knowing of God's Red Sea Highway they followed in hot pursuit in the rear of the moving light. "And the angel of God, which went before the camp of Israel, removed and went behind them; and the pillar of the cloud went from before their face, and stood behind them: And it came between the camp of the Egyptians and the camp of the Israel; and it was a cloud and darkness to them, but it gave light by night to these: so that the one came not near the other all the night."[421] We should never, ever forget that in front of us and behind us there is a watchful God. He will cover our backs. He guided and defended them with the same source, the pillar of cloud which would assume whatever shade God desired at the moment.

After a while Pharaoh and his army found that the dry ground got soggy and operational difficulties set in. The chariots would not run as before. Those well-oiled machines began to break down. Mud created a real problem for the Egyptians' passage. But they were determined to bring the Hebrews back. Pharaoh had so soon forgotten the ten plagues and their blood-curdling effects. But sin is irrational and Pharaoh imprudent, proud, and rebellious. He could run to God, but he could not run from Him. The Egyptians reached the middle of the sea at about the time all Israel had safely reached the other side. Then God looked through the clouds, "and troubled the host of the Egyptians."[422] Pharaoh and his army placed themselves in the line of fire. He tried what no one has ever done and succeeded: to fight against God. Chariot wheels fell off; there was confusion among the military; foot soldiers were trampled; they were confused; men and horses were mired in the mud; they decided to beat a hasty retreat when they discovered that God fought for His people; but it was too late. At God's command Moses stretched his hand over the Red Sea after all Israel and their possessions were safe and accounted for. Pharaoh, his host, the pride and power of Egypt, were swallowed up in the sea. Not one survived. Israel in the meantime stood on the shore that morning and sang songs of triumph and praise and thanksgiving to God for His mighty deliverance. He told them the Egyptians would never be seen again, and true to His word, as God always is, the bodies washed upon the shores with every wave that bathed it. The Red Sea Highway was only for Israel.

Let us never forget that the mighty God, who delivered Israel when they thought only the worst, is our God forever and ever. While the things that frighten, annoy, and distress us are quite different from those of Pharaoh's time, they are just as foreboding, just as real. We do well to remember the words of God through Moses, "The Lord shall fight for you."

"Between Migdol and the sea," "between the rocks and a hard place" was not a trap. The battle belonged to God. God fights for His people, and dare anyone tell Him how to design His affairs or what strategy He ought to employ? With all the wonders of this conflict, one can only "stand still" and say that the drowning of Pharaoh and his army could not be the point of emphasis with God, but rather "that the Egyptians may know that I am the Lord." The display of His power, His glory, His victory, and His ability to stand independent of anything that man may do or wants to do and obedience to His commands were of greater importance than anything else.

A friend of mine gave me a paper entitled, "But God" some time ago. It author is unknown and I have never seen one. But when one's faith gets shaky and doubt assails, it is worth the while to read this document. Drooping faith in God will be revived.

BUT GOD

Here are some interesting facts that will show the greatness of God.

The Bible says that the children of Israel numbered 600,000 men when they left Egypt. If you count a family of five members, that would be approximately 3,000,000 people, not counting the cattle and other animals.

The Bible says they crossed the Red Sea in one night. Walking 5,000 abreast, this would take a space opened up three miles wide. In double file this would make a line 800 miles long and it would have taken 35 days and nights to cross. *BUT GOD!*

For this many people to camp, it would require a space 750 square miles or 2/3 the size of the state of Rhode Island. *BUT GOD!*

They camped and traveled with no food. The amount needed to feed this many people to keep them from starving would come to 1500 tons of food per day. If they were to eat as we do today, it would take 4,000 tons per day. It would take two freight trains one mile long to haul that much food. At today's prices it would cost $5,000,000 per day. *BUT GOD!*

Manna from heaven would need to equal 2,000,000 gallons per day. *BUT GOD!*

It would take 11,000,000 gallons of water per day just for the barest necessities. *BUT GOD!*

If you figure just one quail per family of five, 600,000 quail would have to come walking into the camp every night.

When you think of this, consider also the fact that God did supply the needs of His children daily for 14,600 days, and their clothes and shoes never wore out. *BUT GOD!*

OH YE OF LITTLE FAITH.

The God who told Moses to tell Pharaoh to free His people, in order to lead them as free moral agents to worship Him, and ultimately into the Promised Land, would never leave them "between Migdol and the sea." He keeps His word. That same Jesus has promised us a place in His eternal kingdom. Not from Egypt to the Promised Land, but from earth to heaven. He will carry every believer safely until face to face they shall behold Him in that Promised Land, the eternal city of God, the haven of rest. That day is not far away when all the faithful shall stand on Jordan's peaceful shore. Our darkest nights, our deepest frustrations, our most painful experiences will soon be over, and that eternal daybreak of joy unspeakable and full of triumph will dawn, never again to know night. Our guide, our Lord and Savior Jesus Christ, will throw open the gates of the city, and on the banks of that river of life the redeemed of all ages shall with expressions of cheerfulness, sing songs of praise and gratitude, and shall extol His name forever for His matchless, amazing, sufficient grace. Israel needed only an unwavering trust in God. And just as He brought them out of Egypt with a mighty and outstretched arm, in like manner He will do the same for present-day Israel of God. Their deliverance from Egyptian captivity has as a landmark those two awesome midnights. One, when God saw the blood and passed over; and two, when He saw them through the cloud, and the Egyptians were destroyed in the Red Sea. We have Calvary, that dark day, and the resurrection morning, that glorious day. God in Jesus Christ fought and won our battles. Victory is assured.

The promise for the Promised Land *waiters* is,

I will never, never leave thee,
I will never thee forsake;
I will guide, and save, and keep thee,
For my name and mercy's sake;
Fear no evil, Fear no evil,
Only all my counsel take.

When the storm is raging round thee,
Call on me in humble pray'r;
I will fold my arms around thee,
Guard thee with the tend'rest care:
In the trial, In the trial,
I will make thy pathway clear.

When the sky above is glowing,
And around thee all is bright,
Pleasure like a river flowing,
All things tending to delight;
I'll be with thee, I'll be with thee,
I will guide thy steps aright.

When thy soul is dark and clouded,
Fill'd with doubt, and grief and care,
Thro' the mists by which 'tis shrouded,
I will make the light appear,
And the banner, And the banner,
Of my love I will uprear.

—Unknown

Chapter 8

A COSMIC INTERRUPTION

(Based on Joshua 9–10)

In the remote and incalculable past (and just how far back that is we will only know when we reach the kingdom of God), "the angels which kept not their estate, but left their own habitation,"[423] started a war in God's kingdom. "And there was war in heaven: Michael and his angels fought against the dragon; and the dragon fought and his angels. And prevailed not; neither was their place found any more in heaven."[424] The war created two captains: God's Son Michael and the dragon. Michael is the captain of the Lord's host, the King of kings and Lord of lords. The dragon is that old serpent, the devil and Satan.[425] He and his angels were routed, defeated, and cast out. As a result of that war in heaven each of us must decide who will be our captain.

The battle is real. The fighting arena was transferred from heaven to earth. The devil and the angels who joined him in the rebellion were cast out. The battlefield is not in interstellar space where these evil spirits roam contending with angels in their flight to and from ministering to us. It is right here on earth. The battle is waged on the job, in the church, at the dining table, in the home, everywhere. It is waged whether you are ready for conflict or not. And only God, who reads the hearts and calculates motives, knows how fierce the battle is for each individual. Sometimes in the conflict we listen to the still small voice, sometimes we do not. If we leave it all to our captain, Michael, it's victory, but if we do not, we are overwhelmed and defeated. All the days of our lives, day and night, hour by hour, we are at war. Sometimes we win and sometimes we lose. I read recently that King Ahasuerus had a party at his palace in Shushan for seven days for great and small. Listen to the atmosphere. "There were white, green, and blue hangings, fastened with cords of fine linen and purple to silver rings and pillars of marble: the beds were of gold and silver, upon a pavement of red, and blue, and white, and black, marble."[426] On our journey to the city of God, where holiness dwells, we encounter nothing like that. It is not a mosaic pavement of beautiful inlaid marble. Ah, no it isn't. It is a real warpath, a lifelong journey over treacherous roads. Sometimes we are uncertain. Sometimes we stumble over the same rocks. Sometimes we are like the sheep straying into many detours, lost, looking for the shepherd and not knowing how to get back to the fold. Sometimes we are like the man who went down from Jerusalem to Jericho, only to fall among thieves who robbed, beat him, and left him almost at death's door—but for the Good Samaritan. On the road we fall into many snares and dangers. But if we remain on the path, fighting the good fight, holding on to the Rock of Ages and being loyal, eventually heaven's gates will swing wide open to welcome a weary, worn, tattered traveler. The war seems endless and relentless, but victory will come sooner than later. The power of evil is doing everything to overcome and win the battle, but just as light is stronger than darkness, so is Captain Michael stronger than the dragon. Better still it is assuring to know that whether in heaven or on earth the battle is already won no matter how fierce.

> When Satan had succeeded in winning many angels to his side, he took his cause to God, representing that it was the desire of the angels that he occupy the position that Christ held.
>
> The evil continued to work until the spirit of disaffection ripened into active revolt. Then *there was war in heaven*, and Satan, with all who sympathized with him, was cast out. Satan had warred for the mastery in heaven, and had lost the battle. God could no longer trust him with honor and supremacy, and these, with the part he had taken in the government in heaven, were taken from him.

Since that time Satan and his army of confederates have been the avowed enemies of God in our world, continually warring against the cause of truth and righteousness. Satan has continued to present to men, as he presented to the angels, his false representations of Christ and of God, and he has won the world to his side. Even the professedly Christian churches have taken sides with the great apostate.[427]

Since the fall of man, every generation has been targeted. This battle that occurred during Joshua's time reveals that there has been no cessation. It is still about the cosmic struggle. It was physical. God authorized, He commanded the conflict. This battle is about God releasing weapons of warfare from His arsenal of nature. They are called hailstones. This battle depicts in graphic language the forces at work poised to separate the soul from God. It shows how easy it is to attempt to do God's deeds, in the armor of flesh, without His involvement. In theological language it is called justification by works. This is about spiritual warfare. We dare not go without God. Again we will observe that *the battle is the Lord's*. We will discover that we cannot claim victory and try to share the spotlight with God. If ever a battle is won, be it in Canaan under Joshua or on earth in our lives, victory is assured only through Christ, who is the captain of our salvation.

In this engagement we will observe how sin is dealt with in whatever form it takes. For example, like covetousness in Achan,[428] lies and deceit in the Gibeonites, and the destruction of the five kings at Makkedah[429] whose probation was closed. The cup of their iniquity was already overflowing. They are illustrative of the final outcome of sin and Satan. The threads of gold that will hold this chapter together will be the great facts announced, that to win the battle for the immortal crown, to overcome, to stand successful at last, God must be trusted. He must be consulted at every step in our pilgrimage. We are engaged in a war, but God, who keeps His promises, is involved because while we must fight the war, it really started against Him. If His Word is kept and obeyed, and by His grace the covenant agreement is maintained, life will be one unending song of triumph and victory. The battle, you see, is the Lord's.

This battle has the following twists and turns. Joshua had spies to view Ai, the next city to be conquered after Jericho.[430] The spies reported that Ai could be defeated by a small contingent of three thousand fighting soldiers. They stated that Ai had only a few fighting men and the city itself was small.[431] No one knew that Achan, son of Carmi, the son of Zimri, the son of Zerah, of the tribe of Judah, had violated God's covenant.[432] He embezzled some of the things devoted to God, acted out a lie, and walked freely in the community with God's possessions buried in his tent, hidden from public view. God knew and saw everything. Job said, "for he views the ends of the earth and sees everything under the heavens."[433] As a result of Achan's act, thirty-six men, soldiers in Israel's army, were killed when the three thousand soldiers attacked the city of Ai.[434] Israel was defeated while trying to take a small city like Ai after the spectacular miracle performed on her behalf in her first conquest, Jericho. The sin of covetousness raised its ugly head in the midst of the great celebration of God. The first fruits of the land of Canaan belonged to God. But before we deal with Achan, let us deal with ourselves. Let us be introspective.

> Among church-members 'in good and regular standing,' there are, alas! many Achans… The deadly sin that led to Achan's ruin had its root in covetousness, of all sins one of the most common and the most lightly regarded. While other offenses meet with detection and punishment, how rarely does the violation of the tenth commandment so much as call forth censure… Covetousness is an evil of gradual development. Achan had cherished greed of gain until it became a habit, binding him in fetters well-nigh impossible to break… We are as directly forbidden to indulge covetousness as was Achan to appropriate the spoils of Jericho. God has declared it to be idolatry. We are warned, "Ye cannot serve God and mammon." "Take heed, and beware of covetousness." "Let it not be once named among you.[435]

Joshua tore his robe when Israel was defeated at Ai. The elders of Israel did likewise. They prostrated themselves before the ark of the Lord until evening.[436] Then Joshua blurted out those doubt-ridden, unbelieving, faithless statements.

> And Joshua said, Alas, O Lord GOD, wherefore hast thou at all brought this people over Jordan, to deliver us into the hand of the Amorites, to destroy us? "Would to God we had been content, and dwelt on the other side Jordan! O Lord, What shall I say, when Israel

turneth their backs before their enemies! For the Canaanites and all the inhabitants of the land shall hear of it, and shall environ us round, and cut off your name from the earth: and what wilt thou do unto thy great name?"[437]

Only moments before, God had miraculously delivered Jericho into Joshua's hands. The sounds of the blaring trumpets and the crashing walls of Jericho were still fresh in Joshua's ears. The great ordained leader of God's people, the one to whom God promised success saying, "as I was with Moses so I will be with thee"[438] offered a prayer saturated with doubt and unbelief. For a moment he had not achieved any higher level of spirituality than had Israel. Forty years before, after leaving Egypt, ready to cross the Red Sea on dry ground, by a mighty and outstretched arm, they asked, "Because there were there no graves in Egypt, hast thou taken us away to die in the wilderness?"[439] Just listen to Joshua. His prayer was laced with doubt, despondency, distrust, disbelief, and fear, unbefitting a leader of his stature. If only he had had the privilege of reading the following statement.

Despondency is sinful and unreasonable. God is able and willing "more abundantly" to bestow upon His servants the strength they need for test and trial.[440]

Joshua assumed that God had simply walked off, deserted His people, and abandoned His covenant. He felt he must now manufacture an answer because Israel would turn their backs on God. Since Israel was defeated by their enemies Joshua felt obligated to give a reasonable explanation. Certainly, this was not Joshua's greatest moment. Must he speak for God? Listen to his question. "O Lord, what shall I say, when Israel turneth their backs before their enemies!" Joshua 7:8 God can and will speak for Himself. Joshua was so much like us. Blessed we are by a loving God, but we are possessors of so many human frailties. Our faith disappears when pressed by trials. We lose our sense of perspective. We abandon our faith in God and His Word when we need it most. In the conflict we veer from the path.

It is important for us to know—and Joshua, if only we could draw him into our circle here and now—that there are mountains of success and valleys of disappointments. Those who follow Jesus Christ will go through some tough situations, through blood, sweat, and tears, trials and misfortunes in the war. That is part of the cosmic struggle. But Joshua and every child of God should always bear in mind the fact that the defeat at Ai, the failures in life, do not mean all will be lost. The temptation to selfishness, to injustice, to untruth, to un-charitableness, the failure to bear each other's burdens that got the upper hand does not mean God has disappeared from our lives. Something must be said for the dishonest acts resisted, the falsehoods unuttered, the unkind words left unsaid, every sensual impulse crushed, and deeds of kindness done. They form a part of the victories in the war. They, in and of themselves, will not secure for us a place in the kingdom, but they say that God is operating in our life His good will and pleasure.

My wife and I were blessed with three children. All three did not learn to walk without their share of falling. They would make one or two steps, then down they'd go. Sometimes the more they tried the greater the fall. They never gave up in despair, but tried and tried un-til the knees no longer buckled, and their efforts were rewarded by a steady gait. We are children of God and our walk with Him is achieved through falling and rising, trying again and again until there are no more mistakes and defeats. And as the journey lengthens the trials and errors make for greater confidence in His amazing ability to "keep you [us] from falling."[441]

In our evaluation of human conduct, we are prone to say that the best Christian, the wisest man, the person with the keenest intellect is the one who makes the fewest mistakes. Not true. It is he who turns blunders and slips into succeeding better. Moses tried to get Israel out of their oppressors' hands. In his own strength he failed miserably. Israel rejected him, and he became a fugitive from Pharaoh. Forty long years of tending sheep out in Midian was the price tag of that failure.[442] But the second time around, after the burning bush experience, going at God's direction, following His outline, Israel succeeded in the emancipation process. Joshua too learned lessons from which he profited and victory attended his labors. The Wright brothers did not put a supersonic jet in the air on their first attempt. Inventors try and try and try again. If, in your efforts to be all that God wants you to be, you have failed and failed, again and again, do not give up. Even if life is nothing but a series of spiritual casualties, and losses, do not give up or in.

> Deem not the irrevocable past
> As wholly wasted, wholly vain;
> For, *rising on its wrecks,* at last
> To nobler greatness we attain.[443]

Joshua needed to look up. His God was still on the throne. His resources were still unlimited. The battle was still His. Joshua sounded in his conversation with the Almighty as if he desired to share the spotlight with Him. "What shall I say?"[444] God had not lost control of His universe. God did not promise skies always blue. He still has the last word. God loves when we come boldly into His presence, not whining, complaining, whimpering, and distressed as if He is out of control, and all of a sudden we are orphans. God is truly, incontrovertibly, and unquestionably a God of grace and love. Grace and love among His other virtues are the foundation stones of His dealings with mankind.

A serious look at Joshua's prayer, at first blush, it appears as though he wanted to protect the honor of God. When more closely scrutinized, we can only declare there was absolutely no foundation for this kind of prayer, given all the circumstances. He never consulted God before going to Ai. There was a gentle rebuke for his doubt and assignment of failure to God.

> And the LORD said unto Joshua, Get thee up; wherefore liest thou thus upon thy face? Israel hath sinned, and they have also transgressed my covenant which I commanded them: for they have even taken of the accursed thing, and have also stolen, and dissembled also, and they have put it even among their own stuff. Therefore the children of Israel could not stand before their enemies, but turned their backs before their enemies, because they were accursed: neither will I be with you any more, except ye destroy the accursed thing from among you.[445]

After casting lots, Achan's covetousness was discovered. Honestly and with candor, taking full responsibility, he explained his situation. No mitigating or extenuating circumstances surfaced. He did not repent and sought no forgiveness. The valley of Achor where they stoned him and his family received their bodies. It all seemed so innocent, but the cancer of covetousness took Achan's life, endangered the nation, caused the death of thirty-six men and halted Israel's progress. The recommended cure for Achan's cancerous covetousness was not chemotherapy. It was promptly excised.

Then Joshua detailed the strategy for taking Ai. The ambush was incredible. The army of Ai was annihilated, the king outmaneuvered, and again Israel moved forward. A review indicates that the defeat of Jericho, Israel's first conquest in the Promised Land, was a miracle. Ai was received by stratagem. The battles did not end there. In the continuing cosmic conflict six kings will see God's handiwork and victory will be achieved as God again demonstrates His power.

All the kings who were situated in the direction where Joshua and Israel's conquest would take them were alarmed at Israel's successful approach. The question posed was, who would be next? They hadn't the slightest clue. They knew no part of Canaan was exempt. The better plan, they thought, would be to fight against God. For hundreds of years the Canaanites had lived on probation.[446] God in His great mercy had spared them in the hope that they would have acknowledged Him as the one and only true God. They didn't and now the cup of iniquity had overflowed.

Before engaging in further conquest, Joshua did something awesome. He marched Israel to the center of the land, passing all the Canaanites who were in awe of them. On Mount Ebal he built an altar and sacrificed burnt offerings and peace offerings to the Lord. Then he divided all the people in two. Half went up on Mount Ebal and the other half on Mount Gerizim. He read the law given to Moses on the mount in the presence of the children of Israel, and then blessed them. Basking in the victory at Ai, Israel turned to God with praise and thanksgiving.

> And afterward he read all the words of the law, the blessings and the cursings, according to all that is written in the book of the law. There was not a word of all that Moses commanded, which Joshua read not before all the congregation of Israel, with the women, and the little ones, and the strangers that were conversant among them.[447]

After Ai, Joshua and Israel will take nothing for granted. They will read from the book and bring their lives into conformity with the will of God. Notice, even the children are drawn into a full understanding of the covenant. The covenant relationship will remain intact. It could have been that they had not recalled all the words of God to fulfill the agreement, and therefore Ai's defeat happened. They pledged that another experience like that of Ai would be averted. Everyone heard the terms of the contract, all the blessings and all the cursings. They then rededicated themselves prior to resuming the conquest.

Like the act of Joshua reading God's words and covenants in the hearing of all Israel, it is marvelous to have God's words rehearsed in our hearing, kept before us in our pilgrimage and dutifully obeyed. Lest they forget, those words were to be rehearsed every seven years.[448] Lest we forget, God placed the holy day of rest in the weekly cycle to be that constant reminder of Him as our creator, redeemer, and friend. Every seventh day of the week it is our gladsome privilege to join in fellowship and praise to God, the creator of the heavens and earth. It impacts all of life, and those who joyfully adhere to His will prosper and are blessed.

Can you imagine reading the law given to Moses in the hearing of over three million people between two mountains without any audio equipment, and every word clearly heard and understood? An activity of this magnitude would not go unnoticed by the surrounding nations. The record states that the kings west of the Jordan heard. "And it came to pass, when all the kings which were on this side Jordan... heard thereof;... they gathered... to fight."[449] I imagine some saw what had transpired on Mounts Ebal and Gerizim. Of course, what happened to Jericho and Ai became common knowledge to the surrounding nations. The kings west of Jordan suspected that they were in the line of fire and that calamity would be on their doorsteps soon. So they banded themselves together "with one accord."[450]

Union, concord, and assembling together as one army they considered a vital necessity if they must survive. One cannot but pray that God's elect will find it needful to unite. There is so much in-fighting, so many sparring matches, quarrellings, dissension, wrangling over nonessentials, lack of agreement, striving for the best seat, pre-eminence in social, political, even spiritual power. Holy wars are not a thing of the past. They still exist. A careful examination will reveal that there is a loss of humility and the existence of the spirit of concord and unity. And while all the internal wars are going on, the enemy walks in and carries off that for which the strife ensues.

The Canaanite kings displayed a greater sense of unity than many a follower of God. They sought unity in a time when danger was ahead. We are on the verge of the appearance of our great God and Savior Jesus Christ, on the very threshold of eternity. The world is in disarray and unbelief exists in every corner. Destruction and dismay are everywhere. Souls are hanging in the balances, some waiting only to be garnered in. The devil knows he has only a short time, therefore he is wreaking havoc, seeing how many he can send to Christless graves. At such a time as this some Christians are as divided as east is from west. The upper room experience needs to be revisited and enjoyed again. If only Christians could utilize their energies to fight a common foe, the devil, rather than each other, significant victories could be achieved.

The Canaanite kings had several things in common. I am sure some territorial disputes and other issues divided them, but at this critical juncture they concentrated on those things that united them. What would our world be like if all Christians concentrated only on those things that united them? Those kings knew that Israel was coming to conquer their land. They had a common danger. Israel was a common enemy. Those kings were not in love with Israel. They had a common hate. They decided to set aside their strife and dissatisfaction over tribal or national disagreements, summons their resources, and fight in a common cause, for a common good.

In the political arena, Democrats and Republicans, opposing parties who face off on some issues, will unite as one voice if the subject at hand infringes on the rights of all. Those who choose sides on the various political issues are quick to erase party lines for the good of the entire nation.

The Pharisees and the Sadducees, who did not share either theological agreements or other social issues, converged on the scene of Christ's crucifixion and shouted together, "Crucify Him! Crucify Him!"[451] "His blood be on us, and on our children."[452] Even Pilate and Herod were drawn together by His blood.

While these kings were uniting, the Gibeonites had a different plan. They might have heard God's word read on Mount Ebal, that they were to show no mercy to the Canaanites, to give no quarter in battle, to make no league with them. The Israelites were instructed,

> When the LORD thy God shall bring thee into the land whither thou goest to possess it, and hath cast out many nations before thee, the Hittites, and the Girgashites, and the Amorites, and the Canaanites, and the Perizzites, and the Hivites, and the Jebusites, seven nations greater and mightier than thou; And when the LORD thy God shall deliver them before thee; thou shalt smite them, and utterly destroy them; thou shalt make no covenant with them, nor shew mercy unto them: Neither shalt thou make marriages with them; thy daughter thou shalt not give unto his son, nor his daughter shalt thou take unto thy son.[453]

A review of the following passages indicate that God left no stone unturned, as related to the relationships that ought to exist between Israel and the Canaanites.

> Thou shalt make no covenant with them, nor with their gods. They shall not dwell in thy land, lest they make thee sin against me: for if thou serve their gods, it will surely be a snare unto thee.[454]

Also,

> But thou shalt utterly destroy them; namely…as the LORD thy God hath commanded thee: That they teach you not to do after all their abominations, which they have done unto their gods; so should you sin against the LORD your God.[455]

Permission was granted to make peace with cities that were far off. God in His providential leading, long before the chosen people entered the land, made provision for every single detail.

They would never confront a situation for which conditions were not already in place.

When thou comest nigh unto a city to fight against it, then proclaim peace unto it. And it shall be, if it make thee answer of peace, and open unto thee, then it shall be, that all the people that is found therein shall be tributaries unto thee, and they shall serve thee. And if it will make no peace with thee, but will make war against thee, then thou shalt besiege it: And when the LORD thy God hath delivered it into thine hands thou shalt smite every male thereof with the edge of the sword: But the women, and the little ones, and the cattle, and all that is in the city, even all the spoil thereof, thou shalt take unto thyself; and thou shalt eat the spoil of thine enemies, which the LORD thy God hath given thee. Thus shalt thou do unto all the cities which are very far off from thee, which are not of the cities of *these nations*. But of the cities of these people, which the LORD thy God doth give thee for an inheritance, *thou shalt save nothing alive that breatheth*:[456]

The recorded conversation of the Gibeonites with Joshua and the princes in Israel indicated they were conversant with the word and will of God.

And they went to Joshua unto the camp at Gilgal, and said unto him, and to the men of Israel, *We be come from a far country:* now therefore make a league with us… And they said unto him, *From a very far country thy servants are come because of the name of the name of the LORD thy God:* for we have heard of the fame of him, and all that he did in Egypt,… Wherefore our elders and all the inhabitants of our country spake to us, saying, Take victuals with you for the journey, and go to meet them, and say unto them, We are your servants: therefore now make ye a *league* with us.[457]

How far is this country that is so far away? Did anyone ask for its geographic location? In their conversation with Joshua and the elders, the Gibeonites disavowed any relationship to the Canaanites. They stressed only one fact—they were from a far country. If their clothes were so shredded, tattered, and worn from the one-way trip, and if they were so insightful, what provision did they make for the return trip? Why travel with molded bread? What about those wineskins that wore away on this trip? If they are that far away, Israel would never get that far for sure. Joshua should have asked only a few more questions. Although a better line of questions did not follow, it is evident Joshua and the elders were not quite convinced. The Gibeonites were overreaching themselves in being so smart. Joshua did not press them sufficiently. They were on the verge of a breakthrough, but they refused to go all the way.

> And the men of Israel said unto the Hivites, Peradventure ye dwell among us; and how shall we make a league with you?[458]

What a great lesson we all can learn right here. We should be on guard twenty-four hours per day, seven days a week. In this great cosmic conflict in which we are all engaged, vigilance ought not to be relinquished for a moment. We should remember always, "a book cannot be judged by its cover." The tricks and trades of evil are all around us. To avoid being taken in unwittingly by the craftiness of the evil one or his workers, we must do what the Savior said, "be ye therefore wise as serpents and harmless as doves."[459] The flattering remarks of the Gibeonites had nothing of value, and no specific destination for Israel. What did they really say that so impressed the leaders? Rahab had already testified that every nation feared the approaching Israelites who were under God's leadership. Joshua made an enormous blunder. The reason why Israel blundered needs no research.

> And the men took of their victuals, and *asked not counsel at the mouth of the Lord.*[460]

They did not make it a matter of prayer. They trusted their own wisdom. They went contrary to the plain declarations of God. No spiritual undertaking, no business transaction, no union is too trivial a matter to embark upon without divine approbation. "Be careful for nothing;" said the apostle Paul, "but in everything by prayer and supplication with thanksgiving let your requests be made known unto God."[461] That counsel should be heeded. We ought to worry about nothing, but we should pray about everything. Furthermore, the exhortation is to "Pray without ceasing."[462] Those guidelines in Christian conduct are great in foresight and hindsight. The reality is, as children of God we dare not embark upon one single activity, however seemingly inconsequential, without first inquiring of the Lord. The fact is that too often decisions without God's sanction or participation are made which end in shame and sorrow, disappointment, even second best or a lifelong dissatisfaction. Irrespective of how flawless, how honest the matter, how plain the path may seem, take it to the Lord in prayer.

> The path of men who are placed as leaders is not an easy one. But they are to see in every difficulty a call to prayer. Never are they to fail of consulting the great Source of all wisdom. Strengthened and enlightened by the Master-worker, they will be enabled to stand firm against unholy influences, and to discern right from wrong, good from evil. They will approve that which God approves, and will strive earnestly against the introduction of wrong principles into His cause.[463]

Failure to seek God first resulted in misplaced trust. Let us not forget that an avenue was available to Joshua whereby he need not have made a mistake. It is so clearly stated that we stand in amazement about how this trap snapped and caught Joshua and the elders. God said to Moses,

> Take him to Eleazar, the high priest, and in the presence of the people lay your hands on him to indicate the transfer of leadership. Tell the children of Israel that Joshua will receive *directions from me* through the two stones, the Urim and Thummin, that are on the garments of the high priest. One stone will light up to give a 'Yes' answer or the other one will cloud over to give a 'No' answer. Israel is to move at his command.[464]

The Urim and Thummim were at Joshua's disposal. All he needed was ask Eleazar to find the direction they ought to take. Yet on two occasions now he failed to seek God's counsel. At Ai he sent spies,[465] and with the Gibeonites he trusted his own senses. Before we find occasion to scold Joshua and the leaders for obvious ineptitude, let us remember that the same is true of us although we do not have the Urim and the Thummim. And yet, God has made provision for every child of His to discover what path ought to be followed. He has a thousand ways of which we know not one to direct our steps. In the absence of the Urim and Thummim all we are requested to do is ask for the leadership of God in our lives. He will answer.

Abraham heard a voice saying, "Take now thy son, thine only son."[466] Joseph had dreams.[467] Moses heard a voice from a burning bush, had visions, and witnessed miracles.[468] Joshua had the priest with the Urim and Thummim flashing God's approval or shadowing His disapproval.[469] Gideon had an angel and a piece of fleece.[470] Jonah had sailors who cast lots.[471] Elijah heard the still small voice.[472] Hezekiah had the sundial.[473] Wise men from the east saw a star over Bethlehem's manager.[474] The disciples of Christ had the living Word, the Word made flesh.[475] And praise be to God we have both the written Word and His indwelling Holy Spirit.[476]

The Gibeonites did a psychological job on Joshua and the elders of Israel. It was a classic. It was so serpent-like, it is disgusting. "And they said unto him, From a very far country thy servants are come because of the name of the LORD thy God: for we have heard the fame of him, and all that he did in Egypt."[477] What flattery! What an ego builder. Those men were smooth, cool, and deceptive operators. They were so shrewd. They possessed nerves of steel. They had no reverence for life. What if they were discovered? They were crafty, scheming, guileful men. What they did and what they hid could consume pages. Suffice it to say they demonstrated faith in God. They sincerely believed that in time they would have been destroyed as stated by the God. They gave glory to God even though it was a bad situation. God received their homage. They confirmed that God was central in the previous conquests of Israel. But they presented God's fame as though achieved by the Israelites. The Israelites were only doing His bidding.

Here is another word of caution for all God's children. We ought to get beyond the flattery. Be sure to test the validity of any presentation by God's Word and earnest prayer, rather than emotions and acceptance of the praise of man. Do not get caught up in the euphoria of the moment. Do not become anxious to take credit for the things God has done, even though He used your hands, talents, and resources to accomplish His purposes.

Joshua, a trusting soul, believed the Gibeonites and accepted their statement that they were from a far country. He could not believe they were a part of the Canaanites. He and the Gibeonites entered into a covenant relationship, made a league of friendship, gave a solemn pledge, and just like that the Gibeonites became part of the Israelite community. They were cemented into the Jewish faith. The covenanted agreements made the bonds unbreakable. There was absolutely no way of untying that pledge of loyalty.

Three days later, Joshua and Israel discovered that the men with the molded bread, tattered garments, breaking wineskins came from nearby Gibeon. "The site is now conclusively identified with the present village of *ej-Jib*, 6 mi. (c. 9.5km) northwest of Jerusalem."[478] However, it was too late to make a single adjustment. Israel must now keep the vows made. God's stamp of approval must be upon every conclusion at which we arrive. If so, regret will never darken our steps.

Watch this now. Deceit, lies, trickery, fraud will get by for only a while. "And be sure your sin will find you out."[479] The Gibeonites desired peaceful, neighborly, brotherly relations with Israel, although they spoke of being their servants. Their hopes were of a lifestyle superior to the other Canaanites. They desired freedom, peace and the blessings they heard read from Mount Ebal when all the people responded, "Amen." However, their fraudulent conduct got them no such virtues. The knowledge of what they had done made Joshua fit to be tied. He summoned the leadership and imposed a life of servitude on the Gibeonites for their lies. One can only imagine the strained relationship that existed. They went about a right thing the wrong way. Who knows what would have happened had they just been forthright. Their act of treachery caused Joshua to say,

> Now therefore ye are cursed, and there shall none of you be freed from being bondmen, and hewers of wood and drawers of water for the house of my God.[480]

> Because of this, you will serve our people as you wanted to, but you will not have the same privileges that other foreigners do who have joined us. You and your descendants will cut wood and carry water for the house of our God.[481]

Machiavellianism sooner or later pays its full, dreadful price. The Gibeonites became servants. Dishonesty, like ropes of sand, will bind nothing. And yet,

Do not so blame them as to forget that every fault is a mirror, looking into which each may see some likeness of his own imperfection. You and I are like the Gibeonites in this, that always some bit of evil creeps into and mixes with the good. Such mixtures, in God's mercy, may not be fatal to our welfare, but they will always mitigate it. In this case a less abject and menial form of servitude would have been the result of their submission if they had possessed the courage of their wisdom. Do your good things in a good way.[482]

In all of His dealings with men we can observe a God of love and compassion. God did not destroy the guileful Gibeonites for lying to Joshua. He did not upbraid Joshua for not seeking His counsel. Despite their trickery, known to God, He spared them. God is always conscious of man's need for salvation. In that nation, who would become servants, He undoubtedly saw souls who would accept His salvation. He probably made an evaluation, that anyone who would risk life and limb for self-preservation would not be hesitant to sacrifice all, and then some, to gain eternal life. They were now a part of the economy of Israel. They had responsibilities to perform. Their duties were menial but essential. By the oath they could say like Ruth, "Thy God is our God and your friends are our friends, your enemies are our enemies, your land is our land, your glorious destiny is our glorious destiny." Permit me, I pray you, an opportunity to restate the above mentioned.

The outsmarted, outwitted princes of Israel made an oath. They vowed a vow. It was binding. It had to be honored. It could not be ignored. If a vow was made, it had to be respected with all its obligations and contractual agreements. The inviolability could not be dishonored. While their lives would be spared, a life of servitude would be theirs. It was like a curse resting upon them. Like slaves, with dishonor they would live out their days. As a child, my mother would often quote a few lines to me if she ever felt that I was about to suppress the truth in any manner. It went like this, and I'm quoting her as best I can recall, "Speak the truth and speak it ever, cost it what it will. He who hides the wrong he did does the wrong thing still." It would have been so much simpler for the Gibeonites to have spoken the truth. God could have saved them without deceit, without their lying tongues. But our God is a merciful God. He could have given them a chance although the probation of the

Canaanites was passed. As with Adam and Eve, Ananias and Sapphira, Jacob and Esau, and the Gibeonites' lying lips were an abomination to God. Paul said, "Wherefore putting away lying, speak every man truth with his neighbor: for we are members one of another."[483]

Herein is a marvelous insight. The fact that the oath had to be honored demonstrates that because someone wrongs us, outwits us, or did us in, we are not at liberty to do likewise to them, but "overcome evil with good."[484] The best that Israel could do was to make the Gibeonites hewers of wood and drawers of water for the altar of God and the congregation.[485]

When Satan deceived Eve and Adam, they learned a lesson they never forgot. It was simple: seek God's counsel first. That became a number one priority, I am sure. Ananias and Sapphira's death because of deception shook the early church into truthfulness and honesty. Annanias and Sapphira obtained nothing. They died on the spot. Jacob's lie to his father Isaac[486] was instructive. As he went to his uncle Laban he learned how to wrestle all night with God in prayer at Bethel. Years later when it became necessary to have his soul blessed and forgiven he wrestled all night with God. Sad as it appears, God can turn all our failures, our wrongs, our sins against Him into lessons of watchfulness, total dependence upon Him, lessons of complete trust and humility and spiritual victories.

Solomon in his great prayer at the dedication of the temple said to God, "If they sin against thee... Then hear... And forgive (for there is no man that sinneth not)"[487], a sad but universal truth. Solomon announced a truth and made a request of God which He had and has fulfilled. If only human history had another statement it could make, but the fact is in Scripture that "*All* have sinned."[488] There is hope. The psalmist concurred: "The Lord looked down from heaven upon the children of men, to see if there were *any* that did understand, and seek God. They were *all* gone aside, they were *all* become filthy: there is *none* that doeth good, *no, not one*."[489] This is so far from a congratulatory statement as it relates to human behavior, yet God takes our shortcomings and brings blessings out of them and thus glorifies His name and exalts the person and ministries of our loving Savior Jesus Christ. In spite of our "guileful Gibeonite alliance" league, our tricks of the trade, our sharp dealings, our departures from strict allegiance and integrity to our God and sovereign King, the gifts of repentance, confession, and forgiveness granted by a loving God will turn the curse into a blessing. The ignorant transaction will be turned into a fountain of wisdom, redeeming blood, pardoning grace, everlasting love, healing virtues; complete restoration and redemption will bring glory to God's holy name. Then the kingdom's cause will move onward, for God is never outside of every event in life.

Here is a real example of the operation of God's grace. Here is tangible proof that God accepts us immediately upon His knowledge of our contrition. This is how it happened then, with the Gibeonites, and how it happens today. Permit me to quote from my favorite Christian author.

> It was possible for Adam, before the fall, to form a righteous character by obedience to God's law. But he failed to do this, and because of his sin our natures are fallen and we cannot make ourselves righteous. Since we are sinful, unholy, we cannot perfectly obey the holy law. We have no righteousness of our own with which to meet the claims of the law of God. But Christ has made a way of escape for us. He lived on earth amid trials and temptations such as we have to meet. He lived a sinless life. He died for us, and now He offers to take our sins and give us His righteousness. If you give yourself to Him, and accept Him as your Saviour, *then, sinful as your life may have been, for His sake you are accounted righteous. Christ's character stands in place of your character, and you are accepted before God just as if you had not sinned.*[490]

No sooner had the Gibeonites settled their situation with Israel, when the other five Canaanite kings decided to attack their former colleagues and a sister nation. Obviously, this would not really pose a military problem. They, Adonizedec, king of Jerusalem; Hoham king of Hebron; Piram king of Jarmuth; Japhia king of Lachish; and Debir king of Eglon, knew all there was to know about the Gibeonites' military might, their census, topography, defenses, and war capabilities. Adonizedec sent a message to the other kings.

> Come up unto me, and help me, that we may smite Gibeon: for it hath made peace with Joshua and with the children of Israel.[491]

The Gibeonites had really made peace with God, not Joshua and Israel. What was true of the Gibeonites is also true of God's people everywhere. When one turns to God in response to His great love, it seems as if every stream runs out of course; every river overflows its banks; every day the sun refuses to shine; every highway becomes a cul-de-sac. It seems as if every door is closed; every friend becomes a foe; every calamity strikes; every misfortune comes; persecution, ridicule, hatred, and every cross is made and placed on the shoulder. You will recall that as long as the apostle Paul persecuted the early Christians things went well. The moment he accepted Christ, became an apostle to the Gentiles, the picture changed dramatically. Jesus said trials and persecutions and swords would be the lot of the Christian.[492] We are often prone to think a bed of ease follows an acceptance of Christ. Ah, my friend, not so, "Yea and all that will live godly in Christ Jesus *shall* suffer persecution."[493] One of the marvelous things about our Father in heaven is that when trouble comes, when He allows the furnace fires to be kindled, He never leaves His children to fight a lonely battle. He will come to the Gibeonites' plight.

Immediately, word came from the men of Gibeon that they were going to be attacked by neighboring kings due to their relationship with Israel.

> And the men of Gibeon sent unto Joshua to the camp to Gilgal, saying, Slack not thy hand from thy servants; come up to us quickly, and save us, and help us: for all the kings of the Amorites that dwell in the mountains are gathered together against us.[494]

What trust! What confidence they had in Joshua's leadership. What faith they had to believe that the covenant relationship implied and involved defense. When one accepts Christ, is covered by His blood, pledges allegiance, makes a league, becomes a soldier in the Lord's army, Jesus takes full responsibility. If one has accepted Jesus only moments ago and has a need seconds later, just call upon Him immediately in faith, call with confidence and assurance, call knowing that, "him that cometh to Me, I will in no wise cast out."[495] Then believe that every sincere prayer is heard in heaven.

Columbus discovered America because he believed there was more land beyond Spain. The Pilgrim fathers colonized it because they believed that God would bless their efforts after landing on those rocky shores. We accept our payroll checks because we believe the employer has money in the bank. We eat because we believe we will be satisfied and that there is nutrition to supply growth and development. Faith saves us, for it makes us cling to God. That vital connection is what influences our love for God and draws us into that personal relationship. Faith is the key that opens doors immediately. If we seek pardon, God pardons. If for forgiveness, He forgives. If for assistance, He hears the call for help and responds quickly. Therefore, when assailed by the enemy, be assured of this: angels will be dispatched to fight the battle and win. Be assured that God would rather send every angel in heaven than see one of His children overcome in this cosmic conflict.

The trust that the Gibeonites had in Joshua is what we need in our God. God commands us to have faith in His Son Jesus Christ. It is not a recommendation and therefore we can do so with confidence, and in so doing find salvation so full and so free. It was according to the faith of the Gibeonites, and it is according to our faith that the heart comes in contact with God and salvation. We must complete this great conflict. But my heart refuses to give me leave of this tremendous act of faith on the part of the Gibeonites in contrast to our hesitancy sometimes in taking God at His word. Look. Overnight the Gibeonites had sufficient faith to believe that although they had sinned they were forgiven. Although a servant's place is all they possessed, they would call for help believing that it would come and that it would be adequate for the task at hand. Their faith matured overnight and they asked for no sign or demonstrations to indicate that their request would be immediately granted. They asked, believed, and awaited Joshua's help. If we could, like them, abandon the shores of sight and feelings (the just lives by his faith), and say goodbye to inward feelings, signs, and wonders, and just believe that God will honor His Word for believing in His Son, life would be beautiful and joyous too. We must come to that superior realm. A blind man trusts his seeing-eye dog because he knows his friend can see. Trustingly he goes wherever his guide takes him. In like manner we trust our lives and all we have to Jesus to be to us what we cannot be to ourselves. We trust Him in all things because He tells us what we ought to know. We trust Him because He is our Savior. We trust Him because all His promises are true. The Gibeonites left us a legacy.

Israel and the Gibeonites by virtue of the covenant agreement became allies. God treated them as if they were Israelites. Joshua, great leader that he was, had by now learned his lesson not to run ahead of God, so, he inquired of the Lord. Then God uttered His favorite words, "Fear not."[496] He assured Joshua that those kings were already conquered foes. *The battle is the Lord's*, you see. Joshua was a man of his word. His word would be his bond. He would, with promptitude born out of God's assurance of victory move quickly as demanded by his people in Gibeon. Joshua immediately summoned his men of war, his mighty men of valor, and that night the marshaled host was on their way.

> The distance from Gilgal to Gibeon was about twenty-four miles… "Beth-horon was made up of twin towns comprising the upper and lower cities.… These towns controlled the mountain pass. Joshua and his men pursued the Amorites in a northwest direction to this point. The path descending from Beth-horon Upper to Beth-horon Lower was very rocky and rugged, so steep that steps have been cut in the rock to facilitate the descent. It was here that the Lord sent hailstones upon them. From this point the enemy turned in a southerly direction, toward Jarmuth and Lachish, the home cities of two of the kings.[497]

The war against these five kings outdistances the previous conflicts. The grandeur of this victory in gaining access to the Canaanite territory is impressive and lauds and magnifies the name of God. The steps were as follows:

1. The Gibeonites were grafted in although that conquest was through a pact made in which God was not consulted and it involved guile.
2. The men of Gibeon requested the help of Joshua and Israel.
3. Joshua and his marshaled men of war responded swiftly.
4. There was a surprise attack upon the five Amorite kings. Miracle of miracles, God opened His arsenal of hailstones and killed more men with them than did Joshua's men with swords.
5. God's artillery took precedence. Then wonder of wonders, the sun stood still on Gibeon and the moon in the Valley of Ajalon at Joshua's command.

When the entire account of this battle with all its twists and turns is read in the book of Joshua, we are awed by the suddenness of Joshua's attack upon the five kings at the Gibeonites' request. The battle would be fought over land that was a portion of the Promised Land. It happened just a little earlier because of the Gibeonites. The completeness of the battle reflected God's original intention. Destroy everything. God reminded Joshua that He had already delivered those nations into his hands. The record indicates that God, yes God, slew the inhabitants before Joshua and his army. As Israel chased the enemy, they seemed to be escaping, so God opened the heavens and used His personal ammunition. His hailstones destroyed the fleeing armies. He opened the arsenal and fought on behalf of His children, the Israelites and the Gibeonites. Of course, they were not innocent bystanders because they used their swords to destroy the enemy. God killed more with the hailstones than they did in combat.[498]

It must have been an amazing experience, of sound and sight, as Joshua called upon God to hold the sun and the moon still until he could complete the assignment.[499] He needed some more daylight hours. We can affirm that the heavens and the earth are in God's control.

Since Joshua asked for the sun and the moon to stand still and God responded positively to complete the battle, questions have arisen as to how the sun can stand still when the earth rotates on its axis around the sun. Before spending an enormous amount of time doing mental gymnastics, let us never forget that we serve a God of might and miracles and majesty. He can accomplish wonders for His children as He promised. All the discussions on what might have happened and the impossibilities or possibilities will never satisfactorily answer or quell man's curiosity. The activities of that day transcended science, reason, and argument. The activity on the part of God resides in the realm of faith and faith alone. It is about the sovereignty of God. "Canst thou by searching find out God?"[500] Certainly not.

> Men of the greatest intellect cannot understand the mysteries of Jehovah as revealed in nature. Divine inspiration asks many questions which the most profound scholar cannot answer. These questions were not asked, supposing that we could answer them, but to call our attention to the deep mysteries of God, and to make men know

that their wisdom is limited; that in the common things of daily life there are mysteries past the comprehension of finite minds; that the judgments of God are past finding out, His wisdom unsearchable… Could men fully understand the ways and works of God, they would not then believe Him to be the infinite One. He is not to be comprehended by man in His wisdom, and reasons, and purposes. "His ways are past finding out" [Rom. 11:33].[501]

This I know: that any God who can open a path in the Red Sea,[502] divide the Jordan River for Israel to cross,[503] has my vote for anything He does without a single question. The sun and the moon standing still was simply a display of His overruling power, His providential control. God is known by His deeds. Who else could have accomplished such a feat? The Bible states clearly that, "there was no day like that before it or after it." It was the only one of its kind. Joshua prayed and God's great lights responded to the word of a man.

> And there was no day like that before it or after it, that the LORD hearkened unto the voice of a man: *for the LORD fought for Israel.*[504]

We can understand the hailstones, for God used hail before in Egypt.[505] God has treasures of hail.[506] But for the sun and moon to stand still for Joshua to complete the victory was incredible. At the command of Joshua the sun stood still in its meridian brightness, and the moon with its soft light about an entire day until the people had destroyed their enemies. Joshua 10:12,13. Joshua did not make a request of God to rain down the hailstones which destroyed the enemy and protected his army from calamity while in battle. God answered Joshua's prayer for the sun and moon to stand still. He went over and beyond his requests. He actually engaged in battle, which was more than Joshua expected. God fought for Israel. What a mighty God we serve! We can certainly identify with this operation. With a like faith in God, as a church or as an individual, we have at our disposal unlimited resources and untapped power. When faced with like situations, we can confidently turn to God who has promised to supply our every need. In the process His name will be glorified. Joshua faced formidable obstacles, but he embarked upon the mission with God saying he ought not to fear, and he was ever so conscious of a reservoir of limitless grace to help in every time of need.

Hailstones, a sun and a moon standing still, and the swords of the mighty men of Israel, all cooperated and the battle was won. God promised to deliver Israel's enemies into their hands. He kept His word. One task remained—Joshua had to deal with the five kings who had hidden themselves in a cave at Makkedah.[507] The five kings thought they had escaped with their lives. They imagined it was only a matter of time before they could rebuild their hopes, cities, and dreams. No such thing. The entrance of the cave was barred with stones at Joshua's command.

> And it was told Joshua, saying, The five kings are found hid in a cave at Makkedah. And Joshua said, Roll great stones upon the mouth of the cave, and set men by it for to keep them: And stay ye not, but pursue after your enemies, and smite the hindmost of them; suffer them not to enter into their cities: for the LORD your God hath delivered them into your hand.[508]

At the conclusion of the battle after the fortified cities were taken and the enemies destroyed, Joshua and his men returned to the cave at Makkedah. There remained one piece of unfinished business. Joshua even had a morale builder injected in the warfare. The captains took the five kings out of the cave, placed their feet on their necks; Joshua killed them, and they hung them on five trees until evening. The captains in the presence of all the men of Israel had an opportunity to stand on the necks of their archrivals. Finally, they were buried in the cave where they imagined themselves to have been safe. The victory was complete after those five kings were buried. Only then did Joshua consider the battle won.

As God's children, we must put to death those hidden-in-the-cave sins, the sins of our lives, those thoughts alien to the kingdom of God. We must ask God to reveal whatever hides from view. When told or shown what they are and where they are located and hiding, promptitude in execution must follow. They must be killed by the blood of Christ which gives overcoming power before there can be a proclamation of victory, freedom, deliverance, and salvation. If not, if left to hide in the nooks and crevices of the heart, they will come back to haunt us, demonstrating that victory was not achieved. God will destroy whatever lurks in the soul. Whatever will be a hindrance to an abundant entrance into His eternal kingdom must be trampled underfoot and killed. The assurance is that God will fight for us. His words to Joshua are ours to claim. He said, "Fear not."

In the not-too-distant future God will grant an identical privilege to His saved church. Satan and all his followers, and the enemies of righteousness will be ashes beneath our feet. Neither root nor branch will remain. The church of the living God, like Gibeon, is surrounded by enemy forces. Five kings representing myriad evil are positioned to destroy the soul. Danger lurks everywhere. We live in an evil world. Men's hearts are wicked and vile, and troubles and temptations abound. The object is to crush the church, God's people. Satan and his host would like to destroy and conquer. We "wrestle not against flesh and blood, but against principalities and powers."[509] But hallelujah to the Lamb of God, He who is our Savior will come quickly to our rescue, to save, to help, to destroy. "But of him are ye in Christ Jesus, who of God is made unto us wisdom, and righteousness, and sanctification, and redemption:"[510] God "will avenge his own elect."[511] God "is able also to save them to the uttermost."[512] When we confess our needs and request divine help, not that the sun and the moon stand still, but that God will help, the victory will be complete. The power lies in God's unmerited favor and not in our faith. It is about God. Our faith is only the conduit; God's grace will flow through it. There is only one reason why Jesus came to this sin-cursed world: to save, deliver, free, ransom, and redeem. He came to seek and save that which was lost.[513]

Joshua shared with his men the victory God had given them, so that that spirit of corporate accomplishment would be registered. Each one could find a sense of contributing to the successful engagement of which God was the architect. "And Joshua returned and *all* Israel with him, unto the camp to Gilgal."[514]

Like Moses before the burning bush, barefooted and in absolute amazement, we stand before the closing scene of this confrontation with the foes of God. We can only ask who is a God like our God. Consider this. Take time to evaluate. No Israelite was slain. There were no prisoners of war. No one was injured. None was taken captive, none was missing; every soldier was present and accounted for. Label it a complete and glorious victory. Then Joshua and Israel returned to Gilgal. One can only imagine the celebration that ensued, and rightly so. To be an eyewitness must have been a great spiritual privilege when the sun and the moon stood still. Words of praise and thanksgiving must have rent the heavens as they rehearsed God's supernatural dealings. Their faith reached a new high. Trust in God deepened. The path and plan of God became more attractive and accomplishable. In like manner, as we trust in our Savior Jesus Christ, the road we are traveling to heaven, our ultimate destination, will be rough. Be encouraged. Let us place our feet in the footprints of those nail-pierced feet. The victories He has gained; the battles He has won were for us. One day soon, Canaan, the mansions above will be ours too.

Throughout this military campaign, over and over, there was a word of assurance, comfort, courage, promise, and a pledge from God that He would fight for Israel. There is no delight in the heart of God when His children die. But God gives opportunities to repent and to turn to Him as creator. When those chances are spurned (and the lifestyles of the Canaanites would affect the relationship of Israel to their God), God was left with no other alternative but to destroy His foes.

God in our day has not opened His treasury of hailstones. But there is coming a day when He will. Those who reject His call and refuse to accept Jesus will be exposed to the wrath of God. But to everyone engaged in the battle for life eternal He gives assurance of complete victory, whether you have found victory or are on the way to complete victory, whether you are suffering or have suffered. If you have been buffeted or bruised, had wars within and wars without, been tempted and tried, are in quest of deliverance—whatever your situation, hear the Word of God. "I can do all things through Christ which strengtheneth me."[515] "No weapon that is formed against thee shall prosper."[516] "But thanks be to God, which giveth us the victory through our Lord Jesus Christ."[517]

God could easily have destroyed everyone in that battle. In fact, Joshua and the Israelite army need not have gone. However, He afforded the human instruments an opportunity to participate. Can you see God's hands in this? He indicated to Joshua and to us that divine power in cooperation with human help can work miracles. He demanded a show of their faith, and Israel trusted in God. They believed that victory would come and it did. They engaged in battle out of obedience to God's command. In our situation Jesus has already won our salvation by His death on Calvary. We believe; we do His will; we cooperate with heaven, not to be saved, but because we are saved, and oh the joy of knowing we are His. And soon we will be restored to our Eden home. None will be missing who by faith has accepted Jesus as captain of the Lord's host.

The message of the Gibeonites was, "Slack not thy hand from thy servants; come up to us quickly, and save us, and help us." In this our day of trouble—and its threatening danger can be seen everywhere—it would do us well to offer a like petition to our Savior: "O God, we are your blood-bought children. Come quickly, Lord Jesus, all conquering Christ, save us. Almighty King, help us." He will hear and answer.

Chapter 9

DITCH DIGGERS

(Based on 2 Kings 3)

The fact is that the wine of liberty goes sour unless pains are taken to preserve it. The sweet love of life, invaded by the bacteria of selfishness, can make a potential champion of humanity into a despotic villain, guilty of the destruction of men's rights and happiness and their very lives. We need to discover the microorganism that is responsible for the disease... The place to begin this investigation is not over in China nor in Europe, it is not in the national legislature nor in our next-door neighbor. It is in our own premises and in our own soul.[518]

From times immemorial Israel and Judah had a common enemy— Moab, an inveterate foe of both nations. When the children of Israel were traveling to the Promised Land they came to the southern border of Moab and requested passage through that country. The Moabites promptly refused. That was only a courtesy request. God instructed Moses:

And command thou the people, saying, Ye are to pass through the coast of your brethren the children of Esau, which dwell in Seir; and they shall be afraid of you: take ye good heed unto yourselves therefore:... Meddle not with them; for I will not give you of their land, no, not so much as a foot breadth; because I have given mount Seir unto Esau for a possession...And the LORD said unto me, Distress not the Moabites, neither contend with them in battle: for I will not give thee of their land for a possession; because I have given Ar unto the children of Lot for a possession... Thou art not to pass through Ar, the coast of Moab, this day:.. And when thou comest nigh over against the children of Ammon, distress them not, nor meddle with them: for I will not give thee of the land of the children of Ammon any possession; because I have given it unto the children of Lot for a possession.[519]

The relations between the children of Israel and the Moabites ruptured due to the Balak-Baalam connection. God told Baalam that since he insisted on going to conduct witchery, he could go down to Balak, but that He, God, would speak through him. The Balak-Baalam's plans regarding the curses with criminal intent disintegrated. He issued blessings instead of curses. Subsequently, the arrangement of Israel's seduction into licentiousness and idolatry worked.[520] As a result, God banned the Moabites from the congregation of Israel to the tenth generation. They were cautioned to have no spiritual or social relations with them.

An Ammonite or Moabite shall not enter into the congregation of the LORD even to their tenth generation shall they not enter into the congregation of the LORD for ever: Because they met you not with bread and with water in the way, when ye came from out of Egypt; and because they hired against thee Balaam the son of Beor of Pethor of Mesopotamia, to curse thee. Nevertheless the LORD thy God turned the curse into a blessing unto thee, because the LORD thy God loved thee. Thou shalt not seek their peace nor their prosperity all the days forever.[521]

After decades of slavery in Babylon, the children of God returned and rebuilt the temple that Nebuzaradan, Nebuchadnezzar's personal aide and bodyguard had razed. At the dedication, those very prohibitions were rehearsed in the hearing of the congregation. Those words must have been significant to God and His people. The sting in God's curse that will last for ten generations, a long, long time, was its irreversibleness. They had forgotten a lot of other laws and statutes but recalled with unerring accuracy this particular injunction.

On that day they read in the book of Moses in the audience of the people; and therein was found written, that the Ammonite and the

Moabite should not come into the congregation of God forever; Because they met not the children of Israel with bread and with water, but hired Balaam against them that he should curse them; howbeit our God turned the curse into a blessing.[522]

After Ahab's death, the king of Moab, Mesha, refused to pay his tax to Israel of one hundred thousand lambs and one hundred thousand rams with wool.[523] As a result, Israel, Judah, and Edom became allies.[524] All three had a common enemy—Moab. History documents that as soon as Moab was defeated, the threat discarded, Edom, Israel, and Judah went their separate ways. They thought only of themselves, not the unity of the Hebrew nation. It was not for the welfare and destiny of God's people as a whole that they yoked up, but rather their own interest.

A. W. Spalding was right that "the sweet love of life is invaded by the bacteria of selfishness."[525] A review of Israel, Judah, and Edom's unity to fight the Moabites, reveals clearly that national conceit, who is the greatest, and the terminal sickness of selfishness was the structure on which they pinned their hopes and decisions. They refused to put the welfare of their nations above the egos of Jehoram, king of Israel, Jehoshaphat, the king of Judah and the king of Edom.

God rules in the affairs of men and nations at all times, in all places, and under all circumstances—despite man's attempts of the exclusion of His sovereignty. However, God always reached over and beyond man's selfishness. A classic example of that aspect of God's dealings is tucked away in His dealings with these three kings. This part of Holy Writ presents a display of nature and nature's God, which almost defies description. It appears so simple, yet is so profound in its conclusions. In this battle several significant acts on God's part declare that God moves in mysterious ways His incalculable wonders to perform. In this engagement the heavens would declare the glory of God.[526] God's people were able to defeat the Moabites as a result of some ditches dug, color of soil, mirages, rays of sunlight, water, and reflections. Far beyond human thoughts were God's plans. We stand amazed at God's ways of achieving His ends, ends of which we are totally unaware, have not the slightest idea of the arrangements, and are baffled by His incorporation of man in the successful resolution.

There are three principal characters. Jehoram sometimes referred to as Joram, Jehosaphat, and the king of Edom. A background check on these kings, before considering the battle, might be worthwhile. It will grant a broader vision of the great God of the universe, an insight into the three kings' attitudes to life, and most importantly, their relationship with God.

JEHORAM/JORAM

Jehoram was the offspring of Ahab and Jezebel, two persons contaminated by all the idolatrous corruptions of Baal worship. They were steeped in covetousness and selfish designs. Just inquire from Naboth.[527] The evil influences of Ahab and Jezebel had stained his soul. Jehoram attempted to walk away from idolatry. He seemed to have washed his soul like Pilate who washed his hands to free himself from the guilt of his participation in the condemnation of Christ. He was an interesting character. His footprints we do well to avoid. This terse overview is rather fascinating:

> And he wrought evil in the sight of the LORD; but not like his father, and like his mother: for he put away the image of Baal that his father had made. Nevertheless he cleaved unto the sins of Jeroboam the son of Nebat, which made Israel to sin; he departed not therefrom.[528]

The Word of God sketches Jehoram's lifestyle in a few graphic lines. His Word does not fail to grant a complete and accurate portrait of His children's character. The sad comparison of Ahab and Jeroboam leaves no room for consideration. It is simply admitting that he did not do wrong in worshipping Baal, nor did he do right in worshipping God one hundred percent for he consorted with the worst—Jeroboam. He was not as bad as Ahab for Baal was set aside, but he mimicked Jeroboam. He did not have a clean conscience. The service and worship of the one and only true God did not find expression in anything he said or did. There was no clean break with sin in his life. What good would it serve if Jesus took Lazarus out of his grave but left him dead? Why lead a blind man into the light if he is still blind? It is the will of God that we give God first place, and indicate that fact by conduct. Close is not good enough.

We "cannot serve God and mammon."[529] An individual who will stand up for God cannot have a character that is half right and half wrong; half for God and half for Satan; half true and half false; half committed and half uncommitted; half faithful and half unfaithful; half repentant and half unrepentant. In fact, God said to the church of Laodicea, you are neither hot nor cold.[530] His preference: that they be one or the other. The half for and half against is nauseating to Him. In human relations no fence straddling is ever appreciated. It is best to be a friend or a foe. Nothing is as deadly as hypocrisy. No one can successfully be both with and against at the same time. We cannot compromise with sin, however minor, and hope to receive the favor of God. The externals cannot be shunned while the internals are out of concord with God. If ever one should possess a conscience void of offense before God and man, divine support must be solicited. With His help we can demonstrate that our walk and talk, life and lip, are equal before Him. We are the same in the light as in the dark. What you see is what you get. In that He takes delight. We can almost hear His compassionate voice pleading: All or none at all is My standard.

Jehoram could be described as vacillating. He suffered from infirmity of purpose, inconsistency, changefulness, being half-and-half, double-minded, and half-hearted. God demands all, whatever it is, and you can name it: love, life, family, self, tithe, time, and talent. Idolatry in any form must be removed from the heart and the home. You can never be successful in the conflict against sin or render worship that is suitable to God unless the entire being is consecrated. Offering less than all and less than the best is an insult and unacceptable. If all is not offered from the onset, whatever is given is doomed to failure. It is the responsibility of each Christian to search his/her heart and home, to see what is there. Is it a desire for first place, bad habits, evil thoughts or practices, that which in the least militates against the worship of God or heightens the experience? Uppermost should be a life reflecting the fruits of the Spirit, one that is all about God and His glory.

Jehoram was much like the man who leased his house, and assured the lessee that he had total access to the entire property, with the exception of the one room where he maintained a pet tiger. On the surface Jehoram seemed acceptable. His appearance reflected godliness. He did "put away the image of Baal," but the spirit of Jeroboam's idolatrous lifestyle, so offensive to a holy God, which severed the ten tribes, steeped them in sin, and erased the worship of God was still evident in his life and ingrained in his worship.

Jehoram should not have just "put away the images and groves and altars of Baal" but destroyed them. The Israelites sent back to worship in Jerusalem would have preferred union instead of war. The demolished sanctuaries in Dan and Bethel, and the calf worship of Jeroboam, would have signaled the right message. It could have been concluded that he meant business. Little did Jehoram realize that the shape or place of the altar where they worshipped would not bring an end to idolatrous results. Frequenting the house of God with serious regularity does not make an unrepentant sinner a saint. Changing the language or the way in which wickedness is done or perceived, however beautifully expressed or performed, does not in anywise lessen sin's deadly results. It is always the same—eternal death. There is only one remedy prescribed by the Great Physician, "Ye must be born again."[531] Jehoram and all of God's children must learn that the greatest need is a new heart, regenerated, revived, and renewed.

Amendments to life and character are not achieved by demographics. A transfer from one community to another will in no wise effectively change the heart. Shutting down one idolatrous way of living, but clinging to another did not help Jehoram's situation. Lessons out of Jehoram's life call for a frank admission that God's diagnoses of the human heart are accurate.

> Can the Ethiopian change his skin, or the leopard his spots? Then may ye also do good, that are accustomed to do evil... The heart is deceitful above all things, and desperately wicked: who can know it?[532]

Only by His grace, His love, His forbearance, His call to repentance, His mercy can lives reflect the image that God is looking for. He awaits the reproduction of Christ in the soul. Jehoram was caught in the grasp of some evil hereditary traits of character. Unwillingness to surrender would place him beyond God's reach. But if his heart remained open to the influence of God's Spirit, Christ would help.

> It is the virtue that goes from Christ, that leads to genuine repentance. Christ is the source of every right impulse. *He is the only one that can implant in the heart enmity against sin... There is help for us only in God.*[533]

God could have taken Jehoram and made him totally committed to Him. However, a demonstration of willingness must be registered. The will must be surrendered. God only knocks at the heart's door. The lock on the inside must be opened for the help needed.

JEHOSHAPHAT

Jehoshaphat was a good king. He walked in the ways of God. His father, Asa, a good and successful king, reigned in Judah for forty-one years. Jehoshaphat ascended the throne as king at age thirty-five and ruled for twenty-five years. With the exception of the invasion by the Ammonites, Moabites, and the Menuites, his kingdom days could be described as quiet and peaceful. There were no internecine feuds or civil wars. He refused to worship foreign gods. Many of his subjects worshiped on the high places which were not torn down. He delegated as a spiritual duty that God's law should be taught.[534]

> Also in the third year of his reign he sent to his princes, even to Benhail, and to Obadiah, and to Zechariah, and to Nethaneel, and to Michaiah, to teach in the cities of Judah. And with them he sent Levites, even Shemaiah, and Nethaniah, and Zebadiah, and Asahel, and Shemiramoth and Jehonathan, and Adonijah, and Tobijah, and Tobadonijah, Levites; and with them Elishama and Jehoram priests. And they taught in Judah, and had the book of the law of the LORD with them, and went about throughout all the cities of Judah, and taught the people.[535]

The judges he selected were commanded to rule fairly in the courts of justice. He had the respect of surrounding nations and he even made peace with Israel.[536] God blessed his reign.

And the fear of God was on all the kingdoms of those countries, when they had heard that the LORD fought against the enemies of Israel. So the realm of Jehoshaphat was quiet: for his God gave him rest round about.[537]

His life and reign spoke to the fallibility of good men or great kings in the normal walk of life. He was blessed by God, but not perfect. Jehoshaphat's three serious blunders are documented. God in His wisdom shares the failures of others to be a deterrent and that others might avoid the pitfalls. I cannot recall where I read this comment, but it is so true. It says, "The best of men are men at best."

JEHOSHAPHAT'S THREE BLUNDERS

The first was the marriage of his son Jehoram.

When Jehoshaphat became wealthy and highly respected, he made a marriage alliance between his son Jehoram and Ahab's daughter Athaliah.[538]

The decision to unite with Ahab to fight Benhadad without first consulting God was the second.

So the king of Israel and Jehoshaphat the king of Judah went up to Ramoth-gilead. And the king of Israel said unto Jehoshaphat, I will disguise myself, and will go to the battle; but put thou on thy robes. So the king of Israel disguised himself; and they went to the battle.[539]

A joint venture in constructing a fleet of trading ships was number three.

And he joined himself with him to make ships to go to Tarshish: and they made the ships in Eziongeber. Then Eliezer the son of Dodavah of Mareshah prophesied against Jehoshaphat, saying, Because thou hast joined thyself with Ahaziah, the LORD hath broken thy works. And the ships were broken, that they were not able to go to Tarshish.[540]

It is unsafe, unscriptural, and unsound to judge human character. But in our evaluation of Jehoshaphat he would not measure up to our highest ideal. Should we paint a portrait of a person or describe the one we consider the ideal man, he would be flawless. He would qualify only for extraterrestrial living. From the first day of that ideal person's life to the last, providing he would die, nothing like a dark cloud would come aslant of that life. Yet, if we were honest to the core, we would be compelled to state that at our best moment, what we consider ideal is not in us. Better still, it is not in anyone we know or will know. Our judgment should go no further for we are advised not to judge. Outside of the Lord Jesus Christ, and He is not a part of this discussion, in the entire biblical record we have never found a single person who even appears to fit in the frame of what we consider ideal. For example, we cannot remake Abraham "a friend of God" without his errors; no, not even Moses "the meekest man" without the murder he committed in haste and anger; nor Joshua without his glaring failures to seek God first, and a costly failure resulting in the death of thousands; and for sure we can do nothing to readjust Jehoshaphat and his serious spiritual concerns. An internal look gives us not a chance at being qualified, although some would like to think so.

They, like us, must be received with all their mistakes, shortcomings, errors, failures, and ravished characters. As good as God made us, our humanity leaves gaping holes of undesirable traits. And then, as much as we achieve in this life, without a single exception, everyone bears in his/her body to the dying day, imperfections. Salvation, God's gift, changes the picture. Praise God for imparted and imputed righteousness which all who enter the city must receive. All of us would have been excluded from the kingdom of heaven, but for those graces of God which are new every morning and sufficient.

KING OF EDOM

Regarding the king of Edom, not much information is given. The Edomites were descendants of Esau, Jacob's brother. They were the ones who refused Israel passage through their country when Moses was traveling north to Canaan. Israel was forced to go around Edom. For the battle with Moab, they were strategically located. They occupied the country south of the Dead Sea.

The battle at hand was so strange. Three nations were going all that distance to fight Moab for unpaid taxes. Yet these three kings had not fully yielded their lives to the requirements of a just God. As leaders they had not destroyed every semblance of evil in their sight or that of their citizens. The demand of a holy, righteous God, "Thou shalt have no other gods before me,"[541] was in a rejection phase, a non-compliant conduct mode, and yet they were going to whip the king of Moab and his nation into shape for tax evasion imposed by a mortal man.

> And Mesha king of Moab was a sheepmaster, and rendered unto the king of Israel an hundred thousand lambs, and an hundred thousand rams, with the wool. But it came to pass, when Ahab was dead, that the king of Moab rebelled against the king of Israel. And king Jehoram went out of Samaria the same time, and numbered all Israel. And he went and sent to Jehoshaphat the king of Judah, saying, The king of Moab hath rebelled against me: wilt thou go with me against Moab to battle? And he said, I will go up: I am as thou art, my people as thy people, and my horses as thy horses. And he said, Which way shall we go up? And he answered, the way through the wilderness of Edom. So the king of Israel went, and the king of Judah, and the king of Edom.[542]

A situation of unpaid taxes by the king of Moab created a real crisis for Jehoram. The kings of Judah and Edom agreed to join him in his battle against Moab. Geographically speaking, Israel would join Judah in Jerusalem, they would go south and connect with Edom by the base of the Dead Sea, then proceed north to Moab. Jehoram and his army joined Jehoshaphat and his men in Jerusalem. Later, they traveled south and were joined by the king of Edom. After seven days had passed, the water supply for the army and the cattle was depleted. This caused great concern, especially since they were located out in the wilderness of Edom. Then they cried unto the Lord. Life became a nightmare for them rather than a lovely dream.

> And they fetched a compass of seven days' journey: and there was no water for the host, and for the cattle that followed them. And the

king of Israel said, Alas! that the LORD hath called these three kings together, to deliver them into the hand of Moab![543]

To this point in the battle arrangements, no mention was made of God, yet Jehoram sought to blame God for their dilemma. He never consulted God regarding the conflict he proposed to Jehoshaphat, king of Judah, and the king of Edom. They assured him they would go with him and of the path they would take. Apparently no preparation for eventualities needful for an encounter of this magnitude crossed his mind. He had the backing of the kings of Judah and Edom, but lacked the support, presence, protection, and benediction of the King of kings. He forgot that, "Except the Lord build the house they labour in vain that build it: except the Lord keep the city, the watchman waketh but in vain."[544]

Jehoram acted as though God was absent from His universe. No word of prayer offered to God? How could Jehoram come to the conclusion that God had called three kings to deliver them into the hand of Moab? But isn't that a typical human outcry? Eve blamed God when she surrendered to Satan's lies in the Garden of Eden.

> The Lord visited Adam and Eve, and made known to them the consequence of their disobedience. As they hear God's majestic approach, they seek to hide themselves from his inspection... Adam acknowledged his transgression, not because he was penitent for his great disobedience, *but to cast reflection upon God.* "The woman whom thou gavest to be with me, she gave me of the tree, and I did eat."...Eve answered, "The serpent beguiled me, and I did eat."[545]

Jehoram blamed God when his woes emerged. He had only one thing in mind when he left for Moab: get the taxes owed Israel from Mesha. He had a strategy for the collection, but no plan, no suggestion, no way out of his self-imposed difficulty. Where will water come from for the troops and cattle? In his hopeless, helpless condition he flared up in God's face, and held Him accountable. This reaction reflects human conduct. When man-made proposals come to naught, when friends and family have no solutions, God is blamed for the sad consequences of man's acts. When man must eat the bitter fruits he has planted, in desperation, God is considered responsible.

Another look would be most helpful if Jehoram had the capacity or the resolve to accept responsibility. Jehoram went with two other kings to humble Mesha's pride, and to receive the taxes due. In his travels, God took all his well-laid plans and thwarted them, which should have gained his attention. God can quickly undo man's propositions to teach lessons of sole dependence on Him. Water can come only from God. He made the seas, springs, rivers, and fountains of water. God was showing Jehoram that, "without me ye can do nothing."[546]

Had he caught the vision, had he heard the message, he would have confessed before his visit to Elisha, that in his plight he sought the Lord and He saved him out of his distresses. Jehoram had received a wake up call. It asserted without the slightest controversy, that when troubles come, and they will come, if a diligent search is made, if humility is a characteristic feature of the soul, that God's saving and loving hands can be detected. God rules in the affairs of men and of nations, therefore Jehoram should have admitted, before the conflict commenced, that *the battle is the Lord's*. God will do the fighting or will intervene. Jehoram must not return from his encounter with the Moabites lauding his strategies, diplomacy, techniques, and military might. God placed a cog, a spoke in Jehoram's wheel, before he had an opportunity to destroy himself with pride. He made no admission of his sin in excluding God, or his failure to inquire of the Lord what was His will.

Jehoshaphat went to Jehoram's aid with men, horses and cattle; temporal things. Now that he needed spiritual help, he would be as diligent in granting that support. He reminded Jehoram that God should have been consulted before the mission began. Without hesitation the prophet, the one who speaks for God, must be contacted.

> But Jehoshaphat said, Is there not here a prophet of the LORD, that we may enquire of the LORD by him? And one of the king of Israel's servants answered and said, Here is Elisha the son of Shaphat, which poured water on the hands of Elijah. And Jehoshaphat said, The word of the LORD is with him. So the king of Israel and Jehoshaphat and the king of Edom went down to him.[547]

Jehoshaphat knew, or should have known, that they ought to have sought the Lord before they even entered into this league, before they began the mission, but it is better late than never. The fact that he recognized Elisha as a prophet and had confidence he could speak for God indicated his respect and conviction. One of Jehoram's servants, worshipper of the true and living God, knew where the man of God resided, his name, his parents, and his previous occupation.[548] Like the captive maid, the little girl in Naaman's house, this servant in Israel's army knew Elisha to be the authentic voice of God. It is a sobering thought to know God has His children everywhere, and at the right time, in the right place, under the right set of circumstances, He calls upon them to step forward so His name might be glorified.

God will get the attention of the confederate kings. They will see for themselves the majesty of the true and living God. God will perform an awesome miracle for their deliverance through nature, in answer to His servant's prayer and intercession on their behalf. Before consideration is given to the battle, some lessons prior to the miracle employed in settling the dispute call for immediate discussion because all cannot be analyzed now. However, something needs to be said for Elisha's conduct when called upon by these kings.

First of all, Elisha did not put on his prophetic garb and go to the three kings. Rather, they immediately, upon learning and hearing of his office and connection with the God of heaven, went to him at once.[549] This was a departure from the normal conduct of kings. Normal procedure was that the prophet was summoned into the king's palace. Or, as the case with Elijah who had a message from God for Ahab, he went directly to the king's residence.[550] Two facts rise into prominence instantaneously. They respected him and realized that their present problem demanded a show of humility. "And Jehoshaphat said, The word of the Lord is with him. So the king of Israel and Jehoshaphat and the king of Edom went down to him."[551] What a great scene that was! Three kings, on the horns of a real dilemma, led to Elisha's house. With all their pomp and pageantry there they were. That was significant! Why? The day is not distant, when every king and prince, president, prime minister, governor, and every high-ranking official, and all nations, and kindred and tongues and peoples will stand before the Lord God. Thanks be to God that great day is not far away. It will be a glorious day. We shall stand before the King of kings clothed with His righteousness. It will be a time of rejoicing and gladsome reunion.

Elisha was greatly displeased. The honor and respect due to the Lord God was not given. Without water, all the men and all the animals would soon die. Now that death stared them in the face they sought the Lord. Mesha, king of Moab, would have had a "field day" had they been inside his territory. The battle was Moab's "hands down." Their plight drove them to seek God. They sought the Lord because they found themselves in a bind. Elisha felt that God should not have been a last resort, but a first choice. We all will agree that is easier said than performed. Think of the millions of persons who only when "caught in a pinch," "in a bind," in difficult situations, in failure, in death, when life comes to a dead end, when the purse strings are no more available to be pulled, financial failure, professional calamity, divorce, cancer, some crisis, then and only then, they turn to God. It must be extolled that we have a great and marvelous God who deserves first place. It is regrettable that those three kings, men who governed God's people, did not have a faithful testimony for the populace. It saddened Elisha. His love and devotion for God caused a reaction that said God deserved more.

The conduct evident then, happened numerous times during our Savior's lifetime, and it happens now. Hadn't the Prodigal Son "begun to be in want," his father's house and a servant's job would not have seemed so appealing to him.[552] I feel confident that those kings must have chosen a route for man and beast where water would have been readily available. But God in His providence can allow situations to pop up for which we have no other refuge than Jesus, and no answer can be found but in Him. Had not the wells run dry, these three kings never would have turned to God for help. If pride, stubbornness, vacillation, half-heartedness, and selfishness cause Him to be left out of the picture, He finds a way through the predicaments, trials, and disappointments to come to the rescue. You see, "God sent not his Son into the world to condemn the world; but that the world through him might be saved."[553]

As soon as Jehoram arrived at Elisha's home the prophet addressed him.

And Elisha said unto the king of Israel, What have I to do with thee?
Get thee to the prophets of thy father, and to the prophets of thy
mother.[554]

Those were fighting words. In my childhood days, no one was safe
who talked about someone's mama. Elisha sounded almost like Elijah.
He disdained Jehoram's policy as much as Elijah had contempt for Ahab
and Jezebel, Jehoram's parents. He would not have respect of persons,
be cowed, or be afraid of his office. He would be respectful. He spoke
with holy boldness. He was fully aware of the idolatry still practiced in
Israel and Jehoram's tenacious grasp on the ways of Jeroboam's worship. Elisha would not permit him to hoodwink him into believing that
his pious attitude was due to contrition of heart. His hiding beneath
Jehoshaphat's cloak would not go unnoticed. He recalled Ahab's imprisonment of Micaiah, and Jezebel, his mother's unrelenting search
for Elijah his boss.

Thus saith the king, Put this fellow in the prison, and feed him
with bread of affliction and with water of affliction, until I come in
peace.[555]

Then Jezebel sent a messenger unto Elijah, saying, So let the gods do
to me, and more also, if I make not thy life as the life of one of them
by tomorrow about this time.[556]

Elisha recognized Jehoshaphat. He would seek God on his behalf,
although, as we discussed in the overview of Jehoshaphat, he had some
character flaws and could not be considered blameless. The Scriptures
indicate that in his heart he served God as he knew best. Elisha however,
issued total contempt toward Jehoram. Israel's suffering, their defection
from God and sustained idolatry, he laid squarely at Jehoram's doorstep.
The position he took would not be relinquished. He consulted God
because of Jehoshaphat.

And the king of Israel said unto him, Nay: for the LORD hath called
these three kings together, to deliver them into the hand of Moab.
And Elisha said, As the LORD of hosts liveth, before whom I stand,

surely, *were it not that I regarded the presence of Jehoshaphat the king of Judah, I would not look toward thee, nor see thee.*[557]

The three kings were standing before Elisha. Those were not insulting words, but he was aware that he also stood before the transcendent God. In His presence all fear vanishes. Elisha refused to be intimidated by Jehoram.

God was ready to do something supernatural. But first He always creates the right situations so His name might be glorified. Despite the fact that these men could not claim perfection, did not recognize Him as Lord, could have called upon Him for themselves, He was fully aware that the kings, the armies as well as the beasts, needed His direct intervention. Nothing would hinder the flow of His grace. The sun shines on the just and the unjust and His open hands satisfy the desires of every living thing. It is interesting also to note that the three kings were begging a favor from a man who had just left the plough. The servant in Israel's army said Elisha was Elijah's servant, and that he poured water on his hands. Yesterday a servant at the plough, today promoted by God as a prophet who speaks to God, and to whom God speaks to give direction to His people. The entire army belonged to God. They were His people. If water were plentiful and available, the three kings would have gone to battle with Moab. The God of heaven would have remained unrecognized as stated previously, and Elisha also. Elisha would not have received the slightest recognition. It would have been as if they did not exist. But God would with one simple stroke get their attention, and in His own way include His servant Elisha, give him visibility and recognition as His servant, mouthpiece, and prophet. That is one meaning to the phrase "using one stone to kill two birds;" really there were three.

Look at the three kings with all their military might, thoroughly equipped to subdue the Moabites. They had all the hardware, but were powerless, ineffective, and dying of thirst. Is this a portrait of the church in an age when Jesus is almost here? The church today is structured, organized, fully equipped with the latest technologies, increased riches, millions of members, great talents, influence, with all the evangelistic procedures and programs essential for finishing the work at hand. But could it be that like the three kings it is equipped but helpless? Could it be that the refreshing of the Holy Spirit, which must come from the Father's presence with power, is not present? The writer is soliloquizing.

The three kings wanted Elisha to inquire of the Lord on their behalf. He would because of Jehoshaphat, but before he did, he requested moments of quiet, holy calm. His ruffled spirit, due to righteous indignation, sought solitude. The sight of Jehoram and past reflections created disquietude. He just had to be soothed. Communication with God will be in a spiritual setting.

He made a strange petition. "But now bring me a minstrel."[558] Just what the music was we have not been told, but the words of the hymn by Horatus Bonar (1859) would have been appropriate.

Calm me my God and keep me calm,
Soft resting on Thy breast;
Soothe me with holy hymn and psalm
And bid my spirit rest.

God's voice would be heard in the stillness. The strains of music were effective in edifying him. The psalms and hymns and spiritual songs have their full impact upon the soul. "Music has charm to soothe a savage breast, soften rocks, or bend a knotted oak."[559] Music gives wings to the soul for its flight into God's presence. What did the minstrel play in Elijah's hearing? Could it be?

The Lord is my light and my salvation; whom shall I fear?
The Lord is the strength of my life; of whom shall I be afraid?...
Teach me thy way, O Lord, and lead me in a plain path,
Because of mine enemies.[560]

Or was it?

Bless the Lord, O my soul: and all that is within me, bless his holy name.
Bless the Lord, O my soul, and forget not all his benefits.[561]

We can only speculate. I am confident that only that which was appropriate and right for the occasion filled his heart, his house, and his mind. We are told in Scripture that David played for King Saul when his heart and mind were troubled. On his harp the sweet singer of Israel brought tranquility. When the minstrel played for Elisha it must have shut out the cares and commotion of life and brought peaceful communion with God. Music plays such an important part in the worship of the high and holy God. Is it any wonder that angels ascribe praise and glory and adoration to our God and King? We are told that there will be singing up in heaven. The inclusion of music in the worship will be to praise our God. But over and beyond the redeemed and angels' voices will be that of the Father Himself singing because His children have been rescued from this world of sin. Can you imagine the joy that will be ours to hear God's voice in rapturous songs of joy over us His redeemed? "He will joy over thee with singing," says the prophet.[562]

After the minstrel played, the word of the Lord came to Elisha. The three kings needed a word from God. God answered. Those powerful kings, made powerless by the lack of water, due to an exclusion of Him in their plans, had the power turned on again by a prayerful life. Then God directed Elisha to give the three kings an unusual assignment:

> And he said, Thus saith the Lord, *Make this valley full of ditches*. For thus saith the Lord, Ye shall not see wind, neither shall ye see rain; yet that valley shall be filled with water, that ye may drink, both ye, and your cattle, and your beasts.[563]

Strange was the command to provide a minstrel, when it was a word from God, and not a musical rendition that the kings needed. Stranger still was the word from God to **dig ditches** in a desert place.

When the children of Israel needed water during their wilderness wanderings, it came from a rock, which typified Christ. The three kings had thought of a variety of ways God would or should have provided water for them and their armies and cattle besides **digging ditches**, I'm sure. We have not the faintest idea how God will supply our needs. We are told, "Our heavenly Father has a thousand ways to provide for us, of which we know nothing."[564] Furthermore, the prophet Isaiah records that God said, "For my thoughts are not your thoughts, neither are your

ways my ways, saith the Lord."565 God's ways of supplying man's needs
are so varied. When He provides, all that we can do is stand amazed at
His proceedings and never should we forget to give thanks. Not only
does He provide, but what He gives will be the best always. God uses
the most unlikely persons and goes in the strangest of directions His will
to perform. Can you imagine *digging ditches* to get water in a desert
valley? He realized that they had no equipment to dig a well. God also
wanted ditches dug for He will not waste what He gives. It will come
from the sovereign God and sufficiently. If the water came from a stream
it would run away and be absorbed by the parched land. In this case
it would be ditches full of water. The earth, though parched out there
in the desert, will not absorb the water. Evaporation would not pose
a problem. Conservation, contamination, evaporation, and pollution
were all given full consideration. The water would not be wasted. One
drink would not be all they would receive.

The kings of Israel, Judah and Edom, complied immediately. Not a
word is mentioned of ditch digging as a mundane task, nor were there
complaints of how difficult it would be to dig the trenches in arid land.
They did precisely what God said. The deeper they dug the ditch, the
greater the blessing. Everyone could determine how much blessing they
would accommodate. There were no instructions about depth and width.
Just dig a ditch. Like hearts, I reckon some parts were more difficult to
dig than others. Stones had to be removed. It took time. God is an equal
opportunity employer. Each ditch dug received a full reward. The ditch
digging was their part, the filling with water God's. That's fantastic.
We do our work and leave God to do His. Human and divine efforts
combine to bring glory to God. The water filled the ditches. When we
dig out all that is in the heart, God will fill it to overflowing with His
Holy Spirit, with love, joy, peace, faith and loyalty. God kept His word
then, and will do the same today. The blessings will come. If you do
your work, God will certainly do His, as promised.

Those three nations demonstrated faith in God and trusted His
word delivered through Elisha. They were not disappointed. God spoke
to them plainly and simply. There would be no wind and no rain, but
the valley full of ditches would be filled with water. In fact, Elisha said,
"this is but a light thing in the sight of the Lord."566 If they asked God

how it would happen, it would have shown a lack of trust. They were just to believe. They just had to withdraw the water from overflowing ditches. We have sufficient evidence and testimony that all God has promised He will do.

Those people believed. They dug the ditches without question, and that was marvelous. They were afforded only one step at a time, one day at a time, one act at a time. May God grant us like them the confidence to walk by faith and not by sight. It is so easy to demand a vision of the entire path. We are interested in knowing from the beginning to the end. Mankind is so results oriented. God in love allows only as much as we can see, as much as we have the capacity to grasp and appropriate. He gives just one day at a time.

We have conducted several evangelistic meetings during our ministry. We asked for God's presence and help and had faith to believe that they were granted in every campaign. However, sometimes I yielded to the "results syndrome." I would check with my star Bible worker, my wife, and inquire, "How are the studies coming along?" "What do the baptism totals look like?" The temptation of "outcome" was always present. That occurred although we prayed and trusted God to give a good harvest of souls. So often the trust factor was there, but total surrender to His success might have been absent.

God grant the church and Christians the faith to simply leave the results with God. If we could only do what He demands in love of us we would be on a highway of blessing heretofore unknown. For example, if He requires the seventh day as the day of worship[567] in His house, not one in seven, not at home, but just as asked of us, do it. Take a good look at a calendar and comply with the command. It will be fantastic. "Just dig the ditches." He said that a tenth of all the money earned belongs to Him including an offering.[568] Don't argue the reasonableness of such a contribution. If there is compliance, He said He will open the windows of heaven and pour out blessings there will not be room enough to contain it. "Just dig the ditches." He said He came and died to save sinners. Since you will never in your own strength become good enough to reach heaven on your works of righteousness, then just believe that He saves and keeps. "Just dig the ditches." Faith is our most precious spiritual commodity. Whether we are at war as were the three kings or in our personal lives, it is obvious that faith has to be exercised every moment of every day. Their faith made them dig the ditches. They were rewarded. We will be also if faithful to His Word.

Stop and think about it. God could have brought water from a nearby rock where they had assembled. He could have filled all the vessels they had repeatedly. Instead of many ditches, how about a storage place, a dam? Ah, no! Just dig ditches. They might have reasoned why should we expend the strength, time, and energy needed to fight the Moabites to dig ditches? The answer would have been that was God's way. It is always the right way. A similar reasoning exists today. Why spend time every day reading God's Word, giving thanks for all His blessings, laying all our plans at His feet, putting on the whole armor, listening for His will for our lives when we have a schedule to meet and things to do? "Just dig the ditches."

Greater still was the fact that other blessings will follow on the heels of the one granted simply for compliance with the order given.

> While the harpist was playing and Elisha was praying, the Lord said to him, "This is what I want you to tell the kings: 'by this afternoon, the Lord wants your men to dig ditches all over the valley. Then you'll begin to see the hand of the Lord. There will be no wind or rain, but all the ditches will fill with water and there will be enough for all your troops including your animals. This is something very small for the Lord to do, *and in addition*, He'll give you victory over the Moabites.[569]

God delights in answering our prayers. There was no rain, and there was no wind. The ditches were dug. Then God in His sovereign majesty after the meat offering brought water by way of Edom and filled the ditches. They had an abundant supply of water, enough for man and beast, and then some. As the water came streaming by, the nations were looking at a miracle in answer to the prayer of faith. God made streams of water in the desert. Now if God can receive a call for water, give instructions as to how it can be obtained and provide it, then certainly, if the human heart cries out for salvation, the plan is the same. If the heart pants for salvation, we read in His Word that we are to "believe on the Lord Jesus and thou shalt be saved."[570] The only requirement is pure faith in the merits of Christ. God stands ready to fill our "ditches," our hearts, with His salvation full and free, when we come believing, trusting, and in full assurance. There is no waiting period, for every sincere prayer is heard in heaven. The dying thief on the cross turned to Jesus and asked Him to remember him when He returned in glory. It must have taken a lot of strength to fill his lungs to speak. But amidst the jeering, mocking, cursing, and rejection, he placed his unwavering faith in Jesus who was suffering a like fate, crucifixion. With sincerity and faith he prayed a simple prayer, "Lord, remember me."[571] Jesus did, and now a crown of life awaits him in glory when He comes. That penitent thief's faith saved him. That day did not appear to be the most hopeful. When things are down, dark, discouraging, dismal and seem hopeless, let courage rise with danger, let your faith triumph over the outward circumstances. Jesus is just as close now as He was to the thief that day—only a prayer away. The grace of forgiveness, power to live for Him, assurance of His presence and a place in His kingdom are yours. He ever lives to make intercession.[572] The same God who heard the three kings' prayer request and who heard the thief on the cross is the same God who will be attentive to our cry. If it has to do with salvation, He came to save.

This ditch digging experience is about how God fought for His children. That the battle is His, is understood. The kings of Israel, Judah, and Edom, could not help but declare that, "It is not by might nor by power, but by God's Spirit."[573] His personal intervention means all battles are won. Notice if you please, the announcement of victory before they engaged in combat. The two-fold impact of providing water was for thirst; the other purpose was to destroy the Moabites. That should have summoned highest praise. In answer to Elisha's prayer while the minstrel played, God said the three kings would have "in addition victory over the Moabites." An added blessing derived for doing exactly what God said.

God employed a pillar of fire to guide Israel safely through the Red Sea. The same cloud was used to confound the Egyptians. It darkened their path. Likewise, the water that slaked the thirst of Israel, Judah, and Edom devastated the Moabites. What a day that was! God provided water to quench the paralyzing thirst of His children and their animals.

But the same water viewed by their enemies, the Moabites, appeared as pools of blood. When the sun arose in its splendor and its bright beams illuminated the ditches of water, they appeared red as blood. The Moabites were deluded. The red soil and rays of sunshine in the trenches proclaimed to them that the three kings and their men had fought among themselves and that the devastation was so great there remained only pools of blood. Oh what a mighty God we serve! Our God can do anything. What a subtle conquest.

> And it came to pass in the morning, when the meat offering was offered, that, behold, there came water by the way of Edom, and the country was filled with water. And when all the Moabites heard that the kings were come up to fight against them, they gathered all that were able to put on armour, and upward, and stood in the border. And they rose up early in the morning, and the sun shone upon the water, and the Moabites saw the water on the other side as red as blood: And they said, This is blood: the kings are surely slain, and they have smitten one another: now therefore, Moab, to the spoil. And when they came to the camp of Israel, the Israelites rose up and smote the Moabites, so that they fled before them: but they went forward smiting the Moabites, even in their country. And they beat down the cities, and on every good piece of land cast every man his stone, and filled it; and they stopped all the wells of water, and felled all the good trees: only in Kirharaseth left they the stones thereof; howbeit the slingers went about it, and smote it. And when the king of Moab saw that the battle was too sore for him, he took with him seven hundred men that drew swords, to break through even unto the king of Edom: but they could not. Then he took his eldest son that should have reigned in his stead, and offered him for a burnt offering upon the wall. And there was great indignation against Israel: and they departed from him, and returned to their own land.[574]

War is a terrible thing. Greed is awful. Power corrupts. The Moabites did not even look before they went down to those illusionary pools of blood. All who could put the armor on went out to battle, and it was fierce. They had to retreat and many died. What seemed like great gain became a great casualty. Without a plan for the acquisition of all the plunder they thought available to them, they rushed headlong with the idea, every man for himself, and what a loss. They received the surprise of their lives. The army had not destroyed themselves. God had only created an illusion. Thereupon three kings and their men went into the Moabite cities. They destroyed everything, flushed it with the ground, flat. Every man carried a stone and covered the land. All the wells were stopped up. Fruit trees were cut down although there were instructions by Moses not to engage in that practice.[575] Kirharaseth, according to commentaries, was a fortified, impregnable city, whose apparent elevation made access difficult. However, they had the slingers to fill it with rocks also. The loss of life and property on that day was great.

Mesha king of Moab was absolutely no better than Balak, the former king in Moab. When Mesha and his seven hundred men could not gain a foothold in Edom, he descended to the lowest level. We have an indication why God supported the battle. The three kings should have destroyed them completely from the face of the earth. Mesha took his eldest son, his firstborn, heir to the throne, and sacrificed him to the god Chemosh, as a burnt offering in full view of all the spectators. What a cruel and inhumane act. It demonstrated a revolt against the government of God. It was one of those abominable acts carried on in those pagan religions. God did not, never did, will never require human sacrifice to atone for wrongs against Him or as a means of help in battle. The act sent the three kings away in utter disgust. They could have done more, but frustrated by Mesha's open rebellion, they journeyed back to their respective nations. Constant reminders of how God gave them victory surfaced over and over again. Had they held out, total victory would have been theirs and greater rejoicing. They stopped short because God had promised to hand over the Moabites to them.

The conversation as they traveled home highlighted God's great act of saving grace. They could not help the recollection that unworthy though they were, God mixed His mercy with His justice and brought salvation. Every cup, or glass, or mug, or puddle of water from then on spoke to them of the victory gained by the power of God and their cooperation. The mission of the three kings in going to fight against Mesha king of the Moabites was to obtain the taxes he refused to pay the king of Israel. Yet the encounter closes with the three kings returning to their nations after a bloody battle in which hundreds of lives were mercilessly destroyed with no plunder in hand. The taxes of a hundred thousand lambs and a hundred thousand rams with the wool did not accompany Jehoram back to Israel. Three kings and their armies returned with nothing to show for the trip but God's marvelous intervention. At the outset of the chapter it was mentioned that "The sweet love of life, invaded by the bacteria of selfishness, can make a potential champion of humanity into a despotic villain, guilty of the destruction of men's rights, happiness and their very lives."[576] Selfishness, yes greed, conquered those kings. Observe as they made the homeward trek. How could they block from memory the record of the invasion, the tremendous slaughter, the destruction of towns and villages, the sight of Mesha's firstborn son sacrificed, the wells stopped up, fruit trees cut down, ruined lives and property, and so much more that were uppermost in mind. But God's will will always be done in heaven and on earth.

They left with their own agenda, war, but God intervened. He left indelibly etched on their minds the ditches filled with water that appeared like blood, which won the battle and turned a bad situation into praise for His name. Like blood was the water. It was the sight of blood that made the conquest possible. Only the blood of Christ brings victory. The blood from the cross brings salvation only to some, for all will not accept. It is only an object of ridicule and shame for others. Some declare that Jesus died to save them from sin. Others conclude that He was only a martyr. It is like the water in the ditches. It quenched the thirst of man and beast in Edom. The same water appeared like blood to Moabites and resulted in a battle where they killed each other. We ought to accept the blood of Christ from Calvary as the only means of our salvation.

We are commanded to just dig the ditches, which is man's part, his acceptance. God will fill them with His blood, God's intervention. When He sees the blood, the blood of Christ, not on the lintel but on us, victory will be ours, and God will pass over us, no condemnation and safe passage granted to the Promised Land.

Chapter 10

EARTHQUAKE—
GOD'S AMMUNITION

(Based on 1 Samuel 14; 3:1–8)

Nahash, king of the Ammonites, intended to punish seven thousand men of Gad and Reuben who had escaped and fled to Jabesh in Gilead for sanctuary. King Saul became rather indignant when he heard of the plans of Nahash. He was angry indeed, not for himself, but for the honor of God's people. He became righteously exasperated; his tender compassion ignited when he heard that Nahash covenanted and contemplated gouging out everyone's right eye. It would be his act of showing his kingship. That act of barbarity and inhumanity would drain the tears from the most callous hearted. Can you imagine those besieged citizens becoming a life-long reproach to all their fellow tribesmen, disabled in war, and bearing in their bodies the marks of a most shameful reproach? They would have been one-eyed spectacles. Never can a covenant of peace be made with the enemies of God without suffering great loss. Furthermore, it is unlawful to make any compromise that is contrary to the Word of God. And don't ever forget it; the enemy of us all is so ready to make a covenant if we are willing to part with our spiritual eyesight.

King Saul had just returned from the farm, (although king), when he received the evil tidings of Nahash's intent. Immediately, God's Spirit descended upon Saul and imbued him with divine authority.[577] The city fathers had requested of Nahash one week to consider the terms of his covenant. This gave King Saul enough time to plan his approach.

223

He accepted the challenge to rescue his people. This is what he did. He took his two oxen, killed them, cut them up in pieces and sent the gory pieces throughout all Israel with a serious message. It said that anyone refusing to join Saul and Samuel in battle against Nahash would have their oxen treated like the pieces they were viewing. They were invited to join them in the deliverance of their brothers. It was like a trumpet call from heaven. The nation responded willingly.[578] An army of three hundred and thirty thousand fighting men met him ready to follow instructions.[579] They went to battle against the Ammonites and severely defeated them, "that they which remained were scattered, so that two of them were not left together."[580] Weeping may endure for a night, but joy came for them in the morning.

The Ammonites, like the Philistines, lived in Israel's territory and controlled some of their cities, towns, and borders. The Israelites had directives from God not to fight with the Ammonites except as ordered by Him.[581] However, the Philistines' presence in Israel was due to the fact that they had not destroyed them completely when they should have. Moses and Joshua distinctly instructed Israel not to spare the inhabitants as they came into possession of the Promised Land for they would become a snare.[582] They knew exactly why they gave that counsel. For disobedience and unbelief there can be no excuse. No argument or reasoning can extenuate the guilt of doing what we know to be contrary to the mind, heart, and will of God. We need to constantly remind ourselves that to choose our own way is to choose loss and defeat, just as Israel did.

Sometime after the battle with the Ammonites, King Saul chose three thousand of those fighting men of Israel as bodyguards from the army of three hundred and thirty thousand men. Two thousand stayed with him in Michmash, and one thousand with Jonathan his son who lived in Gibeah, Saul's hometown.[583]

The Philistines who occupied sacred soil were a menace. They delighted in subduing Israel at will. They sensed their broken covenant with God. Then one day Jonathan raided the Philistines at Geba with the one thousand men assigned to him and captured their garrison.[584] Geba was located about four miles northeast of Gibeah.[585] This would be Jonathan's first appearance in battle as the prime mover. The Philistines did not take the defeat, the hit on the chin, turn the other cheek, and simply walk away. They called for reinforcements and advanced against the strongholds of Saul in Bethel and Michmash.[586] The Philistines were a powerful nation and well equipped for war. They were plundering the plains and valleys of Michmash. The struggle was so intense that the Israelites had to hide in caves, pits, and wells to survive.[587] Just about any place that would provide seclusion was considered prime property. The Philistines laid the country waste. Saul and Jonathan knew how difficult it would be to react with limited resources.

Life in Israel could not be considered livable. Jonathan decided to conduct a second campaign. Although attributed to his father, King Saul, it was really Jonathan's exploit. He crushed the Philistines and drove them out of Michmash. This is the battle that attracts our attention. In it, God utilized an earthquake to defeat the enemy. The slain were in large numbers. A fortuitous earthquake terrorized the entire Philistine army, and those who survived went to their own country.

In each of the battles fought by Israel, the question comes: what is God going to do in this encounter? And may I ask you, "Is an earthquake ammunition in war?" It was in *this* engagement. God employs various things of and in nature or celestial messengers to do His bidding. There can be no discussion, for the victory is His to give. Why? Because the glory, His glory, He will not share. He will, however, utilize willing hands, minds, and hearts to show that divine might united with human effort can produce amazing results.

Jonathan, son of King Saul and his armor bearer, his foxhole buddy, had sneaked out of the camp unknown to his father. It was not disobedience or failure to be a team player. The fact is, there are times when God appears to His children and prompts them to do certain exploits that demand secrecy. For example, Abraham took Isaac to Mount Moriah to use as a sacrifice without conferring with his mother or anyone about the demands of God.[588] When situations like that occur, the sole desire must be to comply with God's will. Sensing the call of God as an individual, responsible first to Him, and desirous of demonstrating that salvation through Christ is a personal choice, Jonathan broke from the camp to fulfill his call. His faith overcame any fear that would rise or lurk in his heart.

And Jonathan said to the young man that bare his armour, Come, and let us go over unto the garrison of these uncircumcised: it may be that the LORD will work for us: *for there is no restraint to the LORD to save by many or by few.*[589]

Jonathan's faith in God would be central to his achievements. His faith said that God would fight, be supportive, if it were only himself and the armor bearer. The faith he demonstrated in God would be rewarded, as we will observe. In this conflict with the Philistines, his faith recorded the victory as accomplished, "a done deal," before the first enemy soldier died. We must always remember that if we see it, it is not faith. Faith is something we hope for, and we move forward as if it is achieved. Jonathan must be cited for his bravery, his valiant spirit, but more than anything else, his faith.

The Philistines had what could be described as a seemingly invincible army. Let's look at it.

And the Philistines gathered themselves together to fight with Israel, thirty thousand chariots, and six thousand horsemen, *and people as the sand which is on the sea shore* in multitude: and they came up, and pitched in Michmash, eastward from Beth-aven.[590]

And Saul tarried in the uttermost part of Gibeah under a pomegranate tree which is in Migron: *and the people that were with him were about six hundred men;*[591]

A calculator is not needed to tally Jonathan's army in this war. It was Jonathan and his armor bearer. That's two. Count it: one, two. They faced serious odds in battle. Then let us look at some further obstacles that complicated the planned encounter. These are facts:

It seems that for a time the Philistines enjoyed practically a monopoly in Canaan on the fabrication of iron and possibly other metals. At this time the iron used in Palestine came from Asia Minor, and was imported through the coastal cities. These, of course, were under the control of the Philistines. Thus it was relatively easy for them to enforce what was, from their point of view, a wise policy by which to keep the Hebrews disarmed.

After years of Philistine oppression Saul and Jonathan seem to be the only ones who possessed these metal weapons. The rank and file of the army could have bows and slings—no mean equipment in the hands of experts (see Judges 20:16)—but they could not compete in hand-to-hand combat with the iron weapons of the Philistines. This verse reveals two things: (1) the battle took place before Israel was well organized, probably early in Saul's reign, and (2) the lack of equipment made it evident to both sides that God intervened on behalf of His people. Saul might rebel, and as a result do many foolish things; but God still wrought for Israel in such a way as to encourage individuals to join His kingdom and place their trust in Him.[592]

In human terms this can only be described as great odds. Israel could not buy iron or any other metal. The Philistines had cornered the market, controlling all imported metals. Israel could not make wheels for their chariots, spears, swords, or farming equipment. They had no blacksmiths. Only two swords were in all of Israel, Saul's and Jonathan's. The army was reduced to stones, slingshots, bows, and arrows. The battle was uneven; Israel did not stand a chance. It is like two men in a boxing match. One has his gloves on. He is shadow boxing around the ring, while the other is in his corner with his hands and feet tied. It is unnecessary to ring the bell for the fight to begin. Just announce the winner, for that cannot be considered a contest. In a seemingly hopeless situation God provided Jonathan's servant with the right words at the right time.

Do all that is in thine heart: turn thee; behold, I am with thee according to thy heart.[593]

Jonathan's heart could no longer bear the ridicule and see the land laid waste. Greatly disturbed, he would take God-inspired action.

THE STRATEGY

The strategy set as to how the battle should begin seems almost beyond belief, even trite for an invasion of this magnitude. As you read the conversation between Jonathan and his armor bearer, it literally glows with the light of heaven upon it:

Then Jonathan said, "All right, let's go. We'll make our way down the gorge and when we get near the Philistine camp, we'll let them see us. If they challenge us by saying, 'If you want to fight, stay where you are and we'll come down and teach you a thing or two,' then we'll slip into the shadows and make our way back here. But if they challenge us by saying, 'If you want to fight, show us your courage and come up here,' that will be a sign from the Lord that He'll fight for us and give us the victory." The armor bearer agreed. So when they got near the outpost they let the Philistine guards see them climbing around the rocks down in the gorge. The guards laughed and said, "Look! The Hebrews are scared of us and are crawling out of the holes they've been hiding in." Then they shouted to Jonathan, "If you want to fight, come up here and show us your courage!" Jonathan turned to his armor bearer and said, "That's the sign we've been praying for. Follow me and we'll go up to meet them as they have asked us to. The Lord has already given us the victory.[594]

That was most interesting. The two men would venture into the garrison of the uncircumcised Philistines. Jonathan had his options ready, for God had appeared to him. First, they would reveal themselves to the enemy. If the Philistines said they were coming down, Jonathan and his armor bearer would disappear in a heartbeat back to Gibeah. However, if they were invited to come up to the garrison that would be God's indication to them that the Philistines' army, however large, would be delivered into their hands by the God whose battle they would fight. He and his armor bearer would go, assured of divine intervention. What they would do was infinitesimally small, but they would do it anyhow, for they believed in the divine-human relationship. But really, it must be considered correctly. Jonathan's faith transcended his sight. He had already learned how blind human reasoning was, and how feeble faith becomes when it tries to walk by sight. Yet he knew how sure were God's promises, and how inexhaustible were His resources. Jonathan decided that neither reason nor sense, nor touch, but the solemnly given, clearly stated, perfectly sufficient word of God would be his guiding light.

If the Philistines said they were to come up to the garrison that would be their clue that God had spoken. Included in the invitation was a promise that the Lord would deliver them into their hands.[595] The proposition he made eclipsed Gideon's conduct with the fleece. Jonathan, unlike Gideon, had zero time to wait. It was instantaneous, right away and immediate. He accepted and rested on the divine promise of victory the moment the Philistines said, "Come." Jonathan and his armor bearer had no idea of the outcome, of how God would accomplish the task at hand, but they believed. It was without reservation, full-hearted, and they rested on the word of God. No further questions would be asked, plans laid or options opened, for he was "fully persuaded that God was able also to perform that which He had promised."[596]

To have tokens of God's guidance in all of life's affairs is wonderful. To have them immediately, testifies to a God for whom nothing is too hard. Add to that kind of trust the ability to wait for a clear, unmistakable signal, and it can be said, it is "Enoch-like," or that that individual walks and talks with God. If only we possessed the ability to wait on God's will. Songwriter W. D. Longstaff's hymn characterized Jonathan's relationship with his Lord. He says, "And run not before Him, Whatever betide; In joy or in sorrow, Still follow thy Lord, And, looking to Jesus, Still trust in His Word."

We must admit this sign of the Philistines saying, "Come, climb this mountain with your armor on and we will teach you a lesson you have not yet learned,"[597] is well nigh impossible if speaking in human terms. Then let us not forget these were the people who were plundering all Israel. The Israelites were in hiding, not contesting. An invitation from the enemy to come and tour the military arsenal and might is certainly not the common procedure of battle.

Jonathan and his armor bearer's approach contained two seeming impossibilities: an anticipated invitation from the enemy; and two, scaling Bozez and Seneh.[598] The two sharp rocks, Bozez and Seneh, would be stepping-stones. They were "in the pass to Michmash, between which Jonathan and his armor bearer climbed up when he overcame the Philistine garrison."[599] Their mention is only for topographical reasons. They concealed Jonathan and his armor bearer's approach from the enemy's garrison. On hands and knees they climbed, though it was dangerous to do so to get to the point of combat. On God's errands fear was discarded.

The conflict between the Israelites and the Philistines grants an insight into the battle in which the soldiers of Christ are engaged daily. It is a war against physical and moral evils, the world, the flesh, and the devil. The wrestling match is not against flesh and blood alone, but against wickedness in all places. Just as the Philistines, a warlike, powerful antagonist sought to control God's people and dispossess them; even so we, as members of God's kingdom are engaged in a real warfare. The objective is to dispossess us of the rights and privileges afforded to us through Jesus Christ here and in His coming kingdom. The evil one would like nothing better than to see us hiding from God like Adam and Eve, after cheating us out of our inheritance. But that will not happen. We will follow Paul's counsel and put on the whole armor of God. We will fight like we have never fought before, be courageous soldiers, and by His grace be victorious.

Jonathan's success at Geba and subsequently at Michmash is a foretaste of what will be. God's covenant with Abraham stipulated that Israel would possess the Promised Land, Canaan. Throughout Israel's history, over and over again, idolatrous nations like the Philistines have attempted to thwart God's plan for a peaceful settlement of the whole territory. They wanted a parcel of the property. Likewise, the Christian is engaged in ceaseless warfare with evil men and evil spirits who are attempting to defraud us of our full inheritance. We fight against the visible and invisible forces. The enemy, like the Philistines, is idolatrous, powerful, deceitful, crafty, lawless, an antagonist of God, a hater of good, accuser of the brethren, hard as steel, and cruel as hell. The heavenly Canaan we seek will not come without a struggle. Christians may take courage from the fact that they are not alone in the fray. Jonathan was not left to fight alone. He had the Lord on his side. He was successful in the conflicts he waged. God gave him the victory before the mission began. He fought for him. God rewarded his faith and his dependence on Him before the battle began. The Christian, likewise, is not by himself in battle. Our faith declares that the Lord Jesus Christ has already struck a deathblow to the enemy of our souls. He is the captain of our salvation. His perfect life, death, and glorious resurrection ensure victory to every soldier in His army. Hope of final victory then and now depends more on faith in God than how formidable the enemy has been or is.

Jonathan had a loyal companion as they embarked upon the mission. He proved to be a companion, an associate, a helper, and he spoke God's words. There are chords in our nature that vibrate mysteriously to another's touch. It is a magnetism that works by laws we cannot explain adequately, and we imperfectly understand. The presence and sympathy of a companion braces and enlivens the heart. Though the disparity might be so great—master and servant—it is not even considered when the contribution is that he thinks and feels alike. The friend knows the magic there is in a look, a touch, or a word, to alleviate and quicken a pained or drooping spirit, or to give commendation in a time of great, little, or no success. There is something to be said for and about the fellowship of kindred spirits. There is something awesome about the power of a good friend, a loyal companion. The armor bearer depicts the loyalty and faithfulness Christian soldiers must possess if they will wear the victor's crown. An unflinching loyalty to each other that neither time nor space can erase. It is called comradeship, a brotherhood. It is surprising that homeless drunks know it. They'll share the last drop of cheap wine with each other. Gang members will protect and cover each other. And although the examples cited defy moral conduct, let's not miss the point of comradeship. Everyone needs at least one friend.

God is no respecter of persons, but He has great respect for faith.

He is well pleased when they make the very highest demand upon Him, that they may glorify His name. *They may expect large things if they have faith in His promises.* " [600]

Jonathan and his armor bearer shared a common belief that, "there is no restraint to the Lord to save by many or by few." [601] Jonathan had personally witnessed God's leading and guiding hand in Israel's affairs. The battle between Gideon's three hundred warriors and the Midianites, demonstrating how God works, was fresh in his memory. He recalled with pride of country how Gideon's army of thirty-two thousand was reduced to three hundred and how a few faithful, conscientious, dedicated, and committed persons served God more acceptably than a large complement of vacillating, unsure, in-the-valley-of-indecision weaklings.

One recurring conclusion is that God does not need human resources in battle. He never changes. The battle is always the Lord's. Man's inclusion serves illustrative purposes only. For example, Joshua and Israel walked around the walls of Jericho. They blew trumpets, the people shouted, and the record reads that the walls of Jericho fell. No mind is so dull as to conceive that the sound of the trumpets, the shouts, and the walking around Jericho brought down those massive walls. Israel simply followed the instructions. When we review what happened, it is marvelous. Israel's obedience in following God's orders with exactness, their faith in Him and their participation in this great venture must have delighted God. The divine-human relationship demonstrated God's great heart of love in sharing His ministry with mankind. He made it to appear as if it were a human success story. At times God enlists human support, although He is totally in charge; at other times He defends the honor of His name or His children without their aid. The marvelous thing is, He includes finite man in His undertakings to build their faith and trust. It is evident that God has absolutely no need to call upon man's aid in any of life's situations. Consider the 185,000 soldiers in the Assyrian army who died in one night. "Then the angel of the Lord went out and put to death a 185,000 men in the Assyrian camp. When the people got up the next morning—there were all the dead bodies!"[602] But every now and then there is a divine-human association that more perfectly demonstrates the plan of redemption.

Throughout history, in every conflict where God's power has been displayed, the correlation between the conflict and redemption can be clearly seen whether divine-human or God's signal act. The high water mark of course was when God sent His only begotten son to effect salvation.[603] A casual look will reveal that the human race did not put in a request for help that God honored.

> But God commendeth His love toward us, in that, while we were yet sinners, Christ died for us.[604]

Of His own free choice and great love Jesus came, lived, suffered, bled, died, and rose a victor over death and the grave, securing salvation for all who will believe. The provision was all God's. The victory

Christ achieved over sin, death, and the grave belongs to all mankind as a free gift. It is interesting to note that in the conflict with sin Jesus went alone to gain victory for us. It is something we could not achieve for ourselves. Jesus took our place, died our death, and gave us His life. Man was not present and did not participate in that battle. The merits of that victory God freely offers.

God did not need Jonathan and his armor bearer to free Israel from the tyranny of the Philistines. But He would involve them in the fight. They staged a surprise attack upon the Philistines and twenty of them were slaughtered.[605] Call it whatever you like—the first fruits? And all of a sudden the camp of the Philistines was in total disarray. Jonathan's statement, "that the Lord can save by many or by few," realized its fulfillment almost immediately. God showed His faithfulness to his children. Inwardly they cried that God could be trusted. Jonathan and his companion received God's approval rating for their faith, not their prowess. At the same time, they had the joy of sensing that the inward promptings of God will be perfected if faithfully obeyed. Sometimes the path may be painful and protracted; we might have to scale "Bozez and Seneh," in obedience to that heaven-born call, but the way will be crowded with evidences of His faithfulness, guidance, and love. Can you imagine that at the outset of their mission they could hear and experience, "He which hath begun a good work in you will perform it."[606] Couple that with the fact that, "God is not unjust; He will not forget your work and the love you have shown Him as you have helped His people and continue to help them."[607]

Jonathan started the battle between the two camps, but the chief commander in the invasion was God. Jonathan was the central figure in the human relationship. The two men slew twenty Philistines only after God gave a clear and unmistakable signal to proceed. Then God caused a trembling in the soldiers, in the field, among all the Philistines, the garrison, the spoilers, and the raiders. Panic, fear, and trembling gripped the hearts of the enemy. God shook the earth with a massive earthquake; if you have been in an earthquake, you realize how disorienting that can be. Then this first-time event in a battle created a literal free-for-all. They were killing each other. Usually in battle the commander would have been given specific ideas as to the procedures for war, such as ambush, taking of city, or otherwise. Not so here. Had we not sufficient details it would make Israel seem armed and ready for battle. But the earthquake really caused the disarray in which they found themselves.

> And there was trembling in the host, in the field, and among all the people: the garrison, and the spoilers, they also trembled, and the earth quaked: so it was a very great trembling.[608]

What size it was on the Richter scale? How long did it last? We cannot tell. What we do know for sure is that God was in charge. The infighting of the enemy, providentially ordered, pre-empted Israel from combat. We have before us another glaring demonstration that God carried out His plans. He it was who wanted Israel free, but kind enough to incorporate these men.

> And Saul and all the people that were with him assembled themselves, and they came to the battle: and behold, every man's sword was against his fellow, and there was a very great discomfiture.[609]

Saul got into the act, but we will recall that his commands, support in the invasion, and the victory proclaimed are the direct result of the acts of the prime movers, the initiators—Jonathan and his armor bearer. The Israelites, who were intimidated by the Philistines and reduced to living in dens and in caves, came out of their hiding places, joined in the fray, and the enemy was overthrown with a tremendous slaughter. The Philistines were on the run and Israel pursued them from all sides. The battle should have ended there with the Philistines routed completely, but for Saul's indiscretion, pride, jealousy, and haste in making vows. Instead we read,

> The rest of his life Saul had to fight off the Philistines *because he didn't follow-up on his victory the day the Lord blessed Jonathan.* Whenever Saul saw a strong or brave man, he took him into his army.[610]

Many wonderful lessons surface throughout this amazing earthquake battle. The Holy Spirit indelibly etches on the heart the lessons God transacted through human instruments from which we should profit.

Moses wrote words that were rehearsed by Joshua and passed to succeeding generations. Jonathan read and accepted them at face value.

> How should one chase a thousand, and two put ten thousand to flight, except their Rock had sold them, and the Lord had shut them up.[611]

> …one man of you to chase a thousand: for the Lord your God, He it is that fighteth for you, as He hath promised.[612]

Jonathan and his armor bearer were successful in beginning the rout. They had followed the Spirit's promptings. But, follow me here. It is clear that God does not need our help. But those who by faith surrender to His will actually help themselves. For example, Jesus during His earthly ministry fed five thousand. However, He used the disciples' hands to distribute the meal.[613] Jesus would heal the man at the pool of Bethesda, sick for thirty-eight years, but he had to take up his bed and walk.[614] Participation, an act of faith, on man's part is vital. It is the divine-human relationship of which we speak. In that experience, God gets the glory and man's faith is strengthened and increased.

Another lesson is that God always has a small group that is successful in the conquests He ordains. Elijah was outweighed and outnumbered by the forces of Ahab and Jezebel. However, the real test did not come until the time came for the evening sacrifice to be offered. Then it was that the true and living God came into full focus, and one man, undaunted, faithful, trusting, and reliant, vanquished the gods of Baal.[615] In fact, seven thousand who had not bowed their knees to Baal stood in the shadows.[616] God is never left without a witness. Even today, God's church, small in number, "enfeebled and defective as it may be,"[617] is making a statement to billions of people around the world that Jesus is coming again and soon. All over the globe, through radio, television, missionaries, literature, medical work, schools, colleges, and universities, the message of a crucified, risen and soon-coming Savior is being proclaimed. One day, sometime in 1961, while on my first missionary assignment in Guyana South America, I baptized a small group of believers in the Demerara River. They had accepted Christ and joined the church through the aid of the Holy Spirit, a study of His Word, and the witness of faithful members. I left Guyana in 1963. I had not seen, I did not remember, I never investigated the whereabouts of those who were baptized that memorable day. Thirty-four years later, while at a 1995 religious convention in Urecht, a young man came to me and inquired if I remembered him. I admitted I did not. He kindly recalled for my benefit the year and place that I had baptized him. He now served as president of the Guyana Conference in South America, and was a very successful worker. He informed me that he was one of those baptized that day. Our discussions led me to believe that his ministry had the blessing of God resting upon it. His evangelistic campaigns accounted for hundreds of persons baptized into the church of God. Then he drew an interesting conclusion. He said he would share those baptisms from his personal labors with me, for it was as a result of my sharing in leading him to Christ that he had joined the church and became a worker for the Lord. In that city of thousands where I labored, he alone became a pastor from among those I baptized. As the president of the conference in the country where he was baptized, he felt honored of God to have been an evangelist leading many to Christ. God never leaves Himself without a witness to do exploits for Him. In the eroding leadership of Saul, king in Israel, He had a Jonathan.

So then, the battle is the Lord's, and we ought to learn to wait on the promptings of His Spirit, and He will never reveal all His plans but unfold then in due time; He has a thousand ways to accomplish His will for our peace; He awaits our notes of gratitude for His deliverance of help bestowed.

Before we conclude, let us take another look at Jonathan's armor bearer. He arrests our sense of loyalty and comradeship. God would like for us to see something redeeming. Often in a game of golf the caddy will be seen sharing ideas, giving advice, and encouraging the player along the course. Looking back upon Jonathan and his armor bearer, glimpses of that kind of experience can be seen, although we are discussing matters of an entirely different nature, this being spiritual. Let us recount his words to Jonathan just for the sheer joy of their commitment. "Do all that is in thine heart; turn thee; behold, I am with thee according to thy heart."[618] His trust in his master gave Jonathan freedom to do all that was in his heart. Listen to the Christ-like-sounding expressions of collegiality and comradeship. Servant he was, yes, but in the foxhole the ground became level. Lines of demarcation were gone, obliterated. He said, "I am with thee."[619] What a friendship! It was poised for success. His faith said, "We will win." That was an announcement of unswerving allegiance and devotion. He suggested by his statement that the content of Jonathan's heart was certifiable fidelity, honor, and devotion to God and man. A man who has friends must himself be friendly. Undoubtedly, Jonathan must have been true-blue to inspire his armor bearer to be that kind of person. He was only a reflection. There are a lot of war stories that speak of intimacy in times of great danger. These two men, Jonathan and his armor bearer were joined by a common objective, *to destroy the enemy*, the Philistines. Although it was the people that rescued Jonathan from King Saul, I would like to think that the armor bearer was the first to deny King Saul access to Jonathan.

You will recall, that unknown to Jonathan and his armor bearer, the men with Saul were charged with an oath not to eat until the evening. Jonathan, who came from a different direction in the same battle, stumbled upon a honeycomb, stuck the end of his rod in it and got some. It must have tasted good after the long day's encounter. In time however, Saul discovered that someone had not done as he impulsively proposed. As always they cast lots and it fell on Jonathan who had unknowingly eaten the honey. The lots were cast because God had not answered him by the Urim or Thummim which had to do with something entirely different. Saul, his father, who had rashly imposed this fast, was sinking quickly in his own irreverence. He did not think the matter through. Another reckless show of his unsanctified zeal surfaced, no questions asked, no considerations given. Although a terrible decision, he said Jonathan had to die. Where did parental love disappear that day? The people said Jonathan would not be killed. I like to feel that the armor bearer snatched him away and would possibly have given life and limb for a friend, along with the other soldiers.[620] Beyond them was a gracious and merciful God who would not allow a human sacrifice because of Saul's folly. The cry today is for more such demonstrations, more such glimpses of loyalty to applaud God's ability to plant in the human heart a love which can be given only by Him.

Who is your armor bearer? Moses told God that he could not speak when told to return to Egypt. That was understandable. Pharaoh had him on his most-wanted list. So God provided help in the person of Aaron. Caleb and Joshua had each other. Amidst the cries of defeat and failure and a lack of faith in the camp of Israel, they stood assured, faithful, fearless, and confident. Their argument won. Daniel had Mishael, Hananiah, and Azariah. They fed off each other's courage and enthusiasm. Their faith did not waver when they said, "We will not eat the king's meat... try us ten days... give us time to pray concerning the king's dream... our God whom we serve is able."[621] Peter, James, and John witnessed the transfiguration of Jesus and were never the same.[622] They also had one hundred twenty praying persons. Paul had Timothy,[623] Dr. Luke,[624] Silas,[625] Barnabas,[626] and a praying church. Naomi had Ruth. The lines, "where thou lodgest... I will lodge... thy people... my people... thy God... my God"[627] have declared the depths of commitment. They are immortal words. David had Jonathan. Their souls were knitted together with a love surpassing that of women.[628] We should be loyal to one another. We should be as true as steel in defense of each other. "Love as brethren, be pitiful, be courteous."[629] Jonathan and his armor bearer's relationship speaks volumes. There is so much to emulate. Better still is the love of our Elder Brother who loves us beyond computation. "Having loved His own which were in the world, He loved them unto the end."[630] He is that "Friend that sticketh closer than a brother."[631]

The manner in which God delivered the children of Israel out of the claws of the Philistines is only a matter of record now. But the record reads well. "So the *Lord* saved Israel that day."[632] It is all about God. Saul and Jonathan yes, but "the *Lord* saved Israel *that day.*" Just add all the factors and activities of the battle from the moment Jonathan and his armor bearer left. Then include all that Saul and his men did until victory came, and the conclusion will be the same, *"The Lord saved Israel."*

Sometimes situations seem hopeless like Saul with only six hundred men, and Jonathan and his armor bearer against thousands of Philistines. There is no telling what God will do or how He will win the battle. His ways are too wonderful to grasp, they are past finding out. He never seems to repeat His strategy. He always has another plan. But win He will, militarily or spiritually.

The "Philistines" are still a nuisance to God's people. The attacks, although different in scope, are nonetheless real. The "Philistines" of shattered dreams, stressful situations, broken relationships, broken families, broken homes, Alzheimer's and Parkinson's diseases, failure on the stock market resulting in significant loss, repossessed property, foreclosure, bankruptcy, cancer, or a failed career. "Philistines, Philistines" are everywhere. Be not dismayed. Use the statement of Jonathan and his armor bearer for encouragement. God will and can save by many or with a few. Then when the "Philistines" show up, remember the words of Joshua, "For the Lord your God He it is that fighteth for you."[633] Better still, remember 1 Samuel 14:23: "The Lord saved Israel that day."

In the final analysis this battle has nothing to do with Saul, Jonathan, the armor bearer, and the Israelite army. But it does indicate that we should give the same loyalty, courage, and fellowship to Jesus Christ as was given by the armor bearer to Jonathan, and should stand shoulder to shoulder as did the soldiers when Saul wanted Jonathan dead. If we did, we would see great and awesome accomplishments. This world would be a happier place despite its blights. Isn't it a fact that when the heart is consecrated to Christ, self no longer dominates? Faith will be central to all our dealings and doings. The achievements will be for God. No one will seek preeminence. It will be understood that without Christ the victory is impossible. God's people today, as in the days of Jonathan and Saul, are completely outnumbered. God was their only helper then, and the only helper today. If so, and it is, then we ought to look to Him for victory in all things. It is assured. Through Christ, "all things are possible."[634] The battles here, there, and everywhere are already won. Faith in God will conquer… no, it has already won.

Chapter 11

THE BABYLONIAN CAPTIVITY

(Based on 2 Kings 24–25)

The *If-Then* Philosophy

The Babylonian captivity of Judah was ordained of God. He permitted it as chastisement for their disobedience. He intended to discipline them and in so doing strengthen their spiritual life. God had no plan to abandon them, for a great future was still before them. His plan provided that the scattered nation would eventually return home. Only a remnant did however, because for many the "good life" in Babylon became a snare and many chose to remain. As a result of their captivity, Jewish history demonstrated God's great plan of redemption. Best of all, Christ's restoration of all things, another glimpse of the plan of salvation, and His return as the rightful King would be revealed. Judah's captivity and restoration from Babylon also encourages God's people to wait patiently for release from present Babylon and for the full and complete restoration of all things. Like Judah, all must wait "until He *come* whose right it is."[635] Judah had no longer a succession of kings after the captivity, neither do we, the "Israel of God,"[636] have any other king but Jesus Christ. All creation waits for the stone cut out of the mountain without hands,[637] the coming of the Lord Jesus Christ in matchless splendor.

God in His great love delineated a path of abundant blessings to come upon Israel if they were obedient and severe punishment if disobedient. When Moses went to Pharaoh he said, "The Lord God of the Hebrews hath met with us: and now let us go, we beseech thee, three days' journey into the wilderness, that we may sacrifice to the Lord our God."[638] God insisted that the days of servitude had ended. It was now time for His people to enjoy religious freedom. More than four hundred years had passed since Pharaoh extended the invitation to Joseph to bring his entire family down to Goshen.[639] God would employ the same means, namely Pharaoh, for their departure. Pharaoh invited Jacob and his family to live in Goshen. They ought to be able to leave on their own volition just as when they came years before. God said,

> And thou shalt say unto him, The Lord God of the Hebrews hath sent me unto thee, saying, Let my people go, that they may serve me in the wilderness: and, behold, hitherto thou wouldest not hear.[640]

> Thus saith the Lord, Let my people go, that they may serve me.[641]

> Thus saith the Lord God of the Hebrews, Let my people go, that they may serve me.[642]

> And Moses and Aaron came in unto Pharaoh, and he said unto him, Thus saith the Lord God of the Hebrews, How long wilt thou refuse to humble thyself before me? Let my people go, that they may serve me.[643]

It took ten successive, crippling plagues to get Pharaoh's attention. Ultimately, he acknowledged God's sovereignty and that all the gods of the world are idols. Finally, Israel left Egypt with the hope of enjoying the promise made to Abraham,[644] reiterated to Isaac,[645] believed by Jacob,[646] and to which Joseph held fast,[647]

> "They left Egypt in the month of Xanthicus, on the fifteenth day of the lunar month; four hundred and thirty years after our forefather Abraham came into Canaan, but two hundred and fifteen years only after Jacob removed into Egypt.* It was the eightieth year of the age of Moses, and of that of Aaron three more. They also carried out the bones of Joseph with them, as he had charged his sons to do."[648]

And it shall be when the LORD shall bring thee into the land of the Canaanites, and the Hittites, and the Amorites, and the Hivites, and the Jebusites, which he sware unto thy fathers to give thee, a land flowing with milk and honey, that thou shalt keep this service in this month.[649]

He went further,

And I will set thy bounds from the Red Sea even unto the sea of the Philistines, and from the desert unto the river: for I will deliver the inhabitants of the land into your hand: and thou shalt drive them out before thee.[650]

God promised Israel that He would be their supreme leader. He promised to fight against nations and peoples stronger and mightier than they and in due time Israel would see the fulfillment of the promise He made over four hundred eighty years before. The conquest of Canaan under the capable and efficient leadership of Moses and subsequently Joshua, his successor, happened. However, it took courage, unrelenting effort, constant appeals, and admonitions to be faithful and to trust in God without doubt to get Israel to comply. That seemed like a daily necessity:

And Joshua said unto the children of Israel, How long are ye slack to go to possess the land, which the Lord God of your fathers hath given you?[651]

All Israel or some portion of them doubted, questioned, or disobeyed every requirement or command of God. They should not associate nor make compromises with the inhabitants of the lands conquered or with those who surrendered. They did. In fact, He specifically told them that they should be annihilated. They didn't. They were instructed not to put up the manna overnight except on the sixth day. They did.[652] They were warned also that only explicit obedience to God would result in a binding, loving, personal, covenant relationship. The instructions were clear:

Thou shalt not bow down to their gods, nor serve them, nor do their works: but thou shalt utterly overthrow them, and quite break down their images[653]

God indicated a need for their undivided attention to every detail. If they forsook Him and the path laid out, the results would be tragic. We serve a wonderful God. He never leaves us to trust our memories or judgment. He expressly told Joshua what His expectations were and had him chronicle them:

Be ye therefore very courageous to keep and to do all that is written in the book of the law of Moses that ye turn not aside therefrom to the right hand or to and the left; …For the Lord hath driven out from before you great nations and strong: but as for you, no man hath been able to stand before you unto this day… Take good heed therefore unto yourselves, that ye love the Lord your God. Else if ye do in any wise go back, and cleave unto the remnant of these nations, even these that remain among you, and shall make marriages with them, and go in unto them, and they to you: Know for a certainty that the Lord your God will no more drive out any of these nations from before you; but they shall be snares and traps unto you, and scourges in your sides, and thorns in your eyes, until ye perish from off this good land which the Lord your God hath given you. And, behold, this day I am going the way of all the earth: and ye know in all your hearts and in all your souls, that not one thing hath failed of all the good things which the Lord your God spake concerning you; all are come to pass unto you, and not one thing hath failed thereof. Therefore it shall come to pass, that as all good things are come upon you, which the Lord your God promised you; so shall the Lord bring upon you all evil things, until he has destroyed you from off this good land which Lord your God hath given you.[654]

The instructions were clear. The commandments written with the finger of God and given to Moses on Mount Sinai were in the ark. The unerring witness of the Urim and Thummim could be consulted day or night to secure the right path. God made Himself available to them. Sad to say, Israel like us did not follow God's rules even in light of the warnings and instruments made available to do His will. He specifically said,

> And I will bring the land into desolation: and your enemies which dwell therein shall be astonished at it. And I will scatter you among the heathen, and will draw out a sword after you: and your land shall be desolate, and your cities waste.[655]

> And the Lord shall scatter you among the nations, and ye shall be left few in number among the heathen, whither the Lord shall lead you.[656]

> The Lord shall cause thee to be smitten before thine enemies: thou shalt go out one way against them, and flee seven ways before them: and shalt be removed into all the kingdoms of the earth... And thou shall become an astonishment, a proverb, and a byword, among all nations whither the Lord shall lead thee.[657]

How much more tragic can it get? Can a loving God destroy His own people? Will God stand by and see Judah literally buried in idolatry, become a byword, and not fight for their deliverance? God remained patient. With all their blunders, mistakes, failure to follow, the roller coaster experiences, the idolatry, the rule by judges, prophets, priests, and kings, He exercised patience, loving-kindness, justice, and grace in the hope of a total and unconditional repentance and response. Sad to say, the conditions only got worst. The records show that Judah sank to unprecedented levels in their departure from the true and living God. God had no alternative but to fulfill His word.

God's house of worship, Solomon's temple, conceived by David, but built by his son, should have been a place of worship to display God's glory, a monument of God's expectations, and to grant the world a knowledge of the King of kings and Lord of lords. Like the Queen of Sheba who visited Solomon and went away saying, "The half was not told me!"[658] God expected the world to visit Him in His house. The visitors should leave resigned to do His holy will having been confronted by this great and awesome God, the one and only true and living God, whom the Israelites called their Father, Redeemer, King. It never happened.

Are we faithful representatives? Do friends and family leave God's house where we worship with them, inspired, instructed, committed?

When David became king, he welded into a unit the little nation of three million persons. All twelve tribes had recognized him as their king, and he inaugurated the golden age of God's people.[659] That majestic age did not last longer than he and Solomon, his son, his immediate successor. Emboldened in idolatry, they lost the opportunity to be what God had specifically called them for, despite His personal intervention. May God help us never to lose our mission, our calling, our reason for being. It happened to Israel.

God visited Solomon twice at Gibeon. The first visit occurred at the beginning of his reign.[660] The second appearance came when he finished the construction of the temple, his house, and all he wanted to do.[661] Shut away within his gorgeous home, away from the glitter and the glamor of the temple, away from the flattery of courtiers and company, away from the light of sun, moon, or stars, during the darkness of night and silence, God granted him the greatest favor He could show and bestowed the greatest gift He could give—Himself.

During that nocturnal visit, God Himself, as clearly as He could speak to mortals, gave Solomon the *If-Then* philosophy of life.[662] If loyally adhered to, it would preserve Israel until God restored all things to Himself. Although he was the wisest man who ever lived, God left nothing unsaid for him to grasp. He did not speak in parables. He did not leave him to lean on his own understanding. In mercy He spoke of life and death. He rehearsed the promises and conditions and the consequences if disobeyed:

> And the Lord said unto him, I have heard thy prayer and thy supplication, that thou hast made before me: I have hallowed this house, which thou hast built, to put my name there for ever; and mine eyes and mine heart shall be there perpetually. And *if* thou wilt walk before me, as David thy father walked, in integrity of heart, and in uprightness, to do according to all that I have commanded thee, and wilt keep my statutes and my judgments: *Then* I will establish the throne of thy kingdom upon Israel for ever, as I promised to David thy father, saying, *There shall not fail thee a man upon the throne of Israel.*

But if ye shall at all turn from following me, ye or your children, and will not keep my commandments and my statutes which I have set before you, but go and serve other gods, and worship them: *Then* will I cut off Israel out of the land which I have given them; and this house, which I have hallowed for my name, will I cast out of my sight; and Israel shall be a proverb and a byword among all people: And at this house, which is high, every one that passeth by it shall be astonished, and shall hiss; and they shall say, Why hath the Lord done thus unto this land, and to this house? And they shall answer, Because they forsook the Lord their God, who brought forth their fathers out of the land of Egypt, And have taken hold upon other gods, and have worshipped them, and served them: therefore hath the Lord brought upon them all this evil.[663]

In that conversation God in no uncertain terms spoke of Israel's history. The promise was *"if"* Solomon would walk in the footsteps of the Lord as did his father David, *"then"* he and Israel would prosper world without end. However, *"if"* they elected to leave the path outlined, *"if"* they chose to follow other gods, *"then"* Israel would be a proverb and a byword among all people. Even the house that Psalm 48:3–5 said would catch the world's attention, where God resided in Shekinah glory, would be left in ruins. When the people would inquire why, the answer would be, "because they forsook their God."

We should never get the idea that God was bartering with Solomon. What we have before us can be discussed only in the light of the basic truth of retribution for sin. It was the same wise man Solomon who said, "pride goeth before destruction and an haughty spirit before a fall,"[664] and "the way of transgressors is hard."[665] With the opportunity of being the world's greatest nation in their hands, Israel exchanged those days, days of blessings and prosperity, for times of hardship and adversity. God's expectations were so lofty and achievable, but His people failed Him. Failure to comply with God's demands meant they would go into captivity. Moses had constantly rehearsed it, Joshua did, the prophets Jeremiah, Ezekiel, Hosea, Daniel, others, and Solomon whose words were just quoted. The rehearsals of God's plan effected no change in conduct or character. Neglect, obstinacy, turning a deaf ear to a plain "Thus saith the Lord" resulted in the serious consequence called the captivity. It involved enslavement, famine, the sword, fire, and a memorial, a warning that there is punishment for sin, even if long deferred. The attribute of God known as long-suffering—not willing that any should perish—suspended His wrath and anger against sin for years. The great God who fought for Israel would, and did, fight against His people in a battle they did not win.

Man's best position always is not to presume upon God's grace and mercy. Because Israel was God's chosen people, they were of the opinion that God would ignore their constant rebellion. He would not keep His word they thought. And yet, the reason for the exile, the beginning of it, and Israel's conduct during the allotted seventy years,[666] reveals a God we often fail to portray, a great and merciful God. He entreated Judah. He appealed to her to repent, to turn from her wrong course of action, and serve the Lord. He gave every conceivable chance for her to get right. He will not forsake or forget His children before, during, or after the captivity. In fact, He will demonstrate salvation for all mankind in a special way as a result of that experience. If only it did not get that far.

A small boy, new in the Sabbath school, was greatly pleased with his picture card and its text, "Have faith in God." As he was riding home in the streetcar, the precious possession slipped from his fingers and fluttered from the open window. Immediately a cry of distress arose, "Oh I've lost my 'Faith in God.' Stop the car! Please stop the car!" The good-natured conductor stopped and the card was recovered while the passengers looked on smilingly. One of the passengers said something about the "blessed innocence of childhood," but a more thoughtful person remarked, "There would be many truer and happier lives if only we older ones were wise enough to call a halt when we find ourselves rushing ahead on some road where we are in danger of leaving our faith in God behind us." If only someone could have called out to Judah… will call out to us.

Why the Captivity?

Seventy years seem like a drastic measure. It is important to remember that for centuries Israel and Judah, but particularly Israel, provoked God by immersing themselves in idolatrous worship. For over four hundred years since the temple was built, Judah clung tenaciously to Baal,

Molech, and other gods. The temple wherein God deigned to dwell, where daily sacrifices were offered, where all sanctuary services were performed, and where the Day of Atonement; the Feast of Tabernacles; the Passover, and other high services were celebrated—instead of granting a deeper relationship with the true and living God because of what those services meant—were rejected. Even with the temple in view, the priests on their daily round of ministry with blood to atone for sins committed, Judah had descended into serious idolatry. Instead of accepting God's gift of salvation as He ordained, they offered their children to Molech as sacrifices in the valley of the son of Hinnom. They outstripped the heathen nations in their pagan practices.[667] King Josiah's good reign apparently suspended temporarily Israel's conduct, but did not bring about a cessation and revocation of their ungodliness. Manasseh's fifty-five year reign[668] that created such havoc, and which revived the worship of idols instead of worship to the true and living God, filled the cup of iniquity to overflowing and God punished, exercising His judgment upon a perverse people. God longed for Judah to reach her maximum potential and display His glory, but she refused Him homage.

There are a number of beautiful things about God we have noted and will see. He never acts without warning His people. He told Judah who, what, where, when, why, and how long the captivity would be. In fact, God called King Nebuchadnezzar of Babylon "my servant."[669] God allowed him to bring about the judgment He promised and to fulfill His word. Judah's cup was overflowing. No help was forthcoming from God or the nations like Egypt or Assyria with whom they consorted.

> And the word of the Lord came unto me, saying, Son of man, set thy face toward Jerusalem, and drop thy word toward the holy places, and prophesy against the land of Israel, And say to the land of Israel, Thus saith the Lord; Behold, I am against thee, and will draw forth my sword out of his sheath, and will cut off from thee the righteous and the wicked. Seeing then that I will cut off from thee the righteous and the wicked, therefore shall my sword go forth out of his sheath against all flesh from the south to the north: That all flesh may know that I the Lord have drawn forth my sword out of his sheath: it shall not return any more.[670]

The picture Jeremiah painted declared absolutely no hope for Judah:

> This is what the Lord says: Do not deceive yourselves, thinking, 'The Babylonians will surely leave us.' They will not! Even if you were to defeat the entire Babylonian army that is attacking you and only wounded men were left in their tents, they would come out and burn this city down.[671]

God's will is inevitable whether to save or destroy. Judah would kick against the pricks as did the apostle Paul, only to find them hard and irresistible.[672] After over four centuries since the temple was constructed, and ten since the Exodus, God's children learned that it would have been best, not better, but best to trust and obey. But the tables had already turned on them. They were no more in a position to have God fight for them. When they came out of Egypt, weak, unorganized, no military might, no weapons, God demonstrated how "one man of you shall chase a thousand."[673] Israel, fresh out of slavery, unaccustomed to war, and weak, as they might rightly be described, possessed might to overthrow mighty armies like King Sihon and King Og because God fought for them. The conquest of Canaan rested squarely on His shoulders. God went before them, fought for them, and victory was assured. However, in the process of time, Judah dismissed God. They failed to remain true, faithful, and loyal. God cautioned them repeatedly not to forget Him. He provided for their daily sustenance, the strategy and diplomacy for every engagement to be successful, the possession of the Promised Land, and every blessing gained. Yet He received no honor, respect, reverence, or obedience. Israel easily forgot the *If-Then* principle God so carefully outlined to Moses, reiterated by Solomon, and others. They thought that if they disobeyed, if they refused to do the will of God, it would simply disappear. Sin is a failure to do God's will. It is rebellion against His government. It is choosing another master. It is saying no to God's direct counsel. Based on the experience of Israel and Judah, all of humanity would do well to always remember that God is who He declares He is—the Almighty. Then, as night follows day, our best position is to obey His commands by His grace, unquestioningly, no matter what. It will only prove to be a blessing here and in the hereafter, life eternal. If not, judgment will be on its way.

A survey of God's words reveals no alternate plan of compliance with His will. Only obedience can avert the judgments of God, and yet, at one time or another, all have been like Israel. Irrespective of the position held, standing, nationality, color of skin, whatever, somewhere along the line the individual's will has been flaunted above the divine will, His holy design for human lives, only to discover the approaching "then."

Can you imagine Jerusalem, a beautifully situated city, Judah's pride and joy, the center of worship, a house fit for the King of the universe, a place of God's choosing, a place for the very presence of the infinite God, razed to the earth? Would God really allow the Babylonians to burn down Mount Zion? Would God actually stand by and watch the Babylonians destroy the temple, take thousands captive, permit the brilliant minds and the artisans to be driven from their residences, the poor killed, send famine and the sword? Would Jerusalem's destruction be laid at Judah's doorsteps? God told them if they did not do His will they would become "a hiss and a proverb." 1 Kings 9:7-9

From the thirteenth year of Josiah the son of Amon king of Judah, even unto this day, that it is the three and twentieth year, the word of the Lord hath, come unto me, and I have spoken unto you rising early and speaking; but ye have not hearkened. And the Lord hath sent unto you all his servants the prophets, rising early and sending them; but ye have not hearkened, nor inclined your ear to hear. They said, Turn ye again now everyone from his evil way, and from the evil of your doings, and dwell in the land that the Lord hath given unto you and to your fathers for ever and ever: And go not after other gods to serve them, and to worship them, and provoke me not to anger with the works of your hands; and I will do you no hurt. Yet ye have not hearkened unto me, saith the Lord; that ye might provoke me to anger with the works of your hands to your own hurt. Therefore thus saith the Lord of hosts; Because ye have not heard my words, Behold, I will send and take all the families of the north, saith the Lord, and Nebuchadrezzar the king of Babylon, my servant, and will bring them against this land, and against the inhabitants thereof, and against all these nations round about, and will utterly destroy them, and make them an astonishment, and an hissing, and perpetual desolations. Moreover I will take from them the voice of mirth, and the voice of gladness, the voice of the bridegroom, and the voice of the bride, the sound of the millstones, and the light of the candle. And this whole land shall be a desolation, and an astonishment; and these nations shall serve the king of Babylon seventy years.[674]

Nebuchadnezzar and the Babylonians were also God's servants. God said that even if the soldiers in the Babylonian army were severely injured in battle, they would still be able to take Judah into captivity for those seventy years. God was serious about the fulfillment of His word regarding Jerusalem and Judah. A lack of appeals and calls to repentance, revival, and reformation by the prophets did not precipitate Judah's awful predicament. They had compromised themselves with the surrounding nations. The preservation of the knowledge of God and His truth through the teachings of the sanctuary and its services they buried in traditions. They suspended their high calling for idolatrous practices.

Here is a crucial point. In times past God fought for Israel and in every engagement with the enemy He said, "I will fight for you." Things are not the same at this juncture. God will use Nebuchadnezzar to fight against His children? God called Nebuchadnezzar "my servant?" No correction intended here, but Nebuchadnezzar was not a child of God or servant, in the same sense as David, we will agree. King of Babylon, yes, but a worshiper of God he was not. Call him an oppressor, an idolater, a heathen, one far removed from the household of faith. No Jewish blood coursed through his veins, although God is no respecter of persons. So steeped in idolatry, so brutal and heartless was he that he requested the flames ignited to destroy the three Hebrew young men who did not worship the golden image on the plain of Dura be raised seven times hotter. To indicate that he wanted to witness a swift meltdown, and destruction of life and property, he had them thrown into the fire with their clothes, hats, shoes and socks on.[675] However, his warped, cruel thinking would have been advantageous for the three. Death would have been swifter than a slow, low-burning flame. But God intervened. He was "His servant" and in that case Nebuchadnezzar had boundaries. Evil is often irrational and has no poise.

He darted upon the page of history. He defeated the Egyptians at Carchemish in 605 BC. He captured Jerusalem in 587 BC.[676] Under his reign Babylon became one of the most magnificent and celebrated cities of the ancient world. God gave him control over the world for a time. We know he was an idolater until the account found in Daniel 4:33–37, which describes his return to sanity and an acknowledgment of God. A great conqueror, he would take the whole world captive. He took over the reins of the government in Judah by appointing her kings. He quickly dealt a crushing blow to Jerusalem, the city of God. He occupied the position as God's final executioner of justice. He rendered a service of which he was totally oblivious.

A survey of Babylon's trips to Jerusalem reveals three. The first occurred in 605 BC. when Nebuchadnezzar took some of the temple vessels and deported some of the royal family and nobility to Babylon. Daniel, Hananiah, Mishael, and Azariah were among these captives. In 597 BC thousands of captives were taken in the second deportation, including King Jehoiakim, his mother, wives, sons, palace officials, Ezekiel the prophet, chief men, and craftsmen. In 586 BC Jerusalem was sacked and burned, all the vessels and treasures of the Lord's house were taken, and those not killed by the Babylonians were taken captive and the seventy years began.[677] It is a worthwhile venture to consider Judah's position in light of the fulfilling prophecies given during this time.

The prophet Habakkuk recoiled. He could not understand how a loving God could allow Nebuchadnezzar and the Babylonians to inflict such cruel, inhumane treatment on His people. Neither could he resolve how a righteous and holy God permitted Judah to go unpunished all those years. How can sinners be free from judgment that long? What's more, Judah's idolatry, wickedness, and apostasy, cannot be considered in the same context with Babylon's. Habakkuk passionately demanded an answer from the God of heaven, the great God of justice. He needed to be reminded that God is not indifferent to sin, to the wickedness of nations, even Judah, or to the transgression of individuals. Judah had fallen into deep national corruption. And in times of great crisis, in personal lives, or in the life of the nation, when the results of sin must be confronted or situations come that cannot be easily explained, God can explain every detail as to why—if He so chooses. The content of Habakkuk's heart and God's answer are given:

> Then the Lord said to me, "Keep your eyes on the nations around you, and you will be surprised at what you see. I am about to do something that you will not believe when I tell you about it. I will bring the Babylonians to power, those fierce and the restless people. They're a quick-tempered and ruthless lot. Their troops will sweep across the land and take places not their own. They will spread fear and terror everywhere. They're a law unto themselves and take pride in promoting their own honor. Their horses can outrun leopards, and their riders are fiercer than hungry wolves. Their horsemen are made up of people from distant lands and their horses paw the ground eager for battle. They swoop down from the hills like eagles attacking their prey. Their armies love to taste violence. When their troops approach a city, everyone is terrified. Their advance is like the desert wind. They take away captives like the wind blows sand. They laugh at kings and treat rulers with contempt. They scoff at fortified cities, and no fortress can stop them. They come and build a ramp and take whatever city they want. They sweep through the land and pass on like the wind. They feel no guilt and go on in the strength of their god." O Lord God, you are our God, the Holy One of Israel, the Just One. Will you let us die at the hands of these Babylonians? Have you raised them up and made them strong to come and punish us? Your eyes are too pure to watch such killing. How can you let such violence be done to your people? That's not fair! How can you keep quiet while these Babylonians are killing your own people? Yes, your people have disobeyed you but they're still better than these foreigners. How can you let these Babylonians do what they're doing? They act like animals, like beasts who have no ruler. They use flesh-hooks to catch people as they do to catch fish. They throw their nets over them and then drag them along the streets shouting for joy over their catch. They worship their flesh-hooks and nets and offer sacrifices to their weapons of war. They do this because their weapons bring them the best of everything and allow them to live in luxury. How long will they keep on using their swords and hooks and nets? How long will they keep on destroying nations and people so mercilessly?[678]

Had Nebuchadnezzar, that vengeful king, heard from the lips of God that he would be His chastening rod, I shudder to think how he would have handled all the nations that would be brought under his control, particularly Judah. A close look at what transpired on his three expeditions to Jerusalem, and a walk in the shoes of those captured, gives such a hurting feeling and an understanding of God's disdain for sin. There was starvation, death, humiliation, imprisonment, separation of families, and only the poorest remained in their homeland.[679]

While Nebuchadnezzar's treatment is instructive, close examination reveals just how marvelous God is at all times and under all circumstances. He used a vicious king like Nebuchadnezzar and the Babylonians to fulfill His purposes, but graciously mingled justice with mercy. Habakkuk needed to hear the words of Zechariah before he contended with God:

> Then the Lord gave me another message, saying, "For years I've told my people they must see that justice is done. They must be kind and merciful to one another. I told them over and over and over again not to take advantage of widows, orphans, the alien, who have come to live among them or those who are poor. But they refused to listen, shrugged their shoulders and paid no attention to what I said. They had made up their minds and their hearts became as hard as stone. They refused to take seriously the messages I sent them through the Holy Spirit and prophets. Finally I decided to discipline them. It was because they kept on sinning and refused to listen to me that I did not answer their prayers. I had no choice but to withdraw my protection and let the enemy come in like whirlwind and take them away and scatter them among the nations. The land they left behind became so desolate that no one wanted to pass through it. So they are the ones who laid the Temple in ruins and made this pleasant land desolate, not the Babylonians.[680]

It is so wonderful to know that proud and presumptuous Nebuchadnezzar, who thought he would humiliate Judah, acted under God's will and plan. How humiliating it must have been for Nebuchadnezzar when he imagined himself to be a great, successful king, a mighty monarch, that he really functioned and operated at the behest of the

King of the universe. As God's servant, he emerged on the scene to transact the business God elected him to do. Nebuchadnezzar operated at God's beck and call. It is good to pause, consider, remember, reflect, and be grateful that in every event of life, in every bird's song, every flash of lightning, every roll of thunder, every sunset and sunrise, every river running to the sea, every heart beat, yes, everything and everyone in life, come beneath the will of God, and everything does His sacred bidding. Although ruthless and brutal, treacherous Nebuchadnezzar and his people would execute God's corrective punishment upon Judah. The reasons were their departure from the worship He was due, walking away from His ways and dishonoring His name. He was never unmindful of the covenant He had made with Abraham, Isaac, Jacob, and most recently David. Judah learned that, "Justice and judgment are the habitation of His throne."[681]

God is no respecter of persons. He is God of heaven and of earth. Jews belong to Him. Christians belong to Him. Catholics, Baptists, Presbyterians, Muslims, heathens, irreligious persons, conservatives, Democrats, Republicans, free thinkers, rich, poor, wise, ignorant, intelligent, white, black, atheists, and agnostics are all His. Even if you do not recognize His sovereignty, the incontrovertible fact is that God knows everyone and everything, sees everything, cares about everything and understands everything. He is fully acquainted with every language, every dialect, and every word.

King Nebuchadnezzar of Babylon, vicious, not of Jewish descent, executed God's directives. That fact demonstrated that God can use anyone or anything. And if so, consternation need not be a part of the equation. He used a donkey to speak His will to Balaam. It resulted in an oral conversation between man and beast.[682] At the crucifixion of Jesus, God used Caiaphas.

> And one of them, named Caiaphas, being the high priest that same year, said unto them, Ye know nothing at all, Nor consider that it is expedient for us, *that one man should die for the people, and that the whole nation perish not.*[683]

Unknowingly, Caiaphas spelled out, articulated most precisely, the true mission of Jesus. He was bearing testimony that the sacrificial system was about to end. "For as by one man's disobedience many were made sinners, so by the obedience of one shall many be made righteous."[684] Caiaphas thought he would abort the Savior's purpose by plotting His death. While Caiaphas unconsciously met with the Sanhedrin to fight against God, that proud, cruel tyrant, that overbearing, ruthless, intolerant high priest, hid beneath a cloak of pretended righteousness. Yet he propounded God's divine will. He was condemning the one whose death would bring salvation for him and all mankind. God sent Jesus for that purpose. Classify Nebuchadnezzar as a part of the fact that God can use anyone or anything and then add, according to His schedule.

With Judah God would no longer issue the statement, "I will fight for you."[685] Just picture in your mind's eye this horrible scene. The sacred temple, the celebrated city, Mount Zion, fertile country, a land flowing with milk and honey, a favored people, exiled because God's long-deferred judgment arrived. Rash, fierce, swift, heedless, cruel Babylon with lion-like tendencies, dreadful and terrible, violently taking full possession of God's dwelling place and all its treasures stored up for years. What the Israelites contributed during and after the Exodus, what David gave from his personal resources, and all the kings acquired and stored went to Babylon with the people in captivity. The booty was gone. There was no impediment to Babylon's thrust to make Jerusalem a heap of rubble. Chained like prisoners they were marched to their new dwelling place, Babylon. What a bleak, black picture! Judah had received the shock of their lives. Idolatrous, sinful beings need to be reminded every day of how needful it is to banish sin and serve the living God. Religious experience must rise above form, profession, ceremony, liturgical exactness, and artificiality. Nothing but a humble and contrite heart is acceptable to God. For too long Judah clung to the conventional practices sprinkled with self and sin. The stench of it rose to the nostrils of God. He had no choice but to punish them.

The fact that God used Nebuchadnezzar summons some rather puzzling questions. They must be addressed, understood, and believed. It rises to a new dimension when Nebuchadnezzar knew nothing about God's will or His assignment as "my servant." Nebuchadnezzar never reviewed sacred Hebrew history and discovered that if God's children were disobedient they would be delivered into the hands of their enemies. He never heard a word of the pronouncements of Isaiah, Jeremiah, Ezekiel, and other prophets that Judah would go to Babylon for seventy years. He was totally unaware of the metallic man of Daniel 2 composed of gold, silver, brass, iron, and iron and clay. Although the head of gold represented the Babylonian Empire, he knew nothing of God's arrangement in history. The golden image set up on the plain of Dura further highlighted his ignorance and arrogance regarding God's plan. Nebuchadnezzar simply did his own thing. He wanted to last forever. The conquest of Syria, Egypt, Judah, evil and brutal in scope as it was, fitted hand in glove into God's purpose, as far as chastisement was concerned, and the all mighty, all knowing, and all seeing God allowed it.

Now, we are confronted with an area of God's dealings where, we must confess, we do not know. It is simply beyond our ken. We must tread softly. But we must examine the matter for deeper trust and an opportunity to let God be God. Upon close examination we must agree that God did not approve wicked human conduct and passions that brought pain and suffering to anyone. God certainly did not authorize Nebuchadnezzar's brutality, or will He accommodate anyone else's and then turn around and declare brutal actions good. For example, God did not watch as an innocent bystander when the Babylonians gouged out Zedekiah's eyes and ruthlessly destroyed his family.[686] "The weakness of Zedekiah was a sin for which he paid a fearful penalty."[687] He died as a result of his personal sin. God must not be blamed for his transgression. The same is true of the people during the time of Noah and the Flood. We read in the Bible that many in Noah's day tried to enter the ark as the skies darkened, the fountains of the deep erupted, and showers of rain began, but the rising waters swept them away. It was too late then. God had given that generation sufficient notice; they too died for their sins. Lot's wife perished on the plain. God cannot be held responsible. Man always has a choice.

Nebuchadnezzar will be punished for his inhumane treatment shoveled upon God's children. But in Nebuchadnezzar's dealings with Israel and Judah, God will use the experience to bring them to their senses. God does that on a daily basis with us His children. Judah would pay for their rejection of God. However, God wanted to make it the lightest possible punishment He could dish out. His heart of compassion would lead on a course whereby they would receive only a partial punishment.

> I have made the earth, the man and the beast that are upon the ground, by my great power and by my outstretched arm, and have given it unto whom it seemed meet unto me. And now have I given all these lands into the hand of Nebuchadnezzar the king of Babylon, my servant; and the beasts of the field have I given him also to serve him. And all nations shall serve him, and his son, and his son's son, until the very time of his land come: and then many nations and great kings shall serve themselves of him. And it shall come to pass, that the nation and kingdom which will not serve the same Nebuchadnezzar the king of Babylon, and that will not put their neck under the yoke of the king of Babylon, that nation will I punish, saith the Lord, with the sword, and with the famine, and with the pestilence, until I have *consumed them by his hand.*[688]

In light of the foregoing, we wonder how God could be anymore lenient. But He was:

> And Zedekiah the king said unto Jeremiah, I am afraid of the Jews that are fallen to the Chaldeans, lest they deliver me into their hand, and they mock me. But Jeremiah said, they shall not deliver thee. Obey, I beseech thee, the voice of the Lord, which I speak unto thee: so it shall be well unto thee, and thy soul shall live. But if thou refuse to go forth, this is the word that the Lord hath shewed me: And, behold, all the women that are left in the king of Judah's house shall be brought forth to the king of Babylon's princes, and those women shall say, Thy friends have set thee on, and have prevailed against thee: thy feet are sunk in the mire, and they are turned away back. So they shall bring out all thy wives and thy children to the Chaldeans: and thou shalt not escape out of their hand, but shalt be taken by the hand of the king of Babylon: and thou shalt cause this city to be burned with fire. Then said Zedekiah unto Jeremiah, Let no man know of these words, and thou shalt not die.[689]

Despite all the entreaties from God through the prophet Jeremiah, Zedekiah remained in opposition to the direct appeals.

> Thus even to the last hour, God made plain His willingness to show mercy to those who should choose to submit to His just requirements. Had the king chosen to obey, the lives of the people might have been spared, and the city saved from conflagration; but he thought he had gone too far to retrace his steps. He was afraid of the Jews, afraid of ridicule, afraid for his life. After years of rebellion against God, Zedekiah thought it too humiliating to say to his people, "I accept the word of the Lord, as spoken through the prophet Jeremiah; I dare not venture to war against the enemy in the face of all these warnings." With tears Jeremiah entreated Zedekiah to save himself and his people. With anguish of spirit he assured him that unless he should heed the counsel of God, he could not escape with his life, and all his possessions would fall to the Babylonians. But the king had started on the wrong course, and he would not retrace his steps. He decided to follow the counsel of the false prophets, and of the men whom he really despised, and who ridiculed his weakness in yielding so readily to their wishes. He sacrificed the noble freedom of his manhood, and became a cringing slave to public opinion. With no fixed purpose to do evil, he was also without resolution to stand boldly for the right. Convicted though he was of the value of the counsel given by Jeremiah, he had not the moral stamina to obey; and as a consequence he advanced steadily in the wrong direction. That king was even too weak to be willing that his courtiers and people should know that he had held a conference with Jeremiah, so fully had the fear of man taken possession of his soul. If Zedekiah had stood up bravely and declared that he believed the words of the prophet, already half fulfilled, what desolation might have been averted! He should have said: "I will obey the Lord, and save the city from utter ruin. I dare not disregard the commands of God because of the fear or favor of man. I love the truth, I hate sin, and I will follow the counsel of the Mighty One of Israel." Then the people would have respected his courageous spirit, and those who were wavering between faith and unbelief would have taken a firm stand for the right. The very fearlessness and justice of this course would have inspired his subjects with admiration and loyalty. He would have had ample support; and Judah would have been spared the untold woe of carnage and famine and fire.[690]

The captivity situation did not get simpler, it became more complex. In the midst of a terrible situation God did everything possible to save them without disregarding their freedom to choose. Nebuchadnezzar had options. *If* they would not resist, *then* Babylon would be their destination, their home for the next seventy years. *If* they resisted and sought to make alliances, *then* the punishment would be severe and unyielding, and they would still have to settle in Babylon for the seventy years.

> Now as soon as the king of Babylon was departed from Jerusalem, the false prophet deceived Zedekiah, and said that the king of Babylon would not any more make war against him or his people, nor remove them out of their country into Babylon; and that those then in captivity would return, with all those vessels of the temple, of which the king of Babylon had despoiled the temple. But Jeremiah came among them, and prophesied what contradicted those predictions, and what proved to be true, that they did ill, and deluded the king; that the Egyptians would be of no advantage to them, but that the king of Babylon would renew the war against Jerusalem, and besiege it again, and would destroy the people by famine, and carry away those that remained into captivity, and would take away what they had as spoils, and would carry off those riches that were in that temple; nay, that besides this, he would burn it, and utterly overthrow the city, and that they should serve him and his posterity seventy years, and then the Persians and the Medes should put an end to their servitude, and overthrow the Babylonians; "and that we shall be dismissed, and return to this land, and rebuild the temple, and restore Jerusalem."*—When Jeremiah said this, the greater part believed him; but the rulers, and those that were wicked, despised him, as one disordered in his senses.[691]

The people of Judah had set at naught the commandments of God for over five hundred years. From King David to King Zedekiah, they abused His laws. They were indifferent to His pronouncements.

While God's ways are past finding out, and a bold attempt can be made to exonerate God, as if He needs that, by saying, God used Nebuchadnezzar, called "my servant" to do the "dirty work" for Him. Let us never, ever forget that the infinite God, the ruler of the universe, answers to no one, and whatever He does is always right. God needs no exemption clause, or does a situation involving judgment need to be explained. He already told the human race that the wages of sin resulted in death,[692] and that "whatsoever one sows, he reaps."[693] If an individual or a nation sins and never seeks forgiveness and repentance and dies, the prophet Ezekiel said, "the soul that sinneth it shall die."[694] The Creator has given sufficient warning to justify any act of justice meted out. The fact that judgment came to Judah registered the righteousness and justice of God. He simply at all times and in all places employs whomsoever or whatsoever He wills to fulfill His high and holy demand. The fulfillment declared His power and faithfulness. "You will suffer the penalty for your lewdness and bear the consequences of your sin of idolatry. Then you will know that I am the sovereign Lord."[695] The Lord exercised every available option to save His children. He is doing the same today, as we speak. But there is a line.

From the days in Egypt, while God waited for the cup of the Amorites to be full,[696] showing them, the Amorites, His grace and long-suffering. He also waited for Israel to get it together, to remember His words, "thou shalt have no other gods before Me."[697] From the days in Egypt to the day they entered Babylonian captivity, Israel and Judah drank from the broken cisterns of the degrading idolatrous practices of the surrounding nations.[698] They forsook the living God, their divine benefactor, provider, sustainer, their rightful king; the one to whom they owed every blessing. The historical records are stained, soiled with their straying, imperfections and flaws, unbelief and heinous ingratitude. They were recompensed by servitude and significant loss of prestige and honor. God wanted to impose on them the glory of His presence to testify of His love and might, but they wanted a golden calf.[699] The nations whose corrupt practices they participated in and mimicked, even enjoyed, would be the ones to chasten them.[700] It was the prophet Isaiah who told Hezekiah that the Babylonians would one day return for all of Israel's treasure that he had on display when they arrived to hear about God's great miracle-working power. Instead of giving glory to God for his marvelous recovery from a life-threatening illness, and declaring what faith in a personal, loving God can do, he paraded Israel's possessions.[701] Nebuchadnezzar came and stripped Jerusalem naked just as He said they would. Nebuchadnezzar and his men took everything to Babylon. Her sons, daughters, vessels of and for worship, all the gold and silver, the very best minds, he razed the temple, and only the poor remained.[702] But praise the Lord, a remnant of faithful brothers hid the ark before it got into the hands of the Babylonians.

> Among the righteous still in Jerusalem, to whom had been made plain the divine purpose, were some who determined to place beyond the reach of ruthless hands the sacred ark containing the tables of stone on which had been traced to precepts of the Decalogue. This they did. With mourning and sadness *they secreted the ark in a cave, where it was to be hidden from the people of Israel and Judah because of their sins, and was to be no more restored to them. That sacred ark is yet hidden. It has never been disturbed since it was secreted.*[703]

God waited for Judah to sing Miriam's song again, to give Him praise and glory, obedience, reverence, and unconditional love, but most of all to reveal the relationship that God intended for His people to share. Instead, they sank to lower levels of ingratitude each passing day. They forgot that sin has a price tag. Judah, you, and I are ultimately accountable to God. While we, like them, fail to give due consideration, God will in due time take judgment for acts committed against Him, and oftentimes using the very idolatrous thing to repay. For example, an alcoholic will pay with cirrhosis of the liver. Drug and tobacco users, unbreakable habits but for the grace of God, will suffer from lung disease. The alcoholic, the drug and tobacco users will be enslaved. Instead of heightening hopes, better days, peace and tranquility, the results are disappointed lives, shredded characters, disgrace, and if no repentance is forthcoming, loss of eternal life. There is absolutely no high like the Most High. W. Jones says, "In the righteous government of God punishment is not arbitrarily annexed to sin: It grows out of the sin." Israel and Judah departed from God's commandments and they killed themselves. They clung to their idols. God in His great love for them had the sacrificial system performed daily, in their sight, portraying how the Lamb of God, His only begotten, would die for their sins, how to follow righteousness, and that the blood shed daily was all-sufficient but they denied Him access to their hearts. They spurned His love, grace, and mercy.

The strongest, loudest appeals found no responsive chords. It seems almost unbelievable that the invitations of God are rejected daily as they were in Judah's days. They had the daily sacrifices. We have Jesus seated at the right hand of God making intercession daily, every moment if necessary, willing and able to supply our every need. Salvation is available. It is "without money and without price"[704] and yet it is not accepted. And what is more tragic is the fact that we have the experience of Judah to profit from.

A look at Zedekiah's last encounter with Jeremiah might be helpful today in turning all God's children toward Him. Zedekiah needed to do only one thing and the record would have read entirely differently. Like the apostle Paul in 2 Corinthians 5:20 beseeching the saints in that city to be reconciled to God, Jeremiah in a private meeting with the king pleaded, asked, entreated, begged, requested, cried, solicited of him that he be reconciled to God. "Obey, I beseech thee, the voice of the Lord."[705] For Zedekiah it meant no loss of life, no destruction to the palace, the temple, the walls, the treasures, or anything because God set boundaries beyond which no one can go when there is obedience. The demand was not to obey Nebuchadnezzar or his army, not the Jews, priests, rulers, false prophets, but the Lord. He had one last chance to do the right thing. He recognized Jeremiah as the voice of God. Jeremiah pleaded, "Zedekiah choose right! Do the right thing." Say like Joshua, 'as for me and my house we will serve the Lord.'"[706] Zedekiah was afraid of man—who could destroy the body but not the body and soul.[707] Zedekiah straddled the fence and had no peace. Jesus said, "no one can serve two masters."[708] Zedekiah wanted the best of both worlds.

When the road we travel forks as it did for Zedekiah, and there are only two ways for travelers, you can be assured that God never leaves His children without a clear identity as to the path they must take. Those blood-stained hands, the Via Dolorosa, and a voice pointed, beckoned, and said to Zedekiah, "Obey, I beseech thee." And if ever the road forks, as it does always, indicating a choice has to be made, the exercise of the will, a voice, will always be heard saying, "This is the way, walk ye in it."[709] When the road forks, to wait in the intersection after reading the two distinct choices, and knowing which road is right, reflects doubt, disobedience, vacillation, uncertainty, and irresolution. Delay is danger. Where the road forks unquestioningly, follow the plain "Thus saith the Lord." When the road forks, it is best not to reason about the choices, especially when one path already has God's name stamped on it. Listen to Jeremiah one more time. "Obey, I beseech thee... so it shall be well unto thee, and thy soul shall live."[710] At that fork in the road for Zedekiah he had the *If-Then* philosophy to deal with. The appeal was urgent. It demanded an immediate response. Procrastination, refusal, and disobedience meant death and disaster. Zedekiah came to the fork in the road and the cringing fear of man decapitated him when it might have been well with him.

The great evangelist Robert L. Boothby told a story of what happened during a revival in Detroit Michigan.

> A young man gave a brief account of his conversion. Embarrassed with doubts and difficulties, he had postponed his choosing of Christ until he should have some questions answered. But, moved by the voice of the Spirit, he yielded himself to the truth in a full surrender to God, thinking that he would ask his questions afterward. "But," said he, "I found that after my surrender, I then had no questions to ask." Satan is pleased to becloud men with an atmosphere of unbelief and skepticism, but when they come to Christ, the light of heaven illuminates the darkness into which their minds have been submerged.

Zedekiah, like most of us, forgot that God's way is the right way, the easiest, the most rewarding, the way to life eternal and that God personally will take care of each traveler. Zedekiah parleyed with Jeremiah's "Obey, I beseech thee," then took the highway of his own choosing, the broad road, his own willful, selfish path and the dreadful *Then* happened. The final acts of King Nebuchadnezzar prophesied by Jeremiah occurred. The sons and daughters of Jacob were exiled in Babylon as indicated. If only mortal man could realize that his worst spiritual disaster is in the distance he is from his heavenly Father; that he finds his highest good in the heartfelt worship he offers, in the love he holds dear, in the obedience he renders, in the godlikeness he achieves, to his Savior, master, risen, ascended, living Lord and friend, life would be without an *If-Then*. Henry Drummond wrote a book about love entitled *The Greatest Thing in the World.* Certainly there is nothing greater in the world than the love that prompted Jesus to give His life for you and me. That love will not let us go; it is for real; it is not some emotional outburst, and it cost God's only begotten Son His life.

The Babylonian captivity chronicled more than gloom and doom. When God chastised Judah, Nebuchadnezzar's successive invasions had devastated institutions and people. God had in mind judgment, discipline, and ultimately restoration. Judah should have walked away from the captivity, that extraordinary experience of not being the head, but in subjection to Babylon, not bitter but better. If only they could have reminded themselves that all that was transpiring, God was in it, gone ahead of them, would remove every obstacle, provide every resource and whatever they dreaded He would take care of it, the captivity would have *been a cakewalk.* At the end of the seventy years a restoration would be accomplished and God would be glorified. God had high hopes and great expectations for His children. He said, "I will bring them back to live in Jerusalem; they will be my people, and I will be faithful and righteous to them as their God."[711]

> For I would take you out of the nations; I will gather you from all the countries and bring you back into your own land. I will sprinkle clean water on you, and you will be clean: I will cleanse you from all your impurities and from all your idols. I will give you a new heart and put a new spirit in you; I will remove from you your heart of stone and give you a heart of flesh. I will put my Spirit in you and move you to follow my decrees and be careful to keep my laws. You will live in the land I gave your forefathers; you will be my people, and I will be your God. I would save you from all your uncleanness. I will call for the grain and make it plentiful and will not bring famine upon you. I will increase the fruit of the trees and the crops of the field, so that you will no longer suffer disgrace among the nations because of famine. Then you will remember your evil ways and wicked deeds, and you will loathe yourselves for your sins and detestable practices. I want you to know that I am not doing *this for your sake, declares the sovereign Lord. Be ashamed and disgraced for your conduct, O house of Israel.*[712]

England's monarchs bear with pride the title Fidei Defensor—*Defender of the Faith*. Cyrus, named "my shepherd," God said it, like He did of Nebuchadnezzar, and spoken of one hundred and fifty years before his birth, would be the defender of Israel's faith and would assist in the redevelopment, restoration, and reconstruction of the temple, its walls, and the return of the exiles.[713]

We should never complain when placed beneath the chastening rod. All who live on earth will be tested and tried sooner or later before entering the city of God. God called Job a perfect man.[714] But God allowed total removal of the residue in his life by trials imposed.[715] Job taught us that when the trials come we ought to search for God's mercies. We ought to sing, "Thy way not mine O Lord, however dark it seems."[716] Nothing on earth is permanent; therefore, the trials of life are temporary. If faithfully borne, the results will be of eternal value. Never should we become impatient when the gold is in the refining process. Our heavenly Father sends or allows punishment to remove the dross and to grant a closer, more intimate spiritual walk with Him.

Jeremiah sent a letter from Jerusalem to the exiles in Babylon. It indicated that the events of life were in God's control, beyond human understanding and totally apart from any effort of theirs.

> Thus saith the Lord of hosts, the God of Israel, unto all that are carried away captives, whom I have caused to be carried away from Jerusalem unto Babylon; Build ye houses, and dwell in them; and plant gardens, and eat the fruit of them; Take ye wives, and beget sons and daughters; and take wives for your sons, and give your daughters to husbands, that they may bear sons and daughters; that ye may be increased there, and not diminished. And seek the peace of the city whither I have caused you to be carried away captives, and pray unto the Lord for it: for in the peace thereof shall ye have peace… For thus saith the Lord, That after seventy years be accomplished at Babylon I will visit you, and perform my good word toward you, in causing you to return to this place. For I know the thoughts that I think toward you, saith the Lord, thoughts of peace, and not of evil, to give you an expected end. Then shall ye call upon me, and ye shall go and pray unto me, and I will hearken unto you. And ye shall seek me, and find me, when ye shall search for me with all your heart. And I will be found of you, saith the Lord: and I will turn away your captivity, and I will gather

you from all the nations, and from all the places, whither I have driven
you, saith the Lord; and I will bring you again into the place whence
I caused you to be carried away captive.[717]

The letter clearly placed the judgment of Israel squarely in God's
hands. It revealed His unchanging nature. The seventy years must be
served. He spoke only once. It was unalterable. His compassion would
not grant a reduced sentence. But conditions of life would show His presence. They were to build houses, raise families, at least two generations
of them, have a lot of children, engage in agriculture, commerce, and
trade and like Daniel work for the government, become civil servants.
They were to remain free from idolatry and its contaminating influences, take a stand like Hananiah, Mishael, and Azariah. They should
possess the courage to say, "We will not bow down," maintain dietary
laws, and like Daniel and his friends reject all compromises with food
offered to idols and drinks consumed to blur the senses. Faithfulness to
God would result in His faithfulness to them, the sure hope of restoration for all the countries into which they were scattered and that would
be an absolute reality.

Of all the living conditions laid down for those in captivity while
in Babylon, one concerning their lifestyle piqued my interest because of
its ultimate results. God told them to have a lot of children. I wondered
why. In no uncertain terms God expressed present and future plans.

> And thou, profane wicked prince of Israel, whose day is come, when
> iniquity shall have an end, Thus saith the Lord God; Remove the
> diadem, and take off the crown: this shall not be the same: exalt him
> that is low, and abase him that is high. I will overturn, overturn,
> overturn it: and it shall be no more, *until he come whose right it is;
> and I will give it him.*[718]

Zedekiah, Judah's last king, covenant breaker and his family died
in Babylon. The children of Judah were told to have a lot of children
in exile for the faithful God would keep His word to David regarding
his seed to sit on the throne. Judah would never again have a king over
them, yet from David's lineage, the restoration in its fullest measure

would be accomplished. Christ, David's son and the Son of God accomplished it.

> Not until Christ Himself should set up His kingdom, was Judah again to be permitted to have a king.[719]

God told the exiles to have a lot of children. The reason, the Christ child was yet to be born. God's plan will not be thwarted. God's covenant with David will be kept.

Joshua told the children of Israel that not one of God's promises failed.[720] God's reliability is unquestioned. Every promise is kept, every covenant ratified, every word true and we can depend on Him. The promised restoration happened as God said. However, sad to say, despite all the fulfillment of His word, Israel never accepted His plan. Irrespective of Israel or man's acceptance however, God will honor His word. One day while in the temple, Simeon saw Jesus and cried out:

> And, behold, there was a man in Jerusalem, whose name was Simeon; and the same man was just and devout, waiting for the consolation of Israel: and the Holy Ghost was upon him.
>
> And it was revealed unto him by the Holy Ghost, that he should not see death, before he had seen the Lord's Christ. And he came by the Spirit into the temple: and when the parents brought in the child Jesus, to do for after the custom of the law, Then took he him up in his arms, and blessed God, and said, Lord, now lettest thou thy servant depart in peace, according to thy word: For mine eyes have seen thy salvation, Which thou hast prepared before the face of all people; A light to lighten the Gentiles, and the glory of thy people Israel.[721]

The Son of David and the Son of God is our Lord Jesus Christ. When He came the first time, He came as our Savior.[722] When God said, "I will give it to him,"[723] He did not speak of a continuation of life here as exalted as some of the kings in Judah made worship and the honor to His name. Therefore, He referenced the day when Jesus Christ shall reign as King of kings and Lord of lords. He spoke of that day when Jesus will restore peace and order to this weary, waiting, anxious world.[724] It is the prerogative of God to give the kingdom to whomsoever He desires. When Nebuchadnezzar, whom God called "my servant," strutted his stuff and lifted up his heart, when pride overwhelmed him, thinking that he and his government and kingdom would last forever, God gave him a gentle reminder.

> Until thou know that the Most High ruleth in the kingdom of men, and giveth it to whomsoever he will.[725]

We live in an evil age. There are wars and rumors of wars. The floods, famines, earthquakes, disasters by land and sea, peace treaties attempted apart from the Prince of Peace, men's hearts failing them for fear, the rise and fall of the stock market inducing greater fear, infidelity, crimes unimaginable, the lack of love in and out of the church, wicked and cruel persecutions and the time of Sodom and Gomorrah present. These signs and others assure us that "He whose right it is," is not far away.

There is discussion about commercial cloning, available to anyone wishing it; there is disrespect for God, arguments before the courts about giving equal rights to homosexuals and endless discussions of subjects that exceed our God-given roles. It cannot be much longer until the rightful leader comes and begins His reign of peace. Righteousness will cover the earth as the waters cover the sea. I am sure He will… and soon.

Years ago, theologians viewing the world scene would say, "It is minutes to midnight." I am sure it is now midnight and holding. Angels of God are holding the four corners of earth from strife until His servants are sealed for time and eternity.

After five hundred years Judah's kings failed to correctly lead and serve the true and living God and to abandon idolatry completely. He was compelled to send them into captivity. After another five hundred years God sent Jesus our Savior. This world longed for someone to rule in righteousness. The world except for a few, a remnant, was buried in idolatry of one form or another, captives to sin and shackled by customs and traditions. It is now over two thousand years since the Messiah came to inaugurate the work of complete restoration. Our world like Judah's is buried in sin. The question raised by thinking Christians everywhere is: how far is it to Canaan land?

Jewish captivity in Babylon lasted seventy years and finally restoration came as promised. The rightful King who came two thousand years ago promised that He is coming again to establish the permanent, eternal restoration we seek. I know He is coming again. He said He would, and He is faithful. This present world's faithful, believing, law-abiding, blood-washed, spirit-filled, redeemed saints will experience soon the joy of their choice. Soon all will be delivered forever from sin and have the privilege to enter the glorious kingdom of God, and live in the restored earth.

The same God who delivered Israel out of Egyptian bondage to go and worship (that was the reason Moses gave) is the same God who seeks our deliverance today. Israel left Egypt, emancipated with reparation, not because Moses worked some great miracles, not because they refused to make bricks without straw, not because the leadership negotiated a good contract, not because they killed the lamb, not due to any number of great circumstances, but simply because God Almighty intervened. He said, "When I see the blood I will pass over you."[726] They did not choose God. He chose them, and not because of their greatness or their goodness, for they possessed none, but just because of His great love and a promise.

We, like Judah, will be released from our captivity, emancipated, freed from sin forever, made joint-heirs with Christ, will sit with Him on His throne, Revelation 3:21, be like angels, study war no more, have peace like a river, receive eternal life, not because we love God, but because He loved us.[727] We will be there not because of works we have done, lest anyone should boast;[728] not because of any possessed righteousness, for all our righteousness is like filthy rags,[729] but because of His grace. God chose us. His only begotten Son died for us. The blood of Christ covers us. When God sees the robes of Christ's righteousness over us, upon us, we shall be called "the children of God." And praise God,

Jesus shall reign where'er the sun Does his successive journeys run; His kingdom spread from shore to shore, Till moons shall wax and wane no more.[730]

We have the divine assurance that just as God did not abandon His people during those seventy years in Babylonian captivity, in like manner he shall not abandon us. Today He calls us to leave Babylon. All the covenants and promises made to Israel are ours to embrace. He expects "the Israel of God"[731] to fulfill today His high and holy designs. When the Majesty of heaven and earth returns riding on that white horse[732] it is going be a wonderful day. He will reward His children and fulfill His Word, "that where I am there ye may be also."[733] We can begin to praise Him now. *If* He said it, and He did, *Then* He will do it. The restoration of all things will make it possible that never again will anything mar His new heavens and new earth. In God's great and awesome universe our long-awaited dreams will become reality. That day is not far away. Let us join John the Revelator in his prayer, "Even so, come Lord Jesus."[734]

Chapter 12

THE BATTLE OF ARMAGEDDON

On September 11, 2001 the whole world changed in an instant. It will be recalled as a day of infamy. The Twin Towers in New York City became the Twin Terrors. The United States of America was attacked with cold-blooded savagery masterminded by Osama bin Laden.

Two jet airlines United Airlines Boeing 767, flight 175 with 56 passengers and 9 crew members and American Airlines Boeing 767, flight 11 with 81 passengers and 11 crew members, both leaving Boston's Logan International Airport, one at 7:58 a.m. and the other at 7:59 a.m., plunged into the Towers. American Airlines Boeing 757, flight 77 with 58 passengers and a crew of 6 that departed out of Washington's Dulles Airport at 8:10 a.m. crashed into the Pentagon. United Airlines Boeing 757, flight 93 with 38 passengers and a crew of 7 left out of Newark's International Airport at 8:01 a.m. On that flight, some valiant men attacked the hijackers and ditched the plane into Shanksville, near Pittsburgh, only two miles and seconds away from Shanksville' Stoney Creek School. 501 grades K–12 students were in attendance.[735]

Under the guise of religion, these horrific acts of terrorism and destruction were perpetrated on our nation. Stories of bravery and tragedy captured our attention. Firemen and policemen going into burning buildings to rescue victims; people jumping out of the burning buildings to their deaths; or they were blown out by the explosion; hospitals and health care professionals who went beyond the call of duty are legion. There are those who to this day cannot adjust to what they saw on television, heard on the radio, or saw at the site.

Tuesday, September 11, 2001 will remain etched in our minds as a day of infamy. The horrific images stapled to our minds were committed by four flights that departed within twelve minutes, total. Between 7:58 a.m. when the first flight left Boston and 10:37 a.m. when United Airlines flight 93 crashed in Shanksville Pennsylvania outside of Pittsburgh, thousands died, scores were injured and hospitalized. It left a trail of blood, sweat, and tears behind in terms of the emotional loss, financial loss, and all the allied evils of such a conscienceless act. That data will never, ever be really computed. In fact, six months later bodies were still being found in the wreckage.

In the September 11, 2001 issue of *Time Magazine* writer Lance Morrow wrote, "The police screamed to the people running from the towers, 'Don't look back!'—a biblical warning against the power of the image."

In hastily called religious services, people sang *God bless America*, lit candles, and declared, "This little light of mine, I'm going to let it shine." President George Bush addressed the nation and said, "Freedom itself was attacked this morning by a faceless coward."[736]

After listening to the president of the United States speak in the moment of the crisis, and subsequently discussing with colleagues and friends the events of September 11, I have come to a valid conclusion—this historic event changed the way we do business.

Mr. Morrow said, "The policemen screamed to the people running from the towers, "Don't look back!" And so I write to all who read this and proclaim by voice to all who will listen, "Jesus is almost here, and the battle of Armageddon will be fought soon." That battle will change the whole world. The battle of Armageddon will bring about changes initiated by God Himself.

The war on terrorism will continue until those faceless, nameless cowards are apprehended and brought to justice. But the Battle of Armageddon will bring to a screeching halt life as we know it on earth.

The great God of the universe has an account to settle with the terrorists—mankind who has violated the laws of His government.

Human history will not be settled when the war on terrorism is won, if ever. The largest most profound question yet to be answered is not, "Will the war on terrorism be won?" The question that must be answered, by Osama bin Laden and every human being, is the same question Pilate asked the Jewish top brass: "What shall I do then with Jesus which is called Christ?"[737] That is the question of greatest importance. Human destiny moves toward a resolution of the question as to what will each person do with Jesus. Certainly, it will not be the adjudication or settlement of the war on terrorism, biological or chemical warfare, not weapons of mass destruction, not the extinction of AIDS, cancer, other diseases, or earthly freedoms granted, important and necessary as they are, but what has mankind or what will mankind do with Jesus who is called Christ.

The question raised is not intended to downplay or trivialize the impact of September 11 on the nation, the world, and those intimately involved with all that transpired. But over and beyond September 11 moves a larger figure, whose name is Jesus. He cannot be dismissed now just as He could not be dismissed prior to September 11. September 11 has brought into sharper focus what is ahead of the world and a wake-up call to deal with this priority.

Many have questioned where God was on September 11, 2001. Some have even questioned, why did He not destroy the evil plans of those vicious characters? Is He really a God of love? I answer without a moment's hesitation: He was at the same place when evil men crucified Christ, His only begotten Son on Calvary. Men prompted by the devil have endeavored to make God other than a God of love, one who allows for free choice in all His children. The cross on which Christ died answers all such questions. Christ is the Lamb slain from the foundation of the world. Jesus on the cross won our eternal freedom from death. The Bible tells us that on that fatal Friday when Jesus Christ died, that the veil of the temple was rent in two from top to bottom. It meant that Jesus, once and for all, resolved the problem of sin introduced by our first parents, Adam and Eve. The result is that anyone who accepts Jesus Christ as Savior is free from sin and its penalty. Man is now redeemed, not with the animal sacrifices previously offered, but with the precious blood of Jesus. That is not a maybe, it is a fact. Because Jesus lived a sinless life, died, was buried, and rose again, eternal life is available to all, even Osama bin Laden, if he would turn to God in repentance and ask for the forgiveness of his sins. "For God so loved the world, that He gave is only begotten Son, that *whosoever* believeth in Him should not perish, but have everlasting life."[738]

It is not God's intention for Christ to die so we could have eternal life, and then leave us forever in this world of sin. All that is left to complete what started two millennia ago is the return of Jesus Christ in majesty and glory. He said He would return. The activities of September 11 and what has occurred since then bring the world one step closer to the realization of that fact. Certainly, life cannot continue like it is whether there was a September 11 or not. People everywhere sense that the world is on the brink of something chaotic.

While on earth, just before His crucifixion, the disciples asked Jesus privately as they sat on the Mount of Olives, "Tell us, when shall these things be? And what shall be the sign of thy coming, and of the end of the world?"[739] Jesus enumerated a number of things to indicate that while no one knows the day or the hour,[740] some occurrences found in Matthew 24, such as the dark day, the falling of the stars, conditions as existed in the time of Noah and Sodom and Gomorrah would be helpful in narrowing the field. Jesus gave unmistakable evidences to the disciples, and to us, facts regarding His return. Then, as if that were not enough, He issued a word of warning. To validate the authenticity of His predictions, He said, "Watch therefore: for ye know not what hour your Lord doth come."[741] He demands constant preparedness and vigilance.

We shall see Christ in our day. Reference here is not to the setting of time, but the simple fact that when a person dies the next major event will be eternal life with Christ in the first resurrection or eternal death in the lake of fire with Satan and his followers. Jesus will be met either as Savior, Lord of lords and coming King, or as judge.

This world and its inhabitants are standing on the threshold of something cataclysmic, stupendous, and final—the coming of Jesus Christ in power and great glory. Each day the weatherman reports the forecast based upon the Super Doppler, an instrument employed in giving the temperature. The accuracy is amazing. Every now and then there is a slight difference that is hardly noticeable. Jesus is beyond the Super Doppler. There is no comparison at all. He has given us a last-day events forecast. The list is impressive. Some have already been fulfilled and others are yet to be.

In Matthew 24 He spoke about deceptions and impersonations, wars and rumors of wars. We have had two world wars, the Korean conflict, the Viet Nam War, the end of the Cold War in 1989, the dismantling of the Berlin wall, the Israeli-Palestinian crisis, the wars in Afghanistan and in Iraq, to name a few. He said nation would be against nation and kingdom against kingdom.[742]

Jesus said there would be famines. Every night people go to bed without food. Millions die annually from starvation. To compound the problem there is pestilence, droughts, floods, hurricanes, tornadoes, and earthquakes. Don't be afraid. This is only the beginning. The worst is yet to come. Jesus said it would. False prophets, deceptive dealers, the ascendancy of wrong, iniquity on the increase, and great tribulation such as mankind has never known or witnessed will be normal.

The people of Noah's time contemplated nothing but evil every waking moment.[743] Our world is experiencing a similar situation. There is no reverence for life. In cartoons, music, and movies violence is glorified. Witchcraft, the worship of Satan, psychic phenomena, practicing witches, spiritualism, and demonology are practiced within the borders of these United States, a Christian nation, and around the world.

In the book of Revelation we are told that four angels are holding back the winds of strife.[744] While the picture is bleak, and man and nature seem out of control, angels are preventing much more chaos. Just think what life would be like on earth had not God provided a shield of protection. While there is destruction and chaos on every hand, at the same time there is unprecedented advancement in space and technology. For example, the spacecraft *Columbia* which broke up over Texas in 2003, circled the earth every ninety minutes when on a mission. The computer has more information and can do more things within seconds or minutes of which the mind cannot conceive. Daniel predicted that, "knowledge shall be increased."[745]

In this the worst of times and the best of times, Jesus said the gospel, the Good News of salvation, how men are saved from sin and its penalty, shall be preached in all the world and then the end shall come.[746] So on radio, television, and personally, the Good News is being carried to earth's remotest bounds.

Jesus indicated to His disciples that,

> "Immediately after the tribulation of those days shall the sun be darkened, and the moon shall not give her light, and the stars shall fall from heaven, and the powers of the heavens shall be shaken: And then shall appear the sign of the Son of man in heaven: and then shall all the tribes of the earth mourn, and they shall see the Son of man coming in the clouds of heaven with power and great glory. And he shall send his angels with a great sound of a trumpet, and they shall gather together his elect from the four winds, from one end of heaven to the other."[747]

John the Revelator repeated what Jesus said, that immediately after the everlasting gospel is preached, Jesus would come. In his writings, the end of the world is portrayed as one great spiritual showdown. Revelation 14:6-12 gives a blow by blow account of what will transpire.

We have seen that the first angel carries the everlasting gospel. The second angel addresses the fall of Babylon, and the third issues the severe consequences of worshipping the beast and his image. The call is to worship the true and living God. Failure to do so will bring about this last and final battle called the Battle of Armageddon.

Many are of the opinion that an Israeli-Palestinian breakdown will be the cause for the last great worldwide conflict. The talk of Armageddon is heard everywhere, particularly in religious circles and on religious programs. Many of the discussions seem to say that the Battle of Armageddon will be in the Middle East, for the place called Megiddo is in the plain of Esdraelon in northern Palestine.

It can be established that the Battle of Armageddon will be the final conflict this world will see. The Bible says:

> And the sixth angel poured out his vial upon the great River Euphrates; and the water thereof was dried up, that the way of the kings of the East

might be prepared. And I saw three unclean spirits like frogs come out of the mouth of the beast, and out of the mouth of the false prophet. For they are spirits of devils, working miracles which go forth unto the kings of the earth and of the whole world, to gather them to the battle of that great day of God Almighty. Behold, I come as a thief. Blessed is he that watcheth, and keepeth his garments, lest he walk naked, and they see his shame. And he gathered them together into a place called in the Hebrew tongue Armageddon. And the seventh angel poured out his vial into the air; and became a great voice out all of the temple of heaven, from the throne, saying, It is done.[748]

The Battle of Armageddon is placed between the sixth and seventh seals. It takes place on the sixth, but it is fought under the seventh. In verse 14 it is called "the great day of God Almighty." If so it will not be political; it will not be an Israeli-Arab conflict; it will not be over economic issues; it has nothing to do with geography because location is not the matter under discussion, but **worship** is. God will be personally involved in this last, great religious conflict. It will be the final act in the great drama known as the great controversy. In this controversy there are two sides, and only two sides. God and His people will be on one side, and Satan and his converts will be on the other. It will be good against evil, right against wrong.

In answering the question of His disciples regarding His return, Jesus told them to "watch" for they were not given the day or the hour. John said of Jesus in Revelation, "Behold, I come as a thief."[749] This demands vigilance on the part of God's people; better still, a state of constant preparedness is encouraged. On the heels of the counsel to watch comes Armageddon. The prophet Daniel announced that prior to the return of Jesus, "there shall be a time of trouble, such as never was since there was a nation even to that same time: and at that time thy people shall be delivered, every one that shall be found written in the book."[750] Only God's people will be delivered. In a situation that is beyond description, God will vouchsafe deliverance for all of His children.

The Bible is its own interpreter. We are told where the three unclean spirits came from. One comes from the mouth of the dragon, the other out of the mouth of the beast, and the third from the mouth of the false prophets. They are described as spirits of devils; they work miracles; they go to the kings of the earth and of the whole world; and they "gather them to the battle of that great day of God Almighty."[751] The whole world will be gathered into this place called Armageddon. It is after they are gathered that the seventh angel pours out his vial. Then the voice out of the temple of heaven, from the throne says, "It is done."[752] When the nations are gathered together, man will have reached this climax. The Bible says it will be the whole world. Furthermore, the voice from heaven, the final authority will say it is finished. In this conflict God will step in to administer His wrath upon apostate Babylon. In this Battle of Armageddon God will deliver His people and end the great controversy.

> and great Babylon came in remembrance before God, to give unto her the cup of the wine of the fierceness of his wrath.[753]

Under the seventh angel the following will transpire.

> These shall make war with the Lamb, and the Lamb shall overcome them:[754]

> Rejoice over her, thou heaven, and ye holy apostles and prophets; for God hath avenged you on her.[755]

for he hath judged the great whore, which did corrupt the earth with her fornication, and hath avenged the blood of his servants at her hand.[756]

> The day of God's wrath and the deliverance of His people, the battle of Armageddon, will be an awful time for those who have not accepted Christ.

When the Bible speaks of "that great day of God almighty," and "the fierceness of his wrath," do not associate God's wrath as a divine temper tantrum. He is not a God who loses control. His wrath must not be compared to human passion. Anger in God is not passion, but principle; not antagonism to existence, but to the evils that curse existence. His anger is but love excited against everything that tends to disturb the harmony, cloud the brightness, and injure the happiness of His creation. He is not a God who is mad or has lost His cool. The wrath of God is divine displeasure against sin, resulting in the abandonment of man to the judgment of death. He says, "Fury is not in me."[757] God delights in mercy but, "The wages of sin is death"[758] and "The gift of God is eternal life."[759] All must make a choice—the Savior or sin.

> When God's wrath against sin fell upon Jesus, the precious Lamb slain from the foundation of the world, to be our Savior, His suffering was excruciating. It is the only time He cried out to His Father as God. "My God, My God, why hast thou forsaken me?"[760]

> He felt that by sin He was being separated from His Father. The gulf was so broad, so deep, that His spirit shuddered before it. In this agony He must not exert His divine power to escape. As man He must suffer the consequences of man's sin. As man He must endure the wrath of God against transgression.[761]

> Upon Christ as our substitute and surety was laid the iniquity of us all. He was counted as a transgressor, that He might redeem us from the condemnation of the law. The guilt of every descendant of Adam was pressing upon His heart. The wrath of God against sin, the terrible manifestation of His displeasure because of iniquity, filled the soul of His Son with consternation… The withdrawal of the divine countenance from the Savior in this hour of supreme anguish pierced His heart with a sorrow that can never be fully understood by man. So great was this agony that His physical pain was hardly felt.[762]

One day God will reveal His wrath against all who have rejected His Son, Jesus Christ, who became sin for us that we might be made the righteousness of God in Him."[763] The inevitable results of that choice, the rejection of His love and mercy, will be demonstrated in the wrath of God being poured out. When in love God gave Jesus, He died to redeem *all* mankind, so that *all* might be saved. The rejection of that offer of love places man where God can do no other than reject him.

John the Revelator outlines what the wrath of God is like in Revelation 19.[764] In verses 19 and 20 of the passage, John stated that he saw this massive army, kings of the earth, the beast and their armies poised to do battle. Included in that number were those that had received the mark of the beast and had worshipped his image.

In Revelation 16:13–16 a picture of the battle of Armageddon is given.

> And I saw three unclean spirits like frogs, out of the mouth of the dragon, and out of the mouth of the beast, and out of the mouth of false prophet... And he gathered them together into a place *called in the Hebrew tongue Armageddon.*[765]

The kings and the whole world spoken of in Revelation 16 and 19 are summoned to fight against God. It will be a losing battle for again we read in Revelation 17:12–14,

> And the ten horns which thou sawest are ten kings,... *These shall make war with the Lamb, and the Lamb shall overcome them:* [766]

There are only two sides; those who are loyal, called chosen and faithful, and those who are gathered in that massive army to fight against the Lamb. All kinds of deception and miracles will be performed to win the allegiance of God's elect, but they will have been fortified by the Word of God. If possible, the very elect would have been caught in the trap. But the promise is, "Because thou hast kept the word of my patience, I also will keep thee from the hour of temptation, which shall come upon all the world, to try them that dwell upon the earth."[767]

The prophecy of Revelation 6:15–17 makes it clear that the second coming of Jesus is spoken of under the sixth seal. The kings of earth will have a face-to-face confrontation with Him who sits upon the throne. They will encounter the wrath of the Lamb. The Word declares,

> And the kings of the earth, and the great men, and the rich men, and the chief captains, and the mighty men, and every bondman, and every free man, hid themselves in the dens and in the rocks of the mountains; And said to the mountains and rocks, Fall on us, and hide us from the face of him that sitteth on the throne, and from the wrath of the Lamb: For the great day of his wrath is come: and who shall be able to stand.[768]

Global events of enormous proportions will occur before the Battle of Armageddon. They will involve civil and religious liberty. The book of John the Revelator does not skimp on the details of these prophetic facts especially in Revelation 13. Its reading is a must. Take time to do so now in Revelation 13:1-4, 11-15.[769]

When the Protestant churches shall unite with the secular power to sustain a false religion, for opposing which their ancestors endured the fiercest persecution; when the state shall use its power to enforce the decrees and sustain the institutions of the church—then will Protestant America have formed an image to the papacy, and there will be a national apostasy which would end only in national ruin.[770]

Already preparations are advancing, and movements are in progress, which will result in making an image to the beast. Events will be brought about in the earth's history that will fulfill the predictions of prophecy for these last days.[771]

Prophecy represents Protestantism as having lamblike horns, but speaking like a dragon. Already we are beginning to hear the voice of the dragon. There is a satanic force propelling the Sunday movement, but it is concealed. Even the men who are engaged in the work, are themselves blinded to the results which will follow their movement. Let not the commandment-keeping people of God be silent at this time, as though we gracefully accepted the situation. There is the prospect before us of waging a continuous war, at the risk of imprisonment, of losing property and even life itself, to defend the law of God, which is being made void by the laws of men."[772]

The persecution when the Sunday law is imposed will be fierce during the time of trouble. The imposers will get to the place where if the law is not kept, death follows. But God will intervene on behalf of His people. In fact, when the date is set to exterminate those who hold fast to the Sabbath truth, and have accepted the righteousness of Christ, Michael will stand up.

And at that time shall Michael stand up, the great prince which standeth for the children of thy people: and there shall be a time of trouble, such as never was since there was a nation even to that same time: and at that time thy people shall be delivered, every one that shall be found written in the book.[773]

At that time probation will have been closed. Jesus will have already made his announcement.

> He that is unjust, let him be unjust still: and he which is filthy, let him be filthy still: and he that is righteous, let him be righteous still: and he that is holy, let him be holy still. And, behold, I come quickly; and my reward is with me, to give every man according as his work shall be.[774]

Christ's work of intercession at the Father's right hand, will be over at that time. He has been there with open arms of love, of mercy and grace, pleading the case of every repentant sinner, ready to receive whosoever will accept God's offer of eternal life. Like the high priest in the earthly sanctuary, which was a copy of the heavenly, Jesus, our faithful High Priest, will ultimately discard the robe of mediation, don His royal white robe of victory, and return as a conquering king in majestic splendor to take His waiting church home.

> The saints are exhorted not to fear the plagues at that time, for God will give his angels charge over them, so that no plague shall come nigh their dwellings; but such an exhortation would be useless, if the saints are immortal before the plagues are poured out... But the humble followers of the Lamb have nothing to fear from the terrors of the day of his wrath; for they will be sealed before the plagues are poured out.[775]

> When Jesus no longer mediates, all the signs He gave His disciples will have already been fulfilled. The seven last plagues would have fallen upon the rejecters of God's grace, those who refused the gift of His Son. The four angels holding back the winds of strife would have released them. Because we are living in the last days, this is absolutely no time to be lulled into a state of ease. If ever vigilance were needed, it is now. The last hours of earth's history confronts mankind. When that irrevocable sentence leaves the lips of our Lord, we will witness a time of unprecedented sorrow which no pen can paint. "We are living in the midst of an "epidemic of crime," at which thoughtful,

God-fearing men everywhere stand aghast. The corruption that prevails, it is beyond the power of the pen to describe. Every day brings fresh revelations of political strife, bribery, and fraud. Every day brings its heart-sickening record of violence and lawlessness, of indifference to human suffering, of brutal, fiendish destruction of human life. Every day testifies to the increase of insanity, murder, and suicide... The time is at hand when there will sorrow be in the world that no human balm can heal.[776]

When He leaves the sanctuary, darkness covers the inhabitants of the earth. In that fearful time the righteous must live in the sight of a holy God without an intercessor. The restraint which has been upon the wicked is removed, and Satan has entire control of the finally impenitent. God's longsuffering has ended. The world has rejected His mercy, despised His love, and trampled upon His law. The wicked have passed the boundary of their probation; the Spirit of God, persistently resisted, has been at last withdrawn. Unsheltered by divine grace they have no protection from the wicked one. Satan will plunge the inhabitants of the earth into one great, final trouble. As the angels of God ceased to hold in check the fierce winds of human passion, all the elements of strife will be let loose. The whole world will be involved in ruin more terrible than that which came upon Jerusalem of old.[777]

When the seven angels with the seven last plagues do God's will, it will not be pretty. The ingredients of the wrath of God unmixed contain painful sores, earthquakes; hurricanes will devastate the entire earth; islands and mountains will be moved out of their places. God will use hail as He did during one of Joshua's battles. Skyscrapers will fall from their foundations. The activities of September 11, 2001, when compared to that day, will be like a birthday candle held against a chandelier. Read about all that happens after the seventh angel in Revelation 16 poured out his vial.[778]

In this Battle of Armageddon, the Euphrates is dried up to accommodate the kings of the east. Who are these kings of the east? Although China has the world's largest population, I am sure that is not the east from where these kings come. What are we to understand that the water dried up?

There is also general agreement that the waters of the river Euphrates here represent human beings (cf. ch.17:15)... The waters of the Euphrates would thus be the "many waters" of ch. 17:1–3, 15 on which mystical Babylon sits, "inhabitants of the earth," whom she makes "drunk with the wine of her fornication" (ch.17:2; cf. ch.13:3–4, 7–8, 14–16)... the drying up of the waters of the Euphrates refers to the withdrawal of human support from mystical Babylon in connection with the sixth plague.[779]

If the way of the kings of the east is prepared, Revelation 16:12, and the three unclean spirits go forth to the kings of the earth and the whole world to gather them to the battle of the great day of God Almighty, Revelation 16:13-14, and if there are only two sides in this great controversy, then certainly the kings of the east cannot be from China or elsewhere in the east. What we have before us is the kings of the east and kings of the earth and the whole world gathered for battle. It is called the great day of God Almighty.

Would it be illogical to say then that "the kings of the east" (Revelation 16:12) are Jesus, the Lamb in Revelation 6:1,16,17, and God in Revelation 16:1,7,9? The Battle of Armageddon will be fought. Based on what we have discovered, every person alive will be on one side or the other. World conditions declare that day is not far removed. It will be a battle of immense proportions. There can be no sleeping on guard. The watchword is "Behold, I come as a thief."[780] Like the wise virgins, lamps must be trimmed and burning, and a supply of oil in reserve, available in case of an emergency should the Bridegroom experience a delay, waiting to rescue one more person.

When the Battle of Armageddon begins, and great Babylon comes in remembrance before God to give unto her the cup of the wine of the fierceness of His wrath, every person will be involved. As stated before, all the kings and all the nations of earth will gather to destroy the people of God. The primary reason will be that they refuse to worship the beast and his image. At that juncture the God of heaven will have a showdown with the dragon, all his angels, and all his followers/supporters.

When the defiance of the law of Jehovah shall be almost universal, when His people shall be pressed in affliction by their fellow men, God will interpose. The fervent prayers of His people will be answered.[781]

Babylon will be fully repaid for her deeds. The second angel of Revelation 14:8–9 predicts her fall and the reason. An invitation is extended to come out of Babylon and the reasons why.[782]

Those who accept the invitation and come out of Babylon, and remain faithful to God will not receive Babylon's punishment. If that is true, and it is, then Armageddon has nothing to do with East-West relations, political measures, or with man grasping the reins of government to execute judgment. This obviously is all about God fighting for His people and against His enemies. In Revelation 19:11, Jesus comes the second time on a white horse, "and in righteousness he doth judge and make war." His mission is to fight against the enemies of His people. Revelation 19:14 states, "the armies which were in heaven followed him upon white horses."

The Battle of Armageddon involves the Lord Jesus and His children who will be caught up in the struggles of the time of trouble, a spiritual war, and the forces arrayed against them will deal directly with Him who sits upon the white horse.

Over and over again throughout the Bible and in this book we have validated battles in which God has fought the enemies of His people and single-handedly won. God has had men on the battlefields, but the victories have always been His doing.

The triumph at the Battle of Armageddon will be no less, only of a greater magnitude in that it is worldwide. Victory is assured. He defeated Pharaoh and his army,[783] Sihon and Og, Amorite kings, and their nations,[784] the walls of Jericho came tumbling down,[785] 185,000 soldiers in Senacherib's Assyrian army died in one night,[786] and one day on Calvary, Jesus said, "It is finished,"[787] and won the greatest battle ever fought to win back man's eternal salvation. On that day He defeated Satan. It is over. All is over but for the shouting.

God has some expectations as we face the oncoming Battle of Armageddon. We should not be like the disciples in the Garden of Gethsemane[788] or the ten virgins who while awaiting the bridegroom[789] in a crisis hour fell asleep. Anyone who will be able to sleep while islands are dislodged, great earthquakes are occurring, hurricane winds are howling, and hail is falling from God out of heaven's arsenal deserves to sleep. God is greatly concerned that we ask of the Holy Spirit to be spiritually fortified. We will need Him in the trying hours ahead. Every Christian person should be praying,

> Nearer, still nearer, close to Thy heart
> Draw me, my Saviour, so precious Thou art;
> Fold me, oh, fold me close to Thy breast,
> Shelter me safe in that "Haven of Rest,"
> Mrs. C. H. Morris[790]

Jesus has already defeated Satan at the cross; the victory gained is ours for the asking. Christ's righteousness, will cover our nakedness. But God expects we will wrestle and fight the good fight of faith, and lay hold of eternal life, here and now. He expects that we will be ever so conscious that "we wrestle not against flesh and blood, but against principalities and powers,"[791] that the choices we make moment by moment will be right ones, and that His Word and promises will undergird us in the hour of trial.

A personal relationship with Christ must be developed before the time of trouble arrives. Prayer, communion with God, must be mastered. We are expected to seek Him like hidden treasure, while He may be found—better still, while He is still at the right hand of the Father. "Those who delay a preparation for the day of God cannot obtain it in the time of trouble, or at any subsequent time. The case of all such is hopeless."[792]

God expects that we will remain rooted and grounded in the faith of our fathers. God does not expect that we will be easily swayed from our convictions. We ought to say like the apostle Paul,

> Who shall separate us from the love of Christ? Shall trouble or hardship or persecution or famine or nakedness or sword?…For I am convinced that neither death nor life, neither angels nor demons, neither the present nor the future, nor any powers, neither height nor depth, nor anything else in all creation, will be able to separate us from the love of God that is in Christ Jesus our Lord.[793]

When Jesus no longer intercedes on mankind's behalf, all will interface with a holy God, the Holy Spirit and angels. Prayers will be turned into notes of thanksgiving and praise. But praise the Lord, the comfort and assurance of the Holy Spirit and angels who will "encamp around those that fear the Lord and to deliver"[794] will be right there.

In the Battle of Armageddon, God's children will be cornered, trapped, have no wiggle room, absolutely nothing will be available to them but to stand still and see the salvation of the Lord. That is an enviable position. Their faith and trust in God, based on experience, will help them recall previous deliverances, and recognize that the resources of God are boundless. Furthermore, God has a thousand ways of which they are unaware. The reality that *the battle is the Lord's* will take on new meaning. Helpless and alone, each person must look in faith and in prayer to Him who is mighty to save.

> The "time of trouble such as never was," is soon to open upon us; and we shall need an experience which we do not now possess, and which many are too indolent to obtain. It is often the case that trouble is greater in anticipation than in reality; but this is not true of the crisis before us. The most vivid presentation cannot reach the magnitude of the ordeal. In that time of trial, every soul must stand for himself before God.[795]

> Will the Lord forget His people in this trying hour? Did He forget faithful Noah when judgments were visited upon the antediluvian world? Did He forget Lot when the fire came down from heaven to consume the cities of the plain? Did He forget Joseph surrounded by idolaters in Egypt? Did He forget Elijah when the oath of Jezebel threatened him with the fate of the prophets of Baal? Did He forget Jeremiah in the dark and dismal pit of his prison house? Did He forget the three worthies in the fiery furnace, or Daniel in the den of lions? Can a woman forget her sucking child, that she should not have compassion on the son of her womb? Yea, they may forget, yet would I not forget thee."[796]

God will not forget His people. He never has; He never will. The things He has gone to prepare for His loved ones will be given them someday soon. The great deliverance in the Battle of Armageddon will bring to an end the great controversy. Never again will God have to emancipate us from anything. Christ's sacrifice on Calvary accomplished man's total restoration and redemption forever. Those are the gracious and loving acts of God. There is an abundance of proof that God will deliver His children. This says it best.

> Christ gave His disciples a sign of the ruin to come on Jerusalem, and He told them how to escape: "When ye shall see Jerusalem compassed with armies, then know that the desolation thereof is nigh. Then let them which are in Judea flee to the mountains; and let them which are in the midst of it depart out; and let not them that are in the countries enter thereinto. For these be the days of vengeance, that all things which are written be fulfilled." This warning was given to be heeded forty years after, at the destruction of Jerusalem. *The Christians obeyed the warning, and not a Christian perished in the fall of the city.*[797]

We have read and heard the counsel of our Savior as it relates to His second coming and the preparations needed. With every provision made for our salvation, this generation should exhibit a like faith and by His grace obey His voice and escape the wrath to come. If faithful, everyone whose name is in the book will be delivered.

The strongest language we can muster will be inadequate to express the completeness of the victory we shall ultimately enjoy. Just as Israel witnessed the Egyptians who perished in the Red Sea, as they stood on the shore,[798] and as the multitude mentioned in Revelation shall look on the scene of their former conflict and peril,[799] so shall we, each of the redeemed, be able to look over the past and see the enemies no more. We shall be more than conquerors through Christ. We shall sing the songs of Moses and the Lamb, songs of triumph and victory. Sin, temptation, evil, wrong, dangers seen and unseen, fears within and without, the slippery places for our footsteps, the roaring torrents, the deep waters that inundated our souls, the problems of life, and a voice of tumult will no longer be heard. We shall be overcomers like our Savior, because He triumphed and gave us His victory. On that day, that glorious day, when the saints of all ages sing that song of deliverance from grateful hearts, they will declare that Jesus Christ is Lord.

We are told that He has something special for the redeemed.

Sin and sinners are no more. The entire universe is clean. One pulse of harmony and gladness beats through the vast creation. From Him who created all, flow life and light and gladness, throughout the realms of illimitable space. From the minutest atom to the greatest world, all things, animate and inanimate, in their unshadowed beauty and perfect joy, declare that God is love.[800]

REFERENCES

KJV

NKJV

NIV

Texts credited to NIV are from the *Holy Bible* New International Version 1973, 1978, 1984, by International Bible Society. Used by permission of Zondervan Publishing House.

The Clear Word. 1994 by Jack J. Blanco. Printed and distributed by R & H Publishing Association.

Handfuls on Purpose, five-volume edition, 1971 by William B. Eerdmans Publishing Company.

Fox's Book of Martyrs, 1926. John C. Winston assigned to Zondervan Publishing House, 1967.

Josephus, "Antiquities of the Jews," Book ii, Chapter 16, Paragraph 3, Baker Book House.

Hymns of the Christian Life, edited by Milton S. Littlefield a.s. 1925 & 1928 by Barnes & Company.

SDA Bible Commentary, 7 Volumes, 1953, by the R & H Publishing Association.

SDA Bible Dictionary, 1960, 1979 by the R & H Publishing Association.

SDA Bible Students Source Book, 1952 by the R & H Publishing
    Association.

SDA Church Hymnal, 1941 by the R & H Publishing Association.

Pulpit Commentary, edited by H. D. M. Spence and Joseph S. Exell–
    William B. Eerdmans Publishing Company.

Arthur W. Spalding, *Who Is The Greatest*, R & H Publishing
    Association.

ABBREVIATIONS OF E.G. WHITE SOURCES

COL	=	*Christ Object Lessons*
GCB	=	*General Conference Bulletin*
IHP	=	*In Heavenly Places*
MH	=	*Ministry of Healing*
PP	=	*Patriarchs and Prophets*
PK	=	*Prophets and Kings*
R&H	=	*Review & Herald*
SOP	=	*Spirit of Prophecy Library*
SG	=	*Spiritual Gifts*
SC	=	*Steps To Christ*
TM	=	*Testimony to Ministers and Gospel Workers*
GC	=	*The Great Controversy*
DA	=	*The Desire of Ages*
VOL.1-9T	=	*Testimonies to the Church*
TMB	=	*Thoughts from the Mount of Blessings*

ENDNOTES

Chapter One Endnotes

[1] Deuteronomy 3:12–13
[2] Deuteronomy 2:24; 3:1
[3] Deuteronomy 2:24
[4] Deuteronomy 3:1–3
[5] Deuteronomy 2:34
[6] Genesis 6:5–6
[7] Deuteronomy 29:29
[8] 1 Corinthians 13:12
[9] Isaiah 6:1–2
[10] Revelation 15:3
[11] Genesis 1:13–21
[12] 1 Kings 4:21; 2 Chronicles 9:26
[13] Psalm 89:34
[14] Hebrews 11:8
[15] Romans 11:33, *Clear Word Paraphrase*
[16] Deuteronomy 7:1–9
[17] Exodus 23:32–33
[18] Exodus 34:12–16
[19] Genesis 15:18

20 Exodus 23:31
21 Exodus 34:11
22 Deuteronomy 7:2
23 Deuteronomy 7:2, *Clear Word Paraphrase*
24 Deuteronomy 7:2 NIV
25 Genesis 15:16
26 *SDA Bible Students' Source Book* pp. 195–196
27 *SDA Bible Dictionary* pp.176–178
28 *SDA Bible Dictionary Source Book* p. 195
29 Joshua 2:10
30 PP p. 434
31 *In Heavenly Places* p. 259
32 Galatians 6:16
33 PP p. 434
34 Deuteronomy 2:13–15
35 Deuteronomy 2:17–19
36 Deuteronomy 2:24–25
37 Deuteronomy 2:25
38 PP p. 435
39 Numbers 21:26
40 Romans 12:19
41 Deuteronomy 2:32–36
42 Dr. Porter in *Kitto Biblical Encyclopaedia* 111. 1032
43 Deuteronomy 3:1
44 Deuteronomy 3:3–7
45 Numbers 20:7–12
46 Deuteronomy 3:3
47 PK p. 570
48 Acts 10:38
49 John 5:18
50 Ephesians 6:12
51 1 Timothy 6:12
52 Hebrews 12:1–2
53 Joshua 13:7–8,12; 13:15–33; Deuteronomy 3:1–13
54 PP p. 437
55 PP p. 437

CHAPTER TWO ENDNOTES

[56] 2 Chronicles 20:15
[57] 2 Chronicles 20:17
[58] 2 Chronicles 20:1
[59] 2 Chronicles 20:21
[60] 2 Chronicles 20:22
[61] 2 Chronicles 20:23
[62] 2 Chronicles 20:24
[63] Psalm 50:23
[64] Psalm 90:10
[65] 2 Kings 8:16; 2 Chronicles 20:31
[66] 2 Chronicles 20:32 *Clear Word Paraphrase*
[67] 2 Chronicles 19:2,3
[68] 2 Chronicles 17:7–9; 19:8
[69] 2 Chronicles 17:10–12; 19:1
[70] SC p. 63
[71] 2 Chronicles 18:*1 Clear Word Paraphrase*
[72] 2 Chronicles 18:28-34
[73] *SD ABC* Vol. 3 p. 258
[74] 2 Chronicles 22:10–12
[75] 2 Chronicles 18:12–27
[76] 2 Chronicles 19:2
[77] 2 Chronicles 20:14–15
[78] Genesis 19:30–38
[79] Deuteronomy 2:4–5, 9, 19 (Emphasis added)
[80] Judges 11:17, 25
[81] Deuteronomy 23:3–5 (Emphasis added)
[82] DA p. 640
[83] Matthew 1:5–16
[84] John 1:12
[85] John 3:16
[86] *The SDA Hymnal* #618 RH Pub. Ass'n 1985
[87] Psalm 46:1
[88] DA p. 330
[89] Deuteronomy 2:4–5, 9, 19

[90] 2 Chronicles 20:13
[91] 1 John 5:14,15
[92] IHP p. 82
[93] Hebrews 11:33–34
[94] 2 Chronicles 20:12
[95] Acts 17:28
[96] Augustus M. Toplady, 1776 *Rock of Ages*
[97] 2 Corinthians 12:9
[98] PK pp. 198–199
[99] Psalm 20:7
[100] 2 Chronicles 19:6–11
[101] Acts 4:12
[102] PK p. 202
[103] Helen H.Lemmel (1864-961) *Turn Your Eyes Upon Jesus*
[104] Acts 2:1
[105] 1 John 5:4
[106] Luke 18:8
[107] Hebrews 11:7
[108] Hebrews 11:8
[109] Joshua 6
[110] 1 Samuel 18:45–47
[111] Mark 5:27–29
[112] 2 Chronicles 20:3–5
[113] Isaiah 65:24
[114] 2 Chronicles 20:15, 17 (Emphasis added)
[115] Philippians 2:12
[116] 2 Timothy 1:9–10
[117] J. H. Sammis (1846–1919) *Trust and Obey*
[118] Luke 17:17
[119] 2 Chronicles 20:18–22
[120] 2 Chronicles 20:17
[121] 2 Chronicles 20:21
[122] Joshua 6:12–16
[123] 2 Chronicles 20:22–24
[124] Matthew 28:20
[125] Horatius Bonar, 1857, *Calm Me, My God*

126 Fanny J Crosby *Victory Through Grace*
127 1 Peter 1:7
128 Hebrews 11:6
129 1 John 5:4

CHAPTER THREE ENDNOTES

130 Lamentations 4:6
131 Ecclesiastes 9:12 *Clear Word Paraphrase*
132 Genesis 32:23–24
133 Genesis 32:24
134 Jeremiah 30:7
135 2 Kings 19:9–36; 2 Chronicles 32:21; Isaiah 37:9–37
136 2 Kings 18:1
137 2 Chronicles 29:1
138 2 Kings 18:2
139 2 Chronicles 32:27–29
140 Isaiah 22:10
141 SDABC Vol. 2 p. 968
142 2 Kings 19:9–36
143 2 Kings 16:7–18
144 2 Kings 18:13 to 19:8; Isaiah 36:1–37
145 2 Kings 18:3–6; 2 Chronicles 29:1–31:21; *SDA Bible Dictionary* pp. 48-486
146 2 Kings 18:3
147 2 Kings 18:4
148 2 Kings 18:5
149 2 Chronicles 30:23
150 2 Chronicles 30:3, 23, 26–27; 31:1, 20–21
151 Matthew 23:23
152 "O, for a Closer Walk" William Cowper, *SDA Church Hymnal* 1941
153 2 Kings 18:3
154 *I Would Be Like Jesus*, James Rowe, #10 *Gospel Melodies*, RH 1944
155 Ecclesiastes 7:20
156 Jeremiah 18:4

[157] 1 Corinthians 10:*12 Clear Word Paraphrase*

[158] 2 Kings 18:13–16

[159] DA p.568

[160] IHP p.20

[161] 2 Kings 18:5

[162] Psalm 103:9, 14

[163] 2 Kings 19:3

[164] Proverbs 18:12

[165] Daniel 4:30

[166] Luke 12:20

[167] Proverbs 16:18

[168] Genesis 22:12

[169] 2 Kings 19:14

[170] Psalm 50:15

[171] Matthew 7:7

[172] Matthew 21:22

[173] John 14:13–14

[174] COL p. 174

[175] *I Sing The Mighty Power* Isaac Watts, Hymn *#93 SDA Church Hymnal*, RH 1941

[176] 2 Kings 19:15–19

[177] 2 Kings 19:20

[178] 2 Kings 19:35

[179] James 4:14

[180] GC p. 512

[181] 2 Kings 19:33–34

[182] Daniel 12:4

[183] John 19:30

[184] 2 Chronicles 32:7–8 (Emphasis added)

[185] Psalm 76:1–5

[186] MH p. 72

[187] Luke 18:1

[188] Acts 17:28

CHAPTER FOUR ENDNOTES

[189] Numbers 13:8, 6

[190] Exodus 17:8–13

[191] Exodus 4:14–16

[192] Exodus 24:13 *Clear Word Paraphrase*

[193] Numbers 13:8

[194] Numbers 27:18–23; Deuteronomy 31:14–23 *Clear Word Paraphrase*

[195] Genesis 12:1–2; 13:14–17

[196] Philippians 3:13,14 *Clear Word Paraphrase*

[197] Joshua 1:3

[198] Joshua 1:5

[199] Joshua 1:7

[200] Ibid.

[201] Joshua 1:8

[202] Ibid.

[203] Numbers 14:26–30

[204] Exodus 4:23

[205] Exodus 25:8

[206] Joshua 2:9-11, 24

[207] Numbers 23:19

[208] Joshua 5:12–13

[209] PP p. 488

[210] Hebrews 4:16

[211] Joshua 6:2

[212] PP p. 509

[213] Joshua 6:1–21

[214] 1 Corinthians 1:27-29

[215] Vol.4T p. 163

[216] *SD ABC* Vol.2 p. 994 EGW Comments

[217] Vol.4T pp. 164, 161

[218] 1 Timothy 6:12

[219] Philippians 4:13

[220] Isaiah 55:1

[221] Genesis 12:1–3

222 Genesis 12:11–20
223 Genesis 22:1–19
224 2 Kings 5:14
225 Luke 17:12–14
226 Matthew 17:27
227 Vol.4T p. 163
228 Exodus 3:8
229 Exodus 14:11
230 Jeremiah 31:35–36; 33:20–21
231 Exodus 17:12
232 Exodus 14:27
233 2 Kings 5:14
234 Psalm 119:130
235 Joshua 6:20
236 Joshua 6:22–23, 25
237 Exodus 12:13
238 Exodus 14:16; Joshua 3:17
239 Joshua 2:18
240 Galatians 6:9
241 Joshua 6:22–25
242 *SD ABC* Vol.2 p.199
243 Joshua 2:10
244 Joshua 2:8–15, 17, 18
245 Joshua 2:8
246 DA p.615
247 Galatians 3:28–29
248 Galatians 6:15–16
249 Ephesians 2:14

CHAPTER FIVE ENDNOTES

250 2 Kings 5:5
251 2 Kings 5:3 NKJV
252 2 Kings 5:14
253 2 Kings 6:8–10
254 Hebrews 4:13

[255] 2 Kings 6:12–14

[256] 2 Kings 6:11

[257] Job 22:12-14 *Clear Word Paraphrase*

[258] Psalm 147:4

[259] Genesis 15:5

[260] Job 9:9–10

[261] Luke 18:13

[262] Genesis 11:5

[263] Genesis 9:1

[264] Genesis 117

[265] Genesis 9:13–15

[266] Genesis 25:23

[267] Genesis 27

[268] Jeremiah 23:23–24

[269] Genesis 15:13

[270] Exodus 12:41

[271] Hebrews 4:13

[272] Genesis 16:13

[273] SDABC Vol. 2 p. 884

[274] 2 Kings 6:15

[275] 2 Kings 6:16

[276] Ibid

[277] Genesis 15:1

[278] Genesis 46:3–4

[279] Exodus 14:13

[280] Numbers 14:9

[281] Deuteronomy 1:21

[282] Isaiah 43:1

[283] Luke 12:32

[284] John 14:27

[285] SDABC Vol. 2 p. 884

[286] 2 Kings 6:17

[287] Matthew 28:20

[288] Psalm 27:1

[289] *The Saviour With Me*, Lizzie Edwards, *Christ In Song*, #541

[290] Psalm 46:1

291 Proverbs 18:10
292 2 Kings 6:17
293 2 Kings 6:16
294 Deuteronomy 20:1
295 2 Kings 6:17
296 Psalm 8:4–5
297 Luke 20:34–36
298 Psalm 68:17 NIV
299 Psalm 68:17 *Clear Word Paraphrase*
300 Hebrews 1:14
301 Genesis 28:12–13
302 Psalm 34:7
303 Matthew 18:10
304 DA pp. 693, 694
305 DA pp. 779, 780
306 Genesis 32:1–2
307 Acts 12:1–19
308 Daniel 6:20
309 Daniel 6:22
310 PK p. 587
311 Matthew 21:22 NIV
312 James 5:17
313 2 Kings 6:17
314 2 Kings 6:18
315 2 Kings 6:20
316 2 Kings 6:19
317 2 Kings 6:20
318 2 Kings 6:21
319 Romans 12:17–21 *Clear Word Paraphrase*
320 Matthew 5:39
321 Matthew 5:41
322 Romans 12:20
323 2 Kings 6:22
324 2 Kings 6:21
325 2 Kings 6:23
326 Judges 3:1–4.

[327] *Handfuls on Purpose*, Vol. 2 page 118
[328] Judges 6:2–6
[329] Judges 6:10
[330] Lamentations 3:22–23
[331] DA 266
[332] Psalm 139:9–10
[333] DA 669, 670.
[334] DA 667.
[335] 1 John 4:16
[336] Hosea 11:8
[337] Jeremiah 31:3.
[338] Luke 15:4.
[339] Judges 6:12
[340] Judges 6:15
[341] Judges 6:12
[342] Romans 8:31
[343] Exodus 3:11
[344] 1 Samuel 9:21
[345] 1 Corinthians 1:27
[346] 1 Corinthians 12:10
[347] Judges 6:14
[348] Isaiah 6:8
[349] Judges 9:46
[350] Genesis 3:10
[351] Judges 6:29–31
[352] Matthew 6:24
[353] Judges 6:34–35
[354] Judges 6:36–40
[355] Psalm 103:14
[356] Isaiah 40:29
[357] Psalm 139:23
[358] Judges 7:12
[359] Judges 7:9
[360] Judges 7:13–15
[361] Judges 7:16–22
[362] Judges 7:22

363 Judges 7:12
364 Judges 7:25
365 Judges 8:10
366 Judges 7:20
367 Acts 17:6
368 Zechariah 4:6
369 Proverbs 21:31
370 Judges 7:17–18
371 John 2:5
372 Judges 7:18
373 Judges 8:22
374 *Hymns of the Christian Life* #294, *Lead Me to Calvary* by Jennie Evelyn Hussey

CHAPTER SEVEN ENDNOTES

375 Acts 7:9
376 Exodus 12:27–33
377 Exodus 1:7–12
378 Genesis 39:5
379 Exodus 12:33
380 Exodus 13:17–18
381 Exodus 14:5–8
382 Exodus 14:9–12
383 Romans 15:4
384 Exodus 14:13–14
385 2 Chronicles 20;15–17
386 Exodus 14:13
387 2 Chronicles 20:17
388 Exodus 14:14
389 2 Chronicles 20:15–17
390 Exodus 14:13
391 2 Chronicles 20:15
392 Exodus 14:4
393 Exodus 14:4
394 Exodus 12:37–38

[395] Exodus 9:14 (Emphasis added)
[396] Psalm 24:1
[397] Isaiah 45:5–6
[398] Isaiah 44:8
[399] Isaiah 43:10–11
[400] Exodus 12:31–33
[401] Exodus 5:2 NIV
[402] Psalm 50:23
[403] Exodus 12
[404] Exodus 14:4
[405] Exodus 14:1–3
[406] *Handfuls On Purpose*, Series 2 p. 73
[407] Exodus 14:10–12
[408] Exodus 14:4
[409] TMB pp.15, 105
[410] GC pp. 108-110
[411] Exodus 14:11
[412] Job 13:15
[413] *What a Friend We Have in Jesus*, J. M. Scriven, Hymn # 320 *SDA Church Hymnal*, RH 1941
[414] Exodus 14:2
[415] Psalm 37 & 73
[416] Exodus 5:1
[417] Exodus 14:13–15
[418] Exodus 14:4
[419] Exodus 14:13
[420] Exodus 14:19
[421] Exodus 14:19–20
[422] Exodus 14:24

CHAPTER EIGHT ENDNOTES

[423] Jude 6
[424] Revelation 12:7–8
[425] Revelation 12:9
[426] Esther 1:6

427 RH Jan. 28, 1909 (Emphasis added)
428 Joshua 7:20–21
429 Joshua 9:4; 10:28
430 Joshua 7:2
431 Joshua 7:3–4
432 Joshua 7:1
433 Job 28:24 NIV
434 Joshua 7:5
435 PP pp. 497, 496
436 Joshua 7:6
437 Joshua 7:7–9
438 Joshua 1:5
439 Exodus 14:11
440 PK p. 164
441 Jude 24
442 Exodus 2:15
443 Longfellow's *Ladder of St. Augustine*
444 Joshua 7:7
445 Joshua 7:10–12
446 Genesis 15:16
447 Joshua 8:34–35
448 Deuteronomy 31:10
449 Joshua 9:1
450 Joshua 9:2
451 Mark 1513–14
452 Matthew 27:25
453 Deuteronomy 7:1–3
454 Exodus 23:32–33
455 Deuteronomy 20:17–18
456 Deuteronomy 20:10–16 (Emphasis added)
457 Joshua 9:6, 9, 11 (Emphasis added)
458 Joshua 9:7
459 Matthew 10:16
460 Joshua 9:14 (Emphasis added)
461 Philippians 4:6
462 1 Thessalonians 5:17

[463] PK p. 31
[464] Numbers 27:21 *Clear Word Paraphrase* (Emphasis added)
[465] Joshua 7:2
[466] Genesis 22:2
[467] Genesis 37:5
[468] Exodus 3:2
[469] Numbers 27:21
[470] Judges 6:37
[471] Jonah 1:7
[472] 1 Kings 19:12
[473] Isaiah 38:8
[474] Matthew 2:2
[475] John 1:14
[476] John 14:26
[477] Joshua 9:9
[478] *SDA Bible Dictionary* p. 418
[479] Numbers 32:23
[480] Joshua 9:23
[481] Joshua 9:23 *Clear Word Paraphrase*
[482] *Pulpit Commentary* Vol. 3 p. 159
[483] Ephesians 4:25
[484] Romans 12:21
[485] Joshua 9:21
[486] Genesis 27:20
[487] 1 Kings 8:46, 49–50
[488] Romans 3:23
[489] Psalm 14:2–3 (Emphasis added)
[490] SC p. 62 (Emphasis added)
[491] Joshua 10:4
[492] Matthew 10:34
[493] 2 Timothy 3:12 (Emphasis added)
[494] Joshua 10:6
[495] John 6:37
[496] Joshua 10:8
[497] *SD ABC* Vol. 2 p. 255
[498] Joshua 10:10–11

[499] Joshua 10:12–13
[500] Job 11:17
[501] GCB Feb. 18, 1897
[502] Exodus 14:22
[503] Joshua 3:16
[504] Joshua 10:14 (Emphasis added)
[505] Exodus 9:23
[506] Job 38:22
[507] Joshua 10:16
[508] Joshua 10:17–19
[509] Ephesians 6:12
[510] 1 Corinthians 1:30
[511] Luke 18:7,8
[512] Hebrews 7:25
[513] Luke 19:10
[514] Joshua 10:15
[515] Philippians 4:13
[516] Isaiah 54:17

CHAPTER NINE ENDNOTES

[518] Arthur W. Spalding, *Who is the Greatest*, pp. 22–23
[519] Deuteronomy 2:4–5, 9,18–19
[520] Numbers 22–25
[521] Deuteronomy 23:3–6
[522] Nehemiah 13:1–2
[523] 2 Kings 3:4–5
[524] 2 Kings 3:9
[525] Arthur W. Spalding, *Who is the Greatest*, p. 22
[526] Psalm 19:1
[527] 1 Kings 21:1–14
[528] 2 Kings 3:2–3
[529] Matthew 6:24
[530] Revelation 3:15–16
[531] John 3:7
[532] Jeremiah 13:23; 17:9

[533] SC pp. 26, 31
[534] 2 Chronicles 17:9
[535] 2 Chronicles 17:7–9
[536] 2 Chronicles 18:3
[537] 2 Chronicles 20:29–30
[538] 2 Chronicles 18:1
[539] 2 Chronicles 18:28–29
[540] 2 Chronicles 20:36–37
[541] Exodus 20:3
[542] 2 Kings 3:4–9
[543] 2 Kings 3:9–10
[544] Psalm 127:1
[545] SOP Library Vol. 3 p.18
[546] John 15:5
[547] 2 Kings 3:11–12
[548] 2 Kings 3:11
[549] 1 Kings 3:12
[550] 1 Kings 18:1
[551] 1 Kings 3:12
[552] Luke 15:14–17
[553] John 3:1
[554] 2 Kings 3:13
[555] 1 Kings 22:27
[556] 1 Kings 19:2
[557] 2 Kings 3:13–14 (Emphasis added)
[558] 2 Kings 3:15
[559] William Congreve, *The Mourning Bride*, Act 1, Scene 1
[560] Psalm 27:1, 4–5
[561] Psalm 103:1–2
[562] Zephaniah 3:17
[563] 2 Kings 3:16–17 (Emphasis added)
[564] DA p. 330
[565] Isaiah 55:8
[566] 2 Kings 3:18
[567] Exodus 20:8–11
[568] Malachi 3:10

[569] 2 Kings 3:16–18 *Clear Word Paraphrase*
[570] Acts 16:31
[571] Luke 23: 42
[572] Hebrews 7:25
[573] Zechariah 4:6
[574] 2 Kings 3:20–27
[575] Deuteronomy 20:19–20
[576] Arthur W. Spalding, *Who is the Greatest*, pp. 22, 23

CHAPTER TEN ENDNOTES

[577] 1 Samuel 11:1–6
[578] 1 Samuel 11:7
[579] 1 Samuel 11:8
[580] 1 Samuel 11:11
[581] Deuteronomy 2:19
[582] Deuteronomy 7:1–5
[583] 1 Samuel 13:2
[584] 1 Samuel 13:3
[585] *SD ABC* Vol. 2, p. 507
[586] 1 Samuel 13:4–5
[587] 1 Samuel 13:6
[588] Genesis 22
[589] 1 Samuel 14:6 (Emphasis added)
[590] 1 Samuel 13:5 (Emphasis added)
[591] 1 Samuel 14:2 (Emphasis added)
[592] *SD ABC* Vol. 2 pp. 511, 512
[593] 1 Samuel 14:7
[594] 1 Samuel 14: 8–12 *Clear Word Paraphrase*
[595] 1 Samuel 14:10
[596] Romans 4:21
[597] 1 Samuel 14:12
[598] 1 Samuel 14:12, 4–5
[599] *SDA Bible Dictionary* pp. 160, 1003
[600] DA p. 657 (Emphasis added)

601 1 Samuel 14:6
602 Isaiah 37:36
603 John 3:16
604 Romans 5:8
605 1 Samuel 14:14
606 Philippians 1:6
607 Hebrews 6:10 NIV
608 1 Samuel 14:15
609 1 Samuel 14:20
610 1 Samuel 14:52 *Clear Word Paraphrase* (Emphasis added)
611 Deuteronomy 32:30
612 Joshua 23:10
613 Matthew 14:13-21
614 John 5:1-15
615 1 Kings 18
616 1 Kings 19:18
617 TM p. 15
618 1 Samuel 14:7
619 1 Samuel 14:7
620 1 Samuel 14:24–45
621 Daniel 1–3
622 Matthew 17:1–13
623 Acts 16:1–4
624 2 Timothy 4:11
625 Acts 15:40
626 Acts 15:22
627 Ruth 1:14–19
628 1 Samuel 20:17; 2 Samuel 1:26
629 1 Peter 1:18
630 John 13:1
631 Proverbs 18:24
632 1 Samuel 14:23
633 Joshua 23:10
634 Matthew 19:26

Chapter Eleven Endnotes

635 Ezekiel 21:27 (Emphasis added)
636 Galatians 6:16
637 Daniel 2:45
638 Exodus 3:18
639 Genesis 46:29; 47:11
640 Exodus 7:17
641 Exodus 8:1
642 Exodus 9:1
643 Exodus 10:3
644 Genesis 12:1, 7; 13:14–15; 15:18–23; 17:8
645 Genesis 26:3,4
646 Genesis 28:13–15; 35:12
647 Genesis 50:24–25
648 *Works of Josephus*, Ant. Book 11 Chapter XV.2
649 Exodus 13:5
650 Exodus 23:31
651 Joshua 183
652 Exodus 16:15–21
653 Exodus 23:24
654 Joshua 23:6, 9, 11–15
655 Leviticus 26:32–33
656 Deuteronomy 4:27
657 Deuteronomy 28:25, 37
658 1 Kings 10:7
659 1 Chronicles 11:1–3
660 1 Kings 3:5
661 1 Kings 9:1–2
662 1 Kings 9:4–7
663 1 Kings 9:3–9 (Emphasis added)
664 Proverbs 16:8
665 Proverbs 13:15
666 2 Chronicles 36:21
667 2 Chronicles 33:6, 9
668 2 Kings 21:1–2

[669] Jeremiah 27:4–22

[670] Ezekiel 21:1–5

[671] Jeremiah 37:9–10 NIV

[672] Acts 9:5

[673] Joshua 23:10

[674] Jeremiah 25:3–11

[675] Daniel 3:21

[676] SDABC Vol.4 p. 347

[677] 2 Chronicles 36:18–20; SD ABC Vol. 4 pp.347, 348

[678] Habakkuk 1:5–17 *Clear Word Paraphrase*

[679] 2 Kings 24:14; 25:12

[680] Zechariah 7:8-14 *Clear Word Paraphrase*

[681] Psalm 89:14

[682] Numbers 22:23–35

[683] John 11:49–50 (Emphasis added)

[684] Romans 5:19

[685] Exodus 14:14

[686] Jeremiah 39:6–7

[687] PK p. 458

[688] Jeremiah 27:5–8

[689] Jeremiah 38:19–23

[690] PK pp. 457, 458

[691] Josephus *Book X* Chapter VII para.3

[692] Romans 6:23

[693] Galatians 6:7

[694] Ezekiel 18:4

[695] Ezekiel 23:49 NIV

[696] Genesis 15:16

[697] Exodus 20:3

[698] Ezekiel 23

[699] Exodus 32

[700] Ezekiel 23:20, 24

[701] Isaiah 39:6

[702] 2 Kings 24:13–14

[703] PK p. 453 (Emphasis added)

[704] Isaiah 55:1

705 Jeremiah 38:20
706 Joshua 24:15
707 Luke 12:4
708 Matthew 6:24
709 Isaiah 30:21
710 Jeremiah 38:20
711 Zechariah 8:8
712 Ezekiel 36:24–32
713 Isaiah 44:28
714 Job 1:8
715 Job 23:10
716 Horatius Bonar, 1857 *Thy Way, Not Mine, O Lord*
717 Jeremiah 29:4–7, 10–14
718 Ezekiel 21:25–27 (Emphasis added)
719 PK p. 451
720 Joshua 23:14
721 Luke 2:25-32
722 Matthew 1:21
723 Ezekiel 21:27
724 Revelation 5:12–13; 11:15
725 Daniel 4:32
726 Exodus 12:13
727 1 John 4:10
728 Ephesians 2:8–9
729 Isaiah 64:6
730 Isaac Watts, 1719 *Jesus Shall Reign Where'er the Sun*
731 Galatians 6:16
732 Revelation 19:11
733 John 14:3
734 Revelation 22:20

Chapter Twelve Endnotes

735 *Time* Magazine, September 11, 2001
736 *Time* Magazine, September 11, 2001
737 Matthew 27:22

[738] John 3:16
[739] Matthew 24:3
[740] Matthew 24:36
[741] Matthew 24:42
[742] Matthew 24:7
[743] Genesis 6:5
[744] Revelation 7:1
[745] Daniel 12:4
[746] Matthew 24:14
[747] Matthew 24:29–31
[748] Revelation 16:12–17
[749] Revelation 16:15
[750] Daniel 12:1
[751] Revelation 16:14
[752] Revelation 16:17
[753] Revelation 16:19
[754] Revelation 17:14
[755] Revelation 18:20
[756] Revelation 19:2
[757] Isaiah 27:4
[758] Romans 6:23
[759] Romans 6:23
[760] Matthew 27:46
[761] DA p. 686
[762] DA p. 753
[763] 2 Corinthians 5:21
[764] Revelation 19:11–21
[765] Revelation 16:13–16 (Emphasis added)
[766] Revelation 17:12–14 (Emphasis added)
[767] Revelation 3:10
[768] Revelation 6:15–17
[769] Revelation 13:1–4, 11–15
[770] ST March 22, 1910
[771] RH April 23, 1889
[772] RH January 1, 1889
[773] Daniel 12:1

774 Revelation 22:11, 13
775 *A Word to the Little Flock* p. 3
776 CS pp. 53–52
777 GC p. 614
778 Revelation 16:17–21
779 SDABC Vol. 7 p. 843
780 Revelation 16:15
781 RH, June 15, 1897
782 Revelation 18:4–5
783 Exodus 14:28
784 Deuteronomy 2:32–36; Deuteronomy 3:3–7
785 Joshua 6
786 2 Kings 19:35
787 John 19:30
788 Matthew 26:40
789 Matthew 25:5
790 *The SDA Hymnal*, Hymn 301 RH Pub. Assoc. 1985
791 Ephesians 6:12
792 GC p. 620
793 Romans 8:35–39 NIV
794 Psalm 34:7
795 GC p. 622
796 GC p. 626
797 DA p. 630 (Emphasis added)
798 Exodus 14:30
799 Revelation 15:2
800 GC p. 678

To order additional copies of

THE BATTLE IS NOT YOURS, IT'S GOD'S

Have your credit card ready and call

Toll free: (877) 421-READ (7323)

or order online at: www.winepressbooks.com